Spirits of Earth

WISCONSIN LAND AND LIFE

ARNOLD ALANEN
Series Editor

Spirits of Earth

*The Effigy Mound Landscape
of Madison and
the Four Lakes*

Robert A. Birmingham

The University of Wisconsin Press

The University of Wisconsin Press
1930 Monroe Street, 3rd Floor
Madison, Wisconsin 53711-2059
uwpress.wisc.edu

3 Henrietta Street
London WC2E 8LU, England
www.eurospanbookstore.com

5   4   3   2   1

Printed in the United States of America

Library of Congress Cataloging-in-Publication Data
Birmingham, Robert A.
Spirits of earth : the effigy mound landscape of Madison and
    the Four Lakes / Robert A. Birmingham.
        p. cm.—(Wisconsin land and life)
        Includes bibliographical references and index.
    ISBN 978-0-299-23264-1 (pbk.: alk. paper)
    ISBN 978-0-299-23263-4 (e-book)
        1. Mounds—Wisconsin—Madison Region.   2. Earthworks (Archaeology)—Wisconsin—
Madison Region.   3. Indians of North America—Wisconsin—Madison Region—Antiquities.
4. Madison Region (Wis.)—Antiquities.   I. Title.   II. Series: Wisconsin land and life.
E78.W8B575   2009
977.5´83—dc22
2009011631

Contents

Contents

Illustrations

Illustrations

Preface

Of Megaliths and Mounds, Recognizing a World Wonder

In 1998 I fulfilled a lifelong dream by visiting Ireland, birthplace of some of my ancestors. My surname comes from a once-tiny Saxon village the Normans took during the conquest of England. Some Norman nobles adopted the place name as their family name, bringing it to Ireland in the twelfth century where, through the great upheavals of Anglo-Irish history, the family eventually became absorbed into the impoverished native Irish population.

I was chiefly interested in visiting would-be ancestral castles, but being an archaeologist, I dragged my family to the many easily visited archaeological sites that dot the countryside. Among these are megalithic tombs, structures of large stone slabs erected many thousands of years ago to mark the burial places of notable people. Archaeologists conclude these monumental burial places, found throughout Europe, functioned as ceremonial centers for Neolithic societies adopting a more settled life based on the cultivation of crops and animal husbandry. The construction of large earthen mounds or barrows and megalithic tombs helped integrate small dispersed populations into new and larger social groupings and more permanent settlements. The highly visible and elaborate burial and ceremonial structures defined their physical place in the world by linking notable ancestors to these places.[1]

This pattern was familiar to me. At the time, I was writing the book *Indian Mounds of Wisconsin* with Leslie Eisenberg and was specifically thinking about the effigy mounds, an ancient cultural phenomenon for which scholars could offer only speculation. Some had proposed that mounds also functioned as ceremonial centers or seasonal gathering places for an otherwise mobile people. Moreover, like the megalithic builders, there was also tantalizing evidence that effigy mound people were intensifying food production, eventually taking the first steps toward a farming lifestyle—in this case by growing small amounts of corn. Also like the megalith and burial mound builders of Western Europe, the construction of effigy mound ceremonial centers ceased as the transition to agriculture was completed. As North American Indian people developed more permanent communities, the need for special ceremonial centers that connect small separate groups seemed to be unnecessary.

In thinking about the effigy mound phenomenon, I re-read the works of the eminent archaeologist and anthropologist Robert Hall on mounds and Native American belief systems. Hall has long argued that to understand ancient archaeological phenomena in North America, such as mound building, one must have a general understanding of Native American beliefs, ceremonies, and worldviews. Regarding the effigy mounds, he pointed out that the various effigy forms corresponded to important spirits in the belief structure and clan systems of some modern Indian people. In this light he viewed effigy mound groups as "monumental expressions of the cosmology of their builders," an argument that made little immediate impact on a profession used to working with the more empirical and measurable evidence of pottery sherds and arrowheads.[2]

Examining the many maps of effigy mounds made by a variety of previous researchers, it became clear to me that the groups not only reflected the structure of many Native American belief and social systems but that the builders used the natural terrain to create three-dimensional "cosmological maps," which in many cases explicitly modeled these systems. This idea was reaffirmed by many discussions with a colleague and then office mate at the Wisconsin Historical Society, Amy Rosebrough, who had just begun her own research on effigy mounds and has since become an expert on the topic.[3]

Figure P.1. Poulnabrone megalith site in Ireland.

With these thoughts in the back of my mind, I visited the Poulnabrone dolmen in the stark and beautiful Burren region of west Ireland on a typically moist Irish day (figure P.1). Taking shelter from the drizzle under a large capstone, it occurred to me that while the effigy mound complexes functioned in a similar way to megaliths—integrating people around them into more complex society—the actual meaning of the mounds and mound groups in the midwestern United States is far clearer than the great stone megalithic sites of Europe. In contrast to the mostly blank and silent stones, North American Indians had left behind detailed maps to their beliefs and worldview. In short, the symbolism encoded in the effigy mounds of the Upper Midwest, and particularly Wisconsin, was a superb and perhaps unparalleled case study for scholars of the world studying the formation of new societies and civilizations as they became farmers.

My sense that our effigy mounds, still much ignored by American archaeologists, were of worldwide significance was reaffirmed by a surprising

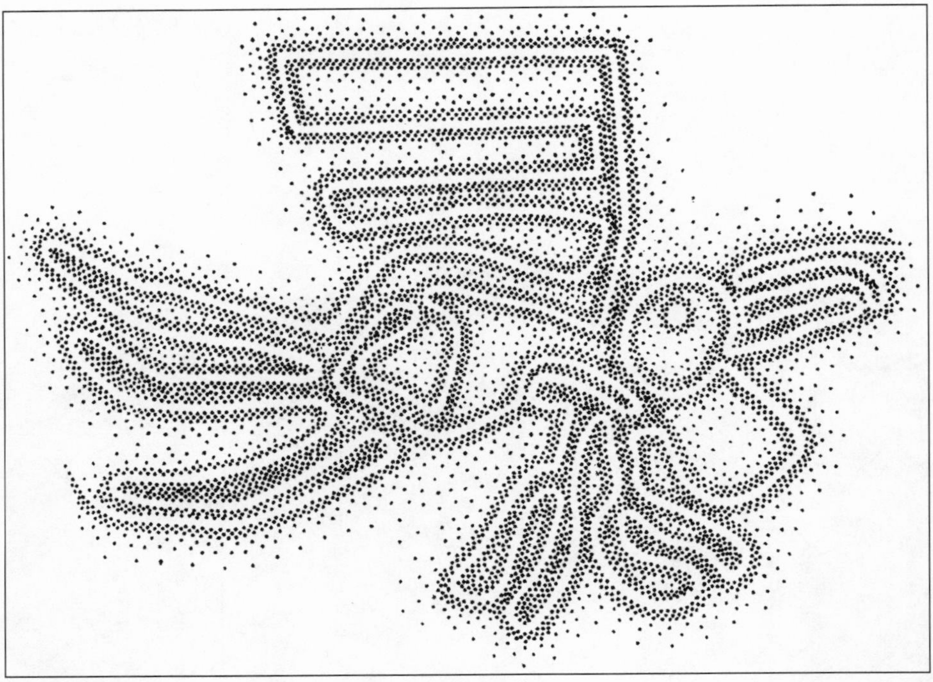

Figure P.2. Huge Nasca ground drawing in Peru.

phone call in 1999 from David Keys, a British archaeology writer and TV consultant. He was working on a documentary on the famous Nasca Lines and geoglyphs of Peru, long lines and immense ground drawings of animals and plants made by clearing the floor of the dry pampas and well comprehended only from the air (figure P.2). He wanted to use other world examples of monumental, symbolic constructions and was looking for effigy mound information and images.

Mound Research and an Ideological Approach

Realizing that the effigy mounds are a wonder with broad application to the study of the formation of new social groups was one of two insights I enjoyed during my mound research. The second was the related lesson that the meaning of the mounds, and by extension other ancient North American archaeological mysteries, is not lost to the ages but is reflected in the worldviews, beliefs, and social systems of Indian people in more recent times, as Robert Hall argued.

The continuity between past and present, a prominent theme of the effigy building itself, is reinforced for me practically every day. Near my home in Madison, Wisconsin, are effigy mounds in small parks, survivors of the once-spectacular mound landscape that is the topic of this book. At one location on Lake Monona, Ho-Chunk artist Harry Whitehorse (Bear Clan), whose family has long resided in the area, carved a tree stump to honor the effigy mound builders (figure P.3). The artist saw in the Madison mounds familiar themes that linked the modern Ho-Chunk Nation to the ancient people. He carved an eagle, bears, and a wolf; important animals in Ho-Chunk beliefs, totems of prominent modern Ho-Chunk clans, and common effigy mound forms. He called the work *Let the Great Spirit Soar.* Above my desk hangs a bear claw necklace given to me some years ago by a Native American friend because of my efforts, during my tenure as Wisconsin state archaeologist, to protect mounds. Among the Ho-Chunk, the Bear Clan is prominent among the earth clans with special responsibilities of keeping order among humans and to the land itself. Indeed, the bear and bear-effigy mounds created a millennium ago seem also closely connected to the earth plane of the cosmos. In 1837, tribal leaders tried unsuccessfully to forestall the sale of their remaining lands by refusing to send members of the Bear Clan, the only ones authorized to conduct land negotiations on behalf of the tribe.[4]

These personal insights led to an ideological approach used in this book. It involves the study of archaeological phenomena within the framework of the worldview and beliefs of the ancient people involved, and the use of ethnography (detailed anthropological studies of societies) as well as ethnohistory (historical descriptions) to inform such study.[5] It is really basic anthropology, combining many lines of evidence on human culture, but it highlights iconography, ideology, and symbolism as a way of understanding the past. It contrasts with the more objective and traditional archaeological approaches that focus mainly on what artifacts people made and what they ate, but it is complementary to this research. It is not a new approach but one that has enjoyed a florescence.

I see this ideological approach as deriving from two assumptions. The first is that relationships to the supernatural, what we would call religion

Figure P.3. The original tree stump sculpture *Let the Great Spirit Soar* by Harry Whitehorse was removed because of deterioration and a bronze replacement was installed in 2009.

today, were not only more important in the ancient world but central to lives of ancient people the world over. For much of the now secular Western world, this worldview changed with industrialization and, accordingly, the tendency since then has been to interpret human behavior in terms of economic relationships between human beings and the environment. Among Native Americans, there were (and for many, still are) no clear boundaries between the natural and supernatural worlds.

Second, basic principles that operate in the religious realm of culture are conservative and do not change rapidly even in the face of much economic, technological, and social change. For example, the underlying structure, sacred beings, ceremonies, and symbols of the great world religions have not changed much in thousands of years even though the material world has changed enormously. As a corollary, ancient worldviews and ceremonial customs of indigenous people of the New World persist, or persisted well into modern times in many areas. Here, insights into ancient belief systems can be gained through stories, myths, oral history, and general belief structures recorded by eyewitnesses, ethnographic accounts, historical documents, and from the people themselves.

For example, Michigan archaeologists make a good case that enigmatic nine-hundred-year-old circular earthworks are linked to the origin story of the Midewiwin or Grand Medicine Society among the Ojibwe, as recounted by members of this important and exclusive organization and depicted on nineteenth-century birch bark scrolls used formerly by Midewiwin priests.[6] The Grand Medicine Society, found among many midwestern native peoples, is composed of specialists or priests rigorously trained in medicinal and spiritual curing and healing. Members are vested with many types of sacred knowledge, and thus the society serves as a vehicle for the transmission of religious and important cultural beliefs. The antiquity of the Grand Medicine Society has long been in question: some scholars have argued that it developed in response to social changes and disease introduced by the Europeans.

Another example is the famous Gottschall Rockshelter in Wisconsin. Robert Hall identified ancient paintings on the cave wall as a story related to a cultural hero, Red Horn, recorded from the Ho-Chunk and Ioway medicine people who had been the special keepers of these stories. Site excavator Robert Salzer views the cave as an important ritual and ceremonial place.[7] The study of traditional belief and ritual systems has increased our understanding of many other ancient rock art sites throughout North America.[8]

An ideological and symbolic emphasis has also generated interest in defining and understanding ancient landscapes where humans built their religious monuments, such as the Nasca Lines and ground drawings in Peru, as well as the arrangements of mounds, megalithic structures, and similar phenomena across the world. The immense Nasca landscapes have long puzzled observers, leading to some outlandish interpretations such as involvement of space aliens. Although still clouded by mystery, recent anthropological investigations interpret the giant symbols and lines as part of an identifiable regional religious system and reflect some the same types of rituals conducted by area people in more recent times. One hypothesis derived from these understandings is that the man-made landscape and related ceremonies concerned the flow of water in the otherwise parched environment of ancient times.[9]

The concept of landscape, then, is an important one and one that has been applied to the arrangements of effigy mounds by various researchers over the last several decades, although what constitutes such a landscape has not been precisely defined.[10] The perspective presented in this book is that effigy mound landscapes are areas, small and large, that were chosen for effigy mound ceremonial construction and ritual activities because of certain spiritual or supernatural characteristics attributed to natural territory. The arrangements of the mounds themselves reflect the structure of the builder's religious and related social world and have the potential to tell us much about the ideological realm.

This kind of landscape is variously called cultural, sacred, or symbolic. I prefer to use the term *ceremonial* since it most clearly communicates to the public the nature of the phenomenon, but it is technically a type of "ideological landscape" as defined by James Sneed and Robert Preucel where a worldview combines place (i.e., characteristics of the environment) and space (i.e., the nature and arrangement of mounds) to produce special meaning for the builders.[11] In the case of effigy mounds, one gets the impression that the man-made constructions were not simply built as static symbols on vacant land, as one might paint religious representations on a blank canvas, but were built to be alive, actively bringing together the natural and supernatural worlds. The natural topography actually animates bird and animal forms and therefore is very much part of the ancient story being told. Following the late Clark Mallam and Robert Hall, I believe that the story is one of ongoing re-creation or renewal of the world.

An ideological approach is not without its critics who rightly maintain that it is highly subjective and really it is not possible to crawl inside the minds of ancient people. Surely, we lack the ability to *prove* anything regarding the motivations of people who left behind no written record. Further, historical, ethnographic, and oral sources are fraught with errors, biases, and misinterpretations and must be used critically.[12]

However, connections between phenomena like the effigy mounds and long-held worldviews and belief systems of Indian people are logical and compelling, and the more we understand the structure of ancient belief systems and worldviews, the clearer the past becomes. At the very least, the approach develops new directions and questions in archaeological research. It is a different way of looking at the past: a past in which there was not a sharp boundary between the supernatural and natural worlds. A past that was not dominated by humans but filled with deities, spirits, powers, and forces, visible and invisible, upon which humans drew for the continuance of life and with which humans communicated through visions, offerings, rituals, and ceremonies, as many traditional people do today. A past where the daily actions of humans were as much dictated by "religious" concerns as by the practical matters of food, shelter, and social interactions.

Effigy Mound Landscapes of Madison and the Four Lakes

As a follow-up to *Indian Mounds of Wisconsin,* this book has two goals. First, it takes a closer look at the spectacular effigy mound phenomenon, and the evolution and meaning of effigy mound landscapes, using the Madison and Four Lakes geographical area as a key example since it was a major center of effigy construction and the subsequent center of intense effigy mound research. Consequently, more is known about the distribution and nature of effigies here than in any other effigy mound center. Further, being in the very center of the effigy mound region, the Madison mound groups best illustrate the fundamental structure of the belief system underlying mound construction and the relationship of the mounds to physical landscape features.

Second, it is a guide to effigy mounds of the Four Lakes since, due to early preservation efforts, many more mounds and mound groups have survived here on public lands than in other areas. This provides an opportunity for readers to examine for themselves the remnants of a world wonder and ponder the mysteries from their own perspectives, perhaps even providing new insights to this short-lived and spectacular phenomenon.

Acknowledgments

I am grateful for the comments on various versions of this manuscript by Robert Boszhardt (formerly of Mississippi Valley Archaeology Center), Robert Hall (professor emeritus, University of Illinois at Chicago), Jay Toth (Seneca, archaeologist for the Ho-Chunk Nation), Janice Rice (Ho-Chunk, University of Wisconsin–Madison), and an anonymous reviewer. I like to thank the excellent and long-suffering University of Wisconsin Press editors and staff, not only for their professionalism and high standards but for their patience.

I am indebted to Amy Rosebrough of the State Archaeology office and state archaeologist John Broihahn for assisting in numerous ways. Amy has long been conducting research on effigy mounds and graciously shared her research information and many of her own maps. Others who contributed to this book in various ways are the late Reid Bryson (UW Climatic Research Center) and his son Robert Bryson (Mojave National Reserve), George Christiansen, Victoria Dirst (Wisconsin Department of Natural Resources, retired), Jeff Durbin, Mark Dudzik (Wisconsin Department of Natural Resources), Fred Finney, Robert Granflaten (Wisconsin Historical Society), Robert Jeske and John Richards (University of Wisconsin–Milwaukee), Amelia Janes, Lisa Marine (Wisconsin Historical Society), David Mollenhoff, Susan Otto (Milwaukee Public Museum), Tom Pleger (UW–Baraboo/Sauk County), Sissel Schroeder (University of Wisconsin–Madison), Philip Salkin (Archaeological Consulting and Services), James Stoltman (professor emeritus, University of Wisconsin–Madison), Woody

Wallace (Earth Information Technology), Dodge County Parks, Effigy Mounds National Monument, Milwaukee Public Museum, Minnesota Historical Society Archives, Mississippi Valley Archeology Center, Ohio Historical Society, Northern Illinois University Press, Mapping Specialists, Ltd., Wisconsin Geological and Natural History Survey, Wisconsin Historical Society Museum Archaeology Program, and the University of Texas Press.

Much love to my wife Nancy and son Kevin for not only putting up with stacks of papers and books around the house but also for help with editing drafts (Nancy), taking photographs (Kevin), and much computer-related work.

Finally, a book like this would not have been possible without the Wisconsin Historical Society, which has been collecting and recording information on mounds and other archaeological sites for more than one hundred years, and the Wisconsin Archeological Society, which has published a truly impressive amount of information for over a century on Wisconsin Indian mounds. I hope this book will reflect well on the efforts of both of these institutions to make material and data available for scholarly and public research.

Despite all this help, I alone bear the responsibility for any errors, omissions, misrepresentations, or mistakes in this admittedly bold interpretation of the effigy mound landscape of Madison and the Four Lakes region.

Spirits of Earth

1 | Spirits of Earth

An Introduction to Effigy Mound Landscapes

WHEN WHITE SETTLERS flooded into what is now southern Wisconsin in the 1830s, many were amazed and perplexed at what they found. Among the hills, parklands, lakes, and rivers it appeared that ancient people had sculpted the terrain into sometimes huge arrangements of birds, mammals, humans, long embankments, and other earthen forms comprising a "multitude of extraordinary figures raised like embossed ornaments over the whole of this country" (figure 1.1).[1] As with other earthworks found in America, the settlers and other visitors found the phenomenon so fantastic and unfamiliar that they could not believe that local Indians, recently pushed off their lands, could have been the originators. The newcomers conjured up instead legends of a superior race lost to history, killed off by the more "primitive" Indians.

As twentieth-century archaeology would reveal, these early observers were right on one account: the Indian people who had recently occupied the land *had not* made these monuments. It was rather their ancient ancestors during a spectacular wave of ceremonial mound building and burial activity more than nine hundred years earlier. Modern research would also justify the amazement of the new people, for they indeed observed a phenomenon unique in the world. Concentrated in the Upper Midwest and centered on what is now southern Wisconsin, the great effigy mound building took place during a comparatively short time, between A.D. 700 and 1100. Further, the vast and mysterious earthworks were not mere representations of wildlife and people of the area but monumental constructions that represented the worldview and religious beliefs of the builders.

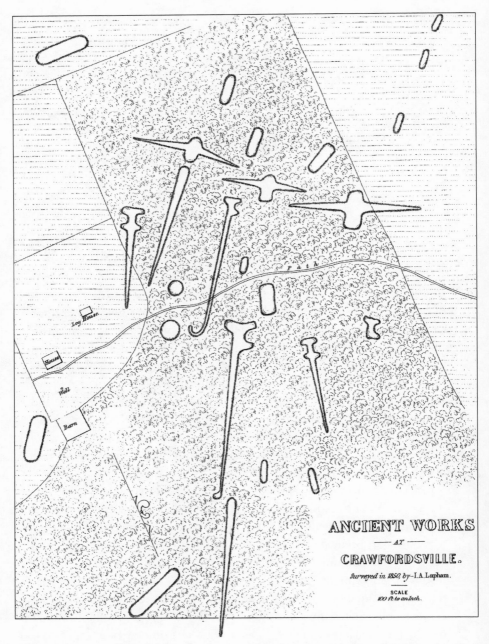

Figure 1.1. Map by Lapham of a mound group on a high hill overlooking the Fox River near present-day Big Bend, Wisconsin.

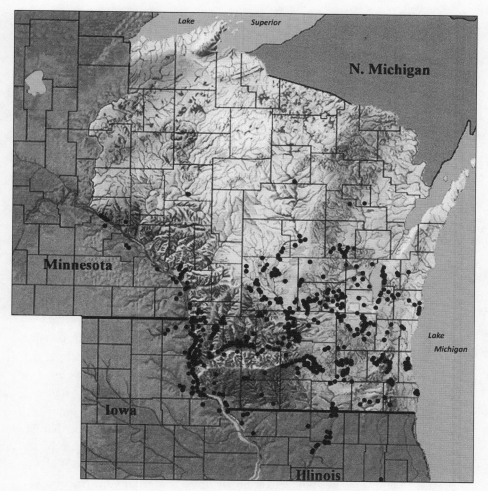

Figure 1.2. The effigy mound region showing location of effigy mounds groups.

Indian people built many thousands of individual mounds in more than a thousand recorded locations during this great wave of ceremonial construction, adding to the hundreds of large conical mounds built previously, often close to or around these early locations (figure 1.2). In Wisconsin, a majority of the more than fifteen thousand recorded mounds are believed to have been constructed over several centuries. While most of the mounds built during this time were conical (round) or linear (long and short straight embankments), the records of the Wisconsin Historical

Society identify over 3,200 as "effigy" mounds because they are in the form of special animals and, occasionally, people.[2]

Comparatively few effigy mounds have been radiocarbon dated, but information to date suggests that effigy mound building ended by A.D. 1100, earlier in some places.[3] Small conical or round mounds continued to be used as tombs in some places for centuries after, but not in the numbers of the previous effigy mound ceremonial era.

The Effigy Mound Region

The effigy mound region covers the whole of southern Wisconsin and small parts of adjacent Iowa, Minnesota, and Illinois. A few outlying effigy mounds are found in northern Wisconsin but not in the large clusters found in the south. The main region closely corresponds to a zone of oak savannas (prairie grasses and scattered oak trees), prairies, forest, and water bodies rich with easily obtained wild food resources, including large deer herds. The productivity of this zone greatly increases when one factors in a favorable environment and climate for corn and other types of agriculture.

The bountiful natural resources allowed for the growth of a comparatively large population and attracted other natives from the south toward the end of the effigy mound era, stimulating massive social change, population relocations, and conflict. Deer were so important to the diet that collapse of the deer herd through overexploitation has recently been proposed as a factor in the demise of the effigy mound culture in western Wisconsin, forcing a greater reliance on horticulture and other adjustments.[4] A concern about deer seems evident from ritual art found in the deepest, darkest cavern of a large cave complex in southwestern Wisconsin, dated to the effigy mound period.[5] The black, charcoal-based paintings depict hunters, pregnant deer, and above a natural fissure what appear to be thunderbirds (figure 1.3). Arrows are quite clearly directed at the fetal deer leading to the interpretation that the paintings represent "hunting magic": an appeal to the spirits for an increase of the herds for future hunts.

Ancient people elsewhere in the Mississippi River drainage system and beyond occasionally made large earthen (and sometimes stone) animal effigies, but nowhere are mounds found in such concentrations as this upper

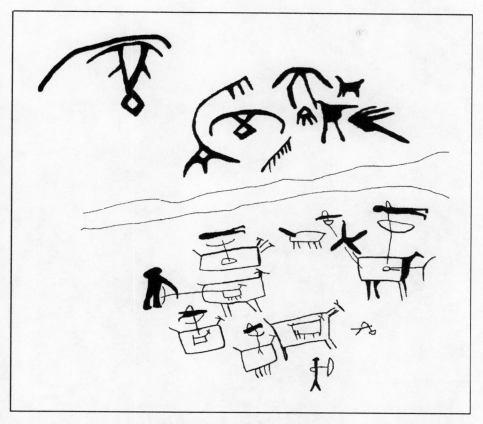

Figure 1.3. Effigy mound era charcoal drawings at Tainter Cave show a deer hunt overseen by remnants of bird-like figures (above natural fissure in bedrock) that represent the upper world of the thunderbirds. The faded drawings are enhanced for clarity but some figures and portions of others have disappeared.

midwestern effigy mound region. Here, the mound groupings occur in large clusters in many key areas and tend to be located on hills, bluffs, and terraces overlooking major rivers, streams, lakes, and large wetlands.

One of the most impressive of the effigy mound complexes was, and remains, in the heart of the effigy mound region in south-central Wisconsin around the present-day city of Madison, the state capital (figure 1.4). Here in the Four Lakes mound district, earthworks were so dense that one early but fanciful map rendered in 1836 gives the impression that mounds visually dominated the landscape (figure 1.5).[6]

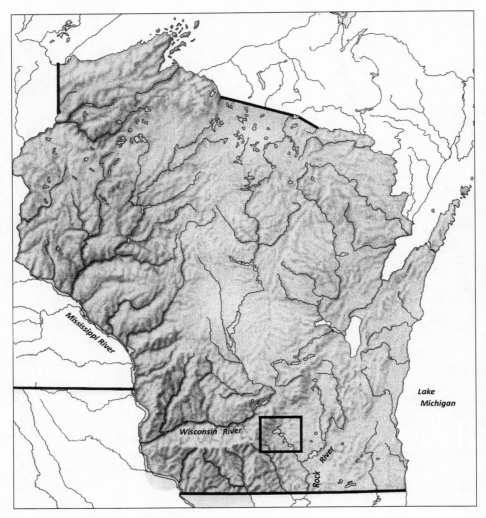

Figure 1.4. Location of Four Lakes mound district.

The four principal lakes of the district, Mendota, Monona, Waubesa, and Kegonsa, are actually widenings in the Yahara River, a tributary of the Rock River, that has its headwaters northwest of Lake Mendota. As white settlers found it, the land was covered mainly by oak savanna and wetlands, with some prairies and forests. The Ho-Chunk expanded into the area in the late eighteenth century and claimed the land as their own until

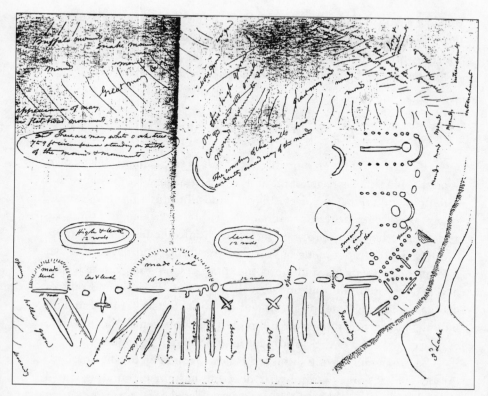

Figure 1.5. Mounds everywhere. Highly impressionistic 1836 map by Samuel Stone and Leandes Judson. "3d Lake" refers to Lake Monona.

treaties in the 1830s turned the land over for white settlement. The Ho-Chunk called this area *Taychopera* or Four Lakes. The name today is often shortened to De Jope. White settlers also called the area "Four Lakes" referring to the principal lakes by number. The individual lakes originally had Ho-Chunk names, but the current euphonic Indian names were selected later by the Wisconsin legislature and have nothing to do with historic associations.[7]

There is actually a fifth lake that figures importantly in the area's mound building history. The small spring-fed Lake Wingra forms part of the headwaters of the Yahara, contributing water through a small stream that flows into Lake Monona. Lake Wingra had a huge number of mounds for such a small lake, but the prominent feature of the lake, its springs, provides a clue to the spiritual significance of the place. Another major effigy mound building center lay along shores of Lake Koshkonong, a large widening of the Rock River southeast of the Four Lakes, most recently described in Hugh Highsmith's *Mounds of Koshkonong and Rock River*.

Origins of the Effigy Mounds

Through more than 150 years of research, much is known about the physical character of mound construction and the locations, distribution, and arrangements of effigy mounds. Information from camps, villages, and rock shelters carefully excavated by archaeologists since the mid-twentieth century provide much insight into the lives of the people involved in the monument building in the form of artifacts, seasonal movements, settlements, and subsistence practices. Ongoing research adds new and important information virtually every year. Even the meaning of many various effigy mound forms and the social function of the mound building itself is becoming clearer. But great questions remain unanswered, as they do for other of the world's ancient monuments and societies.

The iconography, symbolism, and beliefs that pertain to effigy mounds extend far back into antiquity, as does the custom of building burial mounds and other earthworks. But what stimulated people to express their worldview in such a monumental fashion over such a wide area? The flamboyance of this unique ceremonial mound building suggests a strong stimulus in the form of some perceived or real challenges to group identity or lifestyle and their resource-rich territory as populations expanded throughout the Midwest. Thus, monument building, incorporating religious and social symbols, may have emerged to reinforce the identity and territorial heritage of a people in the face of cultural challenges.

Ultimately the answer to this question will come from better understandings of this dynamic and turbulent period in the Midwest, a period when populations dramatically increased and an agricultural revolution took place, giving birth to one of the most complex and expansive pre-Columbian societies north of Mexico—the Mississippian—whose own history is intertwined with that of the effigy mound builders. For now, the true origins of the effigy mound phenomenon are opaque, thus ranking among the great archaeological riddles of North America.

Monumental Constructions of Cosmology

Different interpretations about the effigy mounds have been offered in the past, but the one presented here follows Robert Hall's view of mound groupings as "monumental constructions of the cosmology of the builders."[8] Cosmology here refers to the way people explain the origin and structure of the universe or world. It is the basis of a worldview. As elaborated in *Indian Mounds of Wisconsin* and other works, the effigy mounds form maps of ancient worldviews, beliefs, and even possibly social arrangements in the form of three-dimensional landscapes.[9] The underlying structure of this ceremonialism was a three-part division of the universe into sky, earth, and water realms, with appropriate animals and key supernatural beings or spirits embodying the powers of each of these realms. Within this three-part cosmology, a dualism is often expressed between the opposing yet complementary upper (sky) and lower (earth, water) divisions.

The animals and spirits not only mirrored cosmic order but in some traditions are the very ancestors of humans themselves in the form of clans, transformed into human form after the world was created. I propose here that builders of the effigy mounds periodically re-created and renewed their world by duplicating both its cosmological and social structure in complex but sometimes exquisitely patterned arrangements, the basic concept first introduced in by the late Clark Mallam, a pioneer in research concerning the ideological basis of effigy mound construction.[10]

As believed by Mallam and some subsequent scholars, the effigy mound complexes served as ceremonial centers where groups of people within certain territories gathered in warmer months to engage in mound building, burial of the dead, and other rituals that emphasized common beliefs, kinship, and ancestry. These activities united them into larger social organizations and broader identities. It is easy to image that once built, the effigy mounds served as sacred places where other important ceremonies were held throughout the year and where individuals, including religious specialists and medicine people, could come to draw upon the blessings and powers of the spirits represented.[11]

The area of the mounds perhaps continued to be used as burial places; there are instances where burials occur outside of the mounds, although the mounds themselves remained undisturbed by the effigy mound people after construction. As prominent places became filled with mounds, the mound-building ceremonials shifted to other appropriate and nearby locations, eventually creating vast effigy mound landscapes such as what the early settlers found in the Four Lakes area.

Demise of the Effigy Mound Tradition

The demise of the effigy mound tradition by ca. A.D. 1050 is correlated with dramatic cultural events and perhaps climatic changes that greatly transformed Midwest Indian societies. An important economic change was the introduction of corn horticulture, a process that began during the effigy mound era ca. A.D. 800–900 and ultimately lead to the establishment of large and permanent agricultural villages after the effigy mound period. As mentioned, in some areas this shift may have been stimulated by other economic factors. The consolidation of people into large, year-round village centers would have ultimately eliminated the need for other special gathering places.[12] Second, and most notably, the end of the effigy mound-making tradition is linked to the influence of and actual migration north into a region of new, intensely agricultural and aggressive people, the Mississippians, between A.D. 1050 and 1100. These new people impacted the cultures and distributions of indigenous people in various and dramatic ways and may have contributed to stress on area resources.

Archaeologists trace influence from southern Illinois, homeland of the Mississippians, for some decades prior to the Mississippian migration north, and this may reflect some initial trading or other social contacts. Contact with the intensively agricultural Mississippians introduced new types of pottery-making traditions and undoubtedly accelerated the adoption of corn horticulture. It probably also brought with it a host of sacred traditions, fertility-oriented rituals, and other ceremonies associated with growing of corn.

After the demise of effigy mound building, and the disappearance of the Mississippians themselves in the Midwest ca. A.D. 1250, people abandoned much of the former effigy mound region. This process began earlier in some areas, but the people of the Four Lakes did not entirely leave until about the same time the Mississippians disappeared.[13] By this time, native populations were nucleating at several places, forming a different cultural lifestyle referred to by archaeologists as Upper Mississippian or Oneota. In Wisconsin, the Oneota lived in clusters of large, sometimes fortified, agricultural villages. One Oneota center was Lake Koshkonong, southeast of the Four Lakes.

Some scholars believe that the effigy mound-building people were physically swept aside by people of the Oneota tradition (who may or may not have come from elsewhere), but others conclude that Oneota are none other than former effigy mound builders transformed by the adoption of a farming lifestyle and by various degrees of contact with the briefly dominating Mississippian cultural leviathan.[14] The Oneota farming tradition emerges in areas where the Mississippians were particularly active, and early Oneota pottery and other artifacts in some areas show clear Mississippian influence. In turn, the Oneota in the Upper Midwest almost certainly continued into the historic period as some of the tribes the Europeans first encountered in the same region.

The Effigy Mound Culture and Late Woodland Stage or Period

Reflecting the times and state of knowledge in the nineteenth century, investigators did not know what to make of the effigy mounds except that they were often tombs and that some mound forms resembled clan totems found in many Native American societies. As late as the 1890s, serious mound researchers seemed not to be thoroughly convinced that Indians had made the mounds. The Indians themselves, dislocated and distrusted, were rarely consulted.

Exceptions included the ethnographer Paul Radin, who between 1908 and 1913 worked among the Winnebago or Ho-Chunk in Wisconsin and those who had been removed to a Nebraska reservation, A. B. Stout of the Wisconsin Archeological Society, and Charles E. Brown, director the Wisconsin Historical Society museum from 1908 to 1944. All three men talked to various degrees with native people, mainly the Ho-Chunk, on the meaning of the mounds in the context of native cultural beliefs.

Ho-Chunk gara is the name these people called themselves and is the one used hereafter in lieu of Winnebago, a name given to them by others.

They are one of the Indian nations, along with the Menominee and Da-
kota Sioux, that historical documents and oral traditions identify as occupants of what is now Wisconsin at the time of earliest European contact.
The once-populous Ho-Chunk occupied much of eastern and southern
Wisconsin, perhaps extending into northern Illinois.[15] Other tribes, like
the Ioway, close relatives of the Ho-Chunk and from which the Oto and
Missouria seem to have later split, moved west of the Mississippi River late
in the pre-Contact time. Ho-Chunk and Ioway traditions state that they
were once part of the same tribe, and indeed their languages are very similar. Many other Indian groups moved into Wisconsin from the east in the
early seventeenth century as consequence of the pressures of the fur trade
and intertribal warfare.

Noting great similarities of the effigy mounds to the Ho-Chunk beliefs, among other reasons, Radin, Brown, Stout, and others became convinced that in fact the Ho-Chunk made the effigy mounds in a not-too-
distant past. According to Radin, this view was held by some Ho-Chunk
people themselves at the time of his study.[16] Here and there throughout
the Four Lakes mound district are old historical markers at effigy mound
groups that state this as fact.

Modern research, however, established the great antiquity of the effigy
mounds, eliminating the possibility of construction by Indian people in
recent times. Additionally, in the centuries between effigy mound construction and American settlement, native societies underwent much cultural change and population rearrangement, not the least of which was
massive disruption caused by European contact—population movements,
the fission and fusion of tribal groups, and a massive death toll due to warfare and especially disease spread from the Europeans. Both oral history
and historic documents attest to a massacre of most Ho-Chunk by the Illinois Indians in the seventeenth century, the survivors fleeing to live with
other tribes.[17] Disease in itself was so devastating that entire tribes could
have disappeared, leaving no one left to bear witness to their existence.[18]
Thus, finding a direct one-to-one connection between ancient mound
builders and specific modern Indian Nations would not be expected.

Noting discrepancies between Ho-Chunk explanations of the effigy
mounds and the archaeological record, some early twentieth-century
archaeologists accused Radin especially of telling the Ho-Chunk that

they made the mounds, rather than the other way around, and this view is repeated by some modern archaeologists. There is actually no reason to doubt Radin's claim that some Ho-Chunk did tell him that the mound building was in their ancestry. At the very least, the Ho-Chunk would certainly have recognized in the mound forms the same animals, spirits, and symbols that comprised their world, and in fact many were and are clan totems. There are other perspectives on Ho-Chunk involvement, however: some traditional Ho-Chunk people today have the opinion that the mounds are the result of spirit activities.[19]

It is quite likely that the Ho-Chunk are *among* the descendants of the effigy mound builders and that the widespread construction in the Upper Midwest and effigy mound phenomena represent the formation of a larger social body from which they and related groups sprang in the form of Oneota culture. Direct biological connections have not been made, but perhaps, with the assent of Indian peoples, advances in DNA analysis and technology will help identify the various descendants of the mound builders.

In the meantime, modern archaeology views the effigy mounds as a unique tradition within a broader and widespread archaeological stage, period, or lifestyle called the Late Woodland and dated in Wisconsin roughly between A.D. 500 and 1250—ending earlier in some areas. The Late Woodland people did not live in large settlements, with one later exception at Aztalan. At first they lived in small groups, maintaining seasonal camps and small villages to hunt, fish, and gather wild foods. At intervals, the various small groups or bands in local areas came together in special ceremonial places to carry out the other rituals of mound building, including the burial of the dead.

As the Late Woodland people incorporated the growing of corn into their economy, small farming villages and hamlets appeared with curious housing in the form of small wood-framed and bark-covered "pithouses" partly dug into the ground. These changes were accompanied by new versions of old pottery styles and the end of effigy mound building. In the eleventh century, and many believe after the climax of the effigy mound building, some of the farming villages in the region became fortified, reflecting friction and warfare. Some of these appeared to have been mixed populations of Late Woodland and the new Mississippian people expanding into the effigy mound region from the south. One major town, the great site of Aztalan along the Crawfish River, was built as a veritable fortress by Mississippians with a characteristic Mississippian town plan, but it also included a sizable Late Woodland population.[20]

The similarity of the effigy mound symbolism throughout the effigy mound region, along with similar pottery-making traditions, suggests that a common social identity extended over a wide area. Most likely this was a confederation of closely related tribes, each with mound-building centers that were often large and sprawling. Based on archeological work in western Wisconsin, University of Wisconsin–La Crosse archaeologists James Theler and Robert Boszhardt characterize the Late Woodland itself in the Upper Mississippi Valley as the "beginning of tribes."[21] They identified social boundaries between two archaeological complexes in western Wisconsin based on different types of artifacts, including variations in pottery decoration, as well as different types of effigy mounds. They view the mound groups as elaborate territory markers for the different effigy mound groups. Whatever political form it took, the broader effigy mound society would have shared ties through kinship (e.g., clans), intermarriage, social organizations that cut across geographical and kinship boundaries, as well as shared religious beliefs, institutions, and ceremonies like effigy mound building.

Effigy Mound Construction

Effigy mound groups vary in size from just a few mounds to many hundreds. Many of the groups, however, include a considerable number of conical and linear mounds not recognizable as effigy forms. Isolated individual effigy mounds occasionally occur but are still part of a broader effigy mound landscape as is illustrated for the Four Lakes mounds district. The mounds were constructed over several centuries, expanding into new areas not used in previous times for mound building. This pattern has been identified in western Wisconsin,[22] and the remote, later-dated Nitschke mound complex, discussed below, is a clear example of this expansion for eastern Wisconsin. Some effigy mounds were enormous—many hundreds of feet long—but they are characteristically low, often only three or four feet high, following the natural contours of the land itself and blending seamlessly into the natural terrain. It is often difficult to see where a mound ends and the natural terrain begins. In some recorded cases, public landowners added dirt to effigy mounds to make them more recognizable to visitors. Some erosion over time would be expected, but it also appears that most mounds were built in areas where prairie grasses would have anchored the soil.

This apparent concern for harmony with the natural terrain is also clear by general lack of borrow areas or holes, despite the amount the earth moved to build the giant mounds. Exceptions are occasional effigy intaglios, excavations into the earth in the shape of water spirits and bears, that were also part of the ceremonial landscape. Here, the topsoil seems to have been scraped to mold or sculpt the mounds. In some cases, the first step would have been to clear the topsoil from the area where the mound would be built and then outline the form of the mound. Occasionally, brightly colored sands, clays, and ash were added to the area before the mound was built.[23]

Great feasts attended construction of mounds and burials beneath them. At the Kolterman effigy mound group in eastern Wisconsin, large pits containing food remains were found with several of the mounds, and a similar concentration, including much butchered animal bone, was found above a burial in a mound at the Nitschke I mound group near Juneau, Wisconsin (figure 1.6).[24]

It would be logical to assume that earth-moving involved in mound construction took place during the warmer months and had taken some time. Habitation sites have been found at a few effigy mounds sites. Sometimes they appear to be temporary, but in the Four Lakes area, a small archaeological excavation on the grounds of the north shore of Lake Mendota revealed evidence of what appears to be part of a Late Woodland village near the shoreline on a large level space surrounded on three sides by huge bird mounds (see figure 4.8).[25] A similar situation, where effigy mounds were neatly arranged around a habitation site, is documented for the Eagle Township mound group along the Wisconsin River in western Wisconsin (figure 1.7).[26]

In recent years, University of Wisconsin–Milwaukee archaeologists discovered a camp or habitation area at the base of the remarkable Nitschke I effigy mound group situated on a high glacial drumlin northeast of the Four Lakes and several miles from the great Horicon Marsh. Drumlins are high, oblong hills of sand and gravel created by glaciers.

Figure 1.6. Rock concentrations occasionally found in effigy mounds.

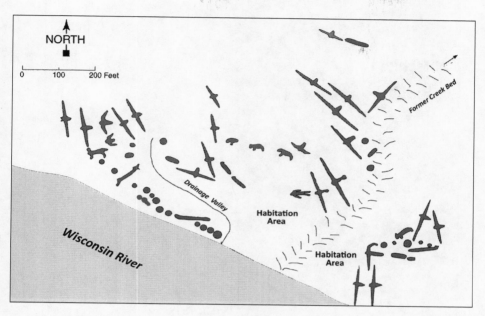

Figure 1.7. Village or camp once surrounded by mounds on the Wisconsin River in southwestern Wisconsin.

Nitschke I is one of two closely spaced and isolated mound groups located at major springs and away from major bodies of water (figure 1.8).[27] W. C. McKern from the Milwaukee Public Museum excavated parts of most mounds in early twentieth century, and one radiocarbon date derived later from excavated material places construction at sometime between A.D. 1027 and 1224, based on a recent calibration.[28] This date range is consistent with later styles of Late Woodland pottery, with its distinctive collars around the rims, found in the mounds and in the newly discovered habitation area. The date and the pottery puts this site at the end of currently postulated time-end of the effigy mound construction and perhaps even later. Ongoing research at the habitation site, which is associated with a small plot of Indian garden beds, will surely provide exciting clues to the cultural changes taking place at this critical juncture in time.

Most people of the effigy mound period appeared to have been buried in mounds. No other cemeteries have been located, although occasionally people were buried in camps or near the mounds themselves. Burials in a variety of forms were placed in pits dug into the land surface or laid into

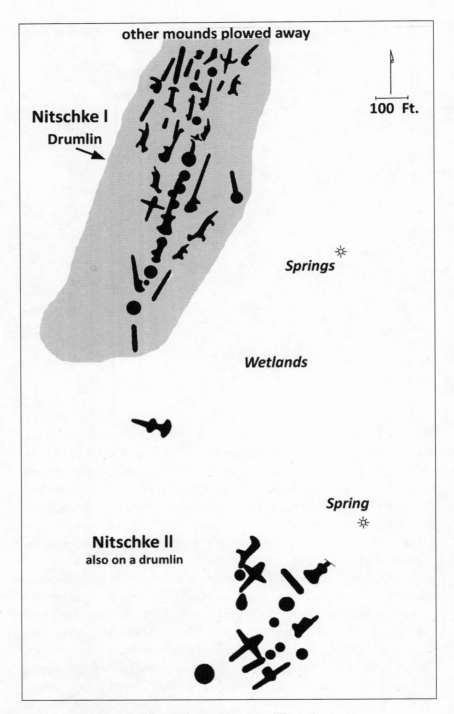

Figure 1.8. Nitschke I and II mound groups in eastern Wisconsin.

the land surface itself, later covered by earthen mounds. Effigy mound burials occur as either single interments or a small number of people all buried at the same time. The interments represent a cross-section of the population, including infants and children. For example, a 1954 excavation of a bird mound on a high hill just north of Lake Mendota, just prior to its destruction for a subdivision, revealed that the large mound covered the grave of a child about nine years old.[29]

But effigy mound groups were more than just exotically formed tombs. Some mounds examined by archaeologists did not contain burials. In some cases this may have been the result of disintegration of human remains, but in other cases there are no grave pits or other clues to suggest that a burial was ever present. The absence of burials in some effigy mounds leads to the interpretation that the mounds were constructed in ceremonials and rituals that transcended the burial of the dead. Remnants of the broader rituals involved at effigy mound sites include the intaglios, rock arrangements, and clay receptacles in mounds even when there are no associated burials (see figure 1.6), feasting pits, and earthen enclosures at some sites that define special ceremonial spaces.

Where burials do occur, the archaeological evidence indicates that mound construction occurred at intervals, rather than as a continuous activity (as for example, immediately after a death). Several types of burials have been identified, but the majority of the many hundreds of burials excavated were in the form of bundles of bones. This indicates that death had occurred sometime earlier and that the cleaned bones, many times only the skull and long bones, had been buried or kept elsewhere until final burial in the mound. Others are flexed in a fetal position so tightly as to suggest that the corpses had undergone some decomposition and the bound bodies were brought to the site for burial or reburial.[30]

Extended or "in the flesh" burials, where little decomposition took place before interment, do occur but are rare. Some interments are in the form of cremated bones, but the significance of this custom, which predates the effigy mounds by thousands of years, is unclear. The combination of bone bundles, flexed burials, and some "in the flesh" burials made not long after death means that the intervals between mound building ceremonies were fairly frequent, perhaps even annual. If death occurred in the winter, the body may have been saved for interment for warm-weather burial ritual.

Several important exceptions to the above-mentioned pattern are conical mounds at several effigy mound groups; here, large mass graves of up to
forty-five people in the form of disarticulated bones were found by early
archaeological excavations.[31] If contemporary with the effigy mounds, as
they seem to be, this suggests the existence of two ritual cycles of burials:
one short and one much longer. Precisely who the people in the mass
burials were is unknown, but sometimes the same people practiced different mortuary customs based on social and kinship differences. Ho-
Chunk people told Paul Radin that in former days, some upper division
clans practiced "sky burial" on specially constructed scaffolds.[32] In historic
times, the custom of aerial burials could be found among numerous midwestern and Great Plains peoples. Periodic and ritual cleaning of decaying
scaffold areas would result in disarticulated bones that then would have
been buried in a mound.

A Complex Society

The very existence of the diverse and sometimes huge
mounds, along with exquisitely patterned mound arrangements, demonstrates the complexity of effigy mound society despite the absence of large
settlements. The construction of some of the larger mounds would have
required coordination of large groups of people. Further, burials in the
many different effigy mounds communicates a status of a certain kind.
The location of many burials in the head or heart of a mound describes an
intimate connection between the people and the mound form in which
they were interred. This has often been interpreted as representing the
existence of animal- and spirit-inspired clans among the effigy mound
people, although there may have been other reasons where individuals are
linked to a particular type of animal or spirit. The head and heart regions
of animals and people figure prominently in the iconography of Indian
people throughout North American in the form of a "heart line"—an
arrow-like line connecting the head and the heart (figure 1.9). In Native
American traditions, these represent the "life force" of special animals,
spirits, and people.

Despite the association between zoomorphic (animal-like) mound
forms and people, the death of an individual seems not to have been

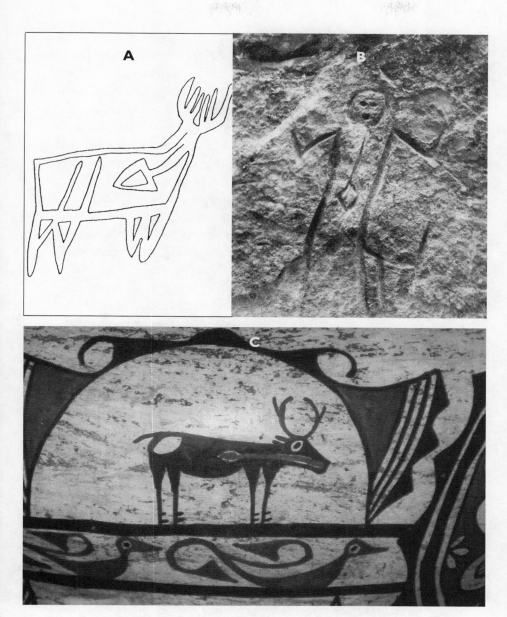

Figure 1.9. Heart lines in Wisconsin and other Indian art: (*a*) antlered animal carving from the Hole-in-the-Wall rock art site in southwestern Wisconsin; (*b*) human figure, interpreted as a religious/medicine specialist commonly referred to as a shaman, from the Gullickson's Glen rock shelter in Wisconsin; and (*c*) animal painted on a relatively modern (ca. 1910) Zuni clay pot from southwestern United States on display at the University of Wisconsin–Waukesha library.

necessary to stimulate the construction of a particular form. Burial may have taken place only if the clan descendents or those otherwise associated with the animal or spirit involved had died during the intervals of mound construction. The interment would be appropriate but not mandatory. This would explain the absence of burials in many of the mounds.

While mounds vary greatly in size, most effigy mound burials themselves do not contain lavish grave goods or notable symbols denoting great differences in social status. Most burials either lack grave items or have fairly simple offerings in the form of tools, arrows, tobacco pipes, or clay pots. Some unusual situations do, however, deserve further study. At the Heller mound group on the east shore of Lake Winnebago in eastern Wisconsin, for example, a complete set of deer antlers was placed across the lower legs of a young woman interred below a long, tapering (snake?) mound. As reported by the site excavator Chandler Rowe in 1953, holes were mysteriously drilled into the lower ends of her femurs.[33] In the eastern part of the North America, deer antler headdresses were worn by special people during ceremonies and rituals in both ancient and more recent times. These are medicine people, frequently referred to as shamans, or even tribal leaders, as among the Iroquois of the Northeast. As we shall see, re-examined evidence from the Four Lakes effigy mound district points to a society even more complex than presently conceived.

The Meaning of Effigy Mounds

Effigy mounds were built in a variety of forms, many of which are recognizable as animals and powerful spirit beings important in many Native American cultures. The most common zoomorphic mounds are both straight- and curve-winged birds resembling eagles and hawks, bears, and long-tailed "water spirits." Others resemble canines (wolf or fox), water birds such as geese and possibly cranes, deer, buffalo, and water mammals such as otter or mink. Some spectacular mounds were in the form of humans. Other shapes, however, elude easy visual identification, such as the ubiquitous linear mounds commonly found with animal effigies. However, the meaning of even these can be inferred from native belief systems, arrangement within the groups, and the physical relationship to key natural landscape features.

Generally speaking, Native Americans traditionally perceived themselves as an integral part of the natural world and active participants in maintaining cosmological order. The activities of humans are closely linked to the forces and powers found in the natural environment—in animals, plants, water, sky, and earth features such as rocks, hills, and mountains—that in a modern European-American worldview are without life or spiritual significance. Among many peoples of the world, the cosmos is perceived to be vertically layered, most often separated into the sky, the earth, and a darker underworld.[34] In many Native American traditions the four sacred directions define a horizontal axis, and a center world connects the vertical layers. Passage from this world to the others can be accomplished by religious specialists or by death. The different parts of the cosmos or world are ruled by certain key spirits or deities, although it is important to note that the distinction between natural and supernatural is largely a modern and Western development.[35]

For example, at the top of the four- or five-layered Ho-Chunk cosmos is Earthmaker, the creator of the world who otherwise stays out of human affairs. Earthmaker in recent times is symbolized by a cross representing the four sacred directions, and such a symbol appears in ancient iconography associated with the Mississippian culture that succeeded the Woodland people. Among the Ho-Chunk, the earth itself is ruled over by Hare, the grandson of Earthmaker, or in some versions a "water spirit" that lives in the center of the earth.[36] In the 1850s, the naturalist, surveyor, and engineer Increase Lapham mapped one huge mound in the form of a cross, oriented in roughly the four principal directions, on a large prairie in south-central Wisconsin (figure 1.10).

In much Native American cosmology, animals, celestial bodies, and spirits embody the forces and blessings contained within the different parts of the cosmos. Within this general framework, a duality is frequently expressed in terms of an upper world and a lower world. The sun, moon, stars, and birds are of the sky or upper world. Common sky spirits are the powerful thunderbirds who are "in control of almost all powers that man can image."[37] Some bird effigy mounds re-create exactly the thunderbird iconography used by more recent Indian people as seen in figure 1.11.

The ubiquitous conical mounds found in effigy mound groups are mostly found within those groups on elevated locations. Some of these date earlier and later than the effigy mounds, but others are clearly built by

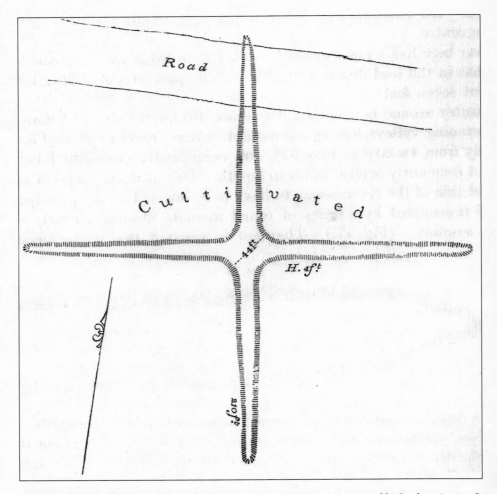

Figure 1.10. Large earthen cross on a prairie in southeastern Wisconsin mapped by Lapham in 1851. It measured 210 feet (north-south) and was four feet high in the center.

the effigy mound people as determined by archaeological research. It is feasible that these conical mounds have upper-world associations as represented by celestial forms such as the sun and moon. Many Native American societies viewed the sun and moon as virtual deities. In later Mississippian iconography, the world itself was represented by a cross (the four directions again) enclosed in a circle.

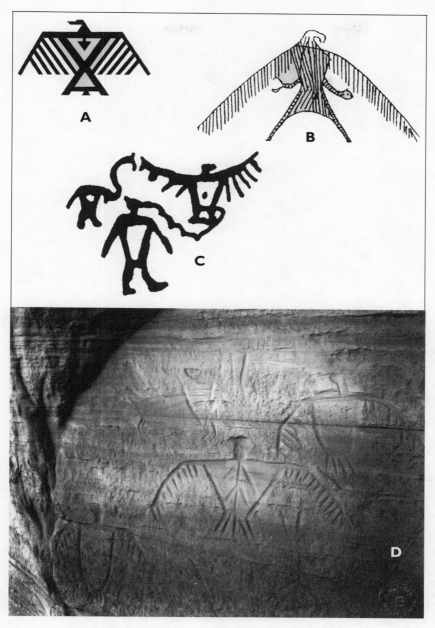

Figure 1.11. Thunderbirds in Indian art: (*a*) drawing of a thunderbird from a nineteenth-century Ho-Chunk woven bag; (*b*) drawing of a thunderbird from a Menominee birch bark scroll; (*c*) humans deriving power from thunderbirds at the Roche a Cri rock art site in Roche a Cri State Park; (*d*) thunderbirds from the Twin Bluffs rock art site in central Wisconsin.

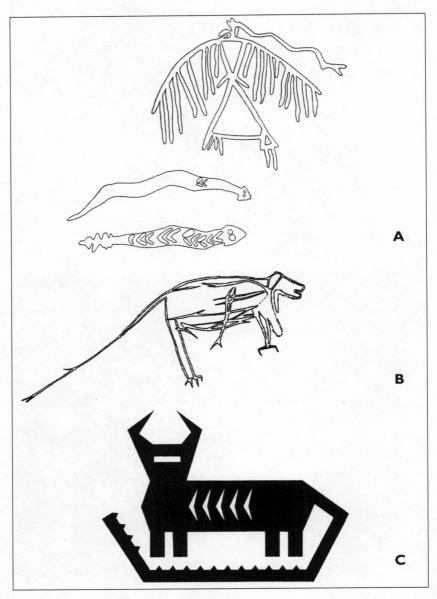

Figure 1.12. Upper- and lower-world iconography in Indian art: (*a*) figures at the La Moille rock art site in Minnesota as drawn by Lewis in 1890; (*b*) a long-tailed water spirit carving from the Samuels Cave site; (*c*) depiction of underground water panther or water spirit similar to that used by several western Great Lakes tribes as a design on bags.

Various animals, including bears, represent the earth, while special supernatural creatures such as various types of snakes, serpents, and long-tailed water spirits represent the lower and watery part of the lower world. Depictions of such a worldview occur in ancient iconography in the Midwest, as with the famous La Moille rock paintings in Minnesota, where an elaborate thunderbird is accompanied by snakes and coil-tailed animals, among other beings (figure 1.12).

Bears, water spirits, and snakes loom especially important in the interpretation of effigy mounds because of their related roles in some traditions as ancestors of human clans and as important figures in the very creation of the world. Effigy mound forms referred to here as "water spirits" belong to a class of powerful long-tailed supernatural beings commonly found in Native American belief systems where they are perceived in various forms. These spirits often have ominous connotations but are also viewed as sources of great medicine and power. In the Midwest, the Menominee and Potawatomi have the Underground Water Panther; the Ho-Chunk equivalent is the horned water spirit; and in some cases the creature is understood to be a composite of features of different animals.

Robert Hall observed that the many long-tailed forms referred to as panthers, turtles, and lizards in popular and archaeological literature are almost all of this class of water spirits.[38] One difference is in perspective. Some, like the so-called panther form, are shown in profile, while the others (turtles, lizards) are flattened as though viewed from above in aerial perspective. Other animals, including bears, are also occasionally presented in this flattened, aerial perspective. The two different forms may be represented in other art. Incised drawings on a broken stone tobacco pipe found by an artifact collector in Minnesota show long-tailed, horned creatures with zigzag "power lines" emanating from the eyes or face on both the sides and the top of the pipe (figure 1.13a).[39] The creatures on the side are panther forms while those on the top of the pipe resemble horned lizards. These may be two different spirits, but decoration details and their positioning suggest that the same creature is being shown in both aerial and profile perspectives, thus matching the two forms of mounds. A similar horned lizard-like creature (also with "power lines") appears on a smoking pipe from western Wisconsin (figure 1.13b) and aerial perspective, horned water spirit mounds have been documented (figure 1.14).

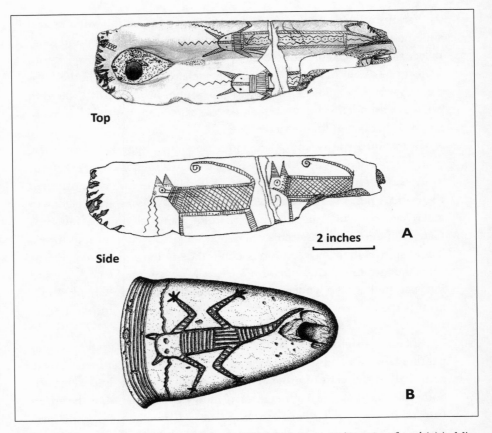

Figure 1.13. Renderings of possible horned water spirits on broken smoking pipes found (*a*) in Minnesota and (*b*) western Wisconsin.

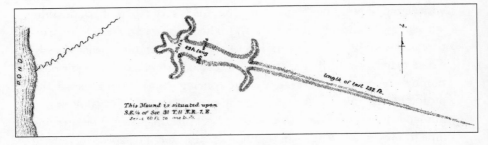

Figure 1.14. Huge horned effigy mound mapped by William Canfield in the nineteenth century in Sauk County, Wisconsin, north of the Four Lakes.

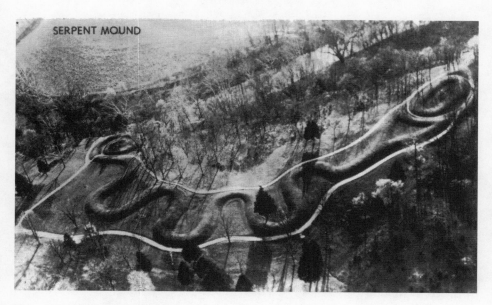

Figure 1.15. The Great Serpent Mound of Ohio.

Here I propose that many of the tapering linear mounds common to the area, as well as occasional curved and serpentine mounds, should also be included as effigies—those of snakes. The most famous snake effigy in the world, the Great Serpent Mound of Ohio, is outside of the effigy mound region but attests to the widespread significance of the creature (figure 1.15). It is currently dated to just after construction of the midwestern effigy mounds.

Curved, bent, wavy, and serpentine-like forms occur throughout the effigy mound region and the Four Lakes mound district, but most of the snake forms are depicted as straight. In different versions of Ho-Chunk world-creation stories, water spirits, bears, and/or snakes secured the corners of the world after its creation by Earthmaker to keep it from spinning out of control—the snakes speared the earth like tent pegs.[40] The association of snakes with this securing role in creation may account for the frequent straight, stake-like form in effigy mounds.

The concept of complementary yet opposing upper and lower forces is widespread throughout the cultures of the world, a metaphor for the contrasts of light/dark, life/death, order/chaos. This dualistic view of the world may be a cultural universal, deeply embedded in human consciousness. Native people throughout the Americas expressed this theme as a struggle of great supernatural celestial birds with lower-world creatures. Far afield of the effigy mound region, the Mexican national flag bears an ancient Aztec emblem that depicts this tension: an eagle struggling with a serpent.

Much closer to the Four Lakes is Devil's Lake, which occupies a rock-strewn basin in the Wisconsin Baraboo Hills, created, according to one Ho-Chunk legend, by a battle between the thunderbirds and water spirits. In some stories, the lake itself is the residence of a powerful water spirit and was called Sacred or Holy Lake by Indian people, a connotation misunderstood and thus changed by the new settlers.[41] Effigy mounds found here include a forked-tail bird or bird-man at the south end of the lake and a water spirit on the north end. Interestingly, the water spirit pipe from Minnesota mentioned earlier was made of Baraboo Pipestone, a purple stone found adjacent to Devil's Lake, and is of a style thought to date earlier than the effigy mounds.

Effigy Mounds and Social Structure

In Native American ideology, the structure of the world and the structure of human society are closely related. Many Indian people traditionally believe they are descended from key animal spirits in the form of clans, taking on the powers and roles of the animals in balancing and maintaining social and cosmic order. Most animal-like effigy mounds have parallels in the various animal-based clans of the diverse Algonquian- and Siouan-speaking peoples that inhabited the Upper Midwest in the historic period. Robert Hall noted a particular correspondence between Ho-Chunk clans and effigy mounds, although other forms, such as geese and other water birds and water mammals, are not found among Ho-Chunk clans—at least not in modern times.[42] The early Ho-Chunk ethnographer Paul Radin reported that thunderbird, bear, and water spirit clans were among the most important among the Ho-Chunk. Significantly, birds, bears, and water spirit forms are the most common of the ancient effigy mounds according to archaeological records.[43] While this correlation does not prove that the Ho-Chunk are descendants of the effigy mound builders, it does demonstrate the longevity of this symbolic arrangement in the

Upper Midwest, despite enormous cultural changes, and suggests that Ho-Chunk and effigy mound people may have had similar social patterns.

Like the cosmos itself, Native American societies are sometimes divided into two divisions or moieties representing the upper sky realm and the lower earth/water realm. In these cases social cohesion is maintained by the custom of exogamy—people must marry a member from the opposite moiety. Each moiety is subdivided into a number of clans, many with their own origin stories. Among the Ho-Chunk, the most important in the upper division is Thunderbird Clan, and it is this clan that still supplies the traditional chief of the Ho-Chunk Nation. The lower division is further subdivided by clans of the earth, headed by Bear, and clans of the water, headed by Water Spirit but including Snake. Similar sky/earth divisions are also found among diverse North American tribes, including the Menominee of Wisconsin, who have a moiety system very similar to the Ho-Chunk, their ancient neighbors.

In the Midwest, the existence of dual upper and lower moieties has been traced back at least two thousand years as indicated by dual burial mound customs in Illinois. A dual mortuary ritual—one mound and other unmounded—is suggested by recent discoveries for about the same time along the Mississippi River in Wisconsin.[44] A dual social division of the later Mississippian society at the ancient city of Cahokia in southern Illinois is also reflected by Mound 72, a spectacular mortuary facility dated to ca. A.D. 1050. Here, an unusually important individual, probably a paramount chief associated with the upper world, was found interred on a hawk- or falcon-shaped bed of shell beads. Another burial underlay this one—that of an individual oriented in the opposite direction—and buried face down.[45] This man possibly represents someone from the lower world moiety.

In some Native American origin stories, tribes formed after the creation of the world, as the animals and spirits were transformed into humans and these clans gathered at certain places. The Menominee of northeastern Wisconsin explain that the first human among them was transformed from a white copper-tailed bear that lived beneath the earth, forming the Bear Clan people.[46] Bear was later joined by Thunderbird and the Thunderbird Clan. The Bear Clan is prominent among the Menominee's earth-related clans, as it is with the Ho-Chunk.

One creation story among the Ho-Chunk recounts how a thunderbird alighted on a tree and became human, the progenitor of the Thunderbird

Clan. After some waiting and anticipation, a white, horned water spirit emerged from a small nearby lake and "became human and walked," giving birth to the Water Spirit Clan, prominent among the water-related clans.[47] Other animals became human at other places, but all joined together to form the Ho-Chunk Nation.

World Creation and Renewal

Effigy mounds clearly symbolize the three natural realms—air, earth, and water—that "provide the resources on which humans depend."[48] Mallam theorized that the mounds were built to maintain balance and harmony to the natural world and those places to which people returned again and again for the purpose of renewing the world and lifeways of the people. Cyclical re-creation or renewal of the world is a common theme in traditional Native American religious beliefs. The birth-death cycles of nature are observed through many types of rituals and laid one basis for ordering life. These are linked to the cycle of human life and death, which can be traced far back into antiquity. By examining the contents and arrangement of two-thousand-year-old mounds and mounded cemeteries found on both elevations and lower on floodplains in Illinois, the archaeologists Jane Buikstra and Douglas Charles concluded that not only a two-part social organization (moiety) existed but that the mortuary and mound building activities "re-created the cosmos, vertically and horizontally differentiated."[49]

The periodic ritual re-creation of the world by communal monument building is a common feature of the human story. European stone monuments such as Stonehenge and Avebury in England and the mounded New Grange site in Ireland clearly mark the cyclic birth and death of the seasons, and both served as burial places. Research at the Stonehenge monument reveals the observation or commemoration of annual solar cycles and perhaps a much longer lunar cycle.[50]

Here, it is important to note that the physical modeling of the world and the structure of human society was not unique to mound building. In fact, it was quite common among Native Americans in more recent times as expressed in other types of landscapes such village layouts and in architecture. For example, several late-nineteenth-century Ho-Chunk related to

Radin that the old villages were laid out to mirror the clan arrangement, with upper-world clans living on the southwest and earth clans oriented toward the northeast.[51] Elsewhere, the Osage are said to have been divided into two groups "just as the cosmos is divided into earth and sky" and that the clans in Osage villages were "organized as mirror images of the cosmos" with an east–west road—the path of the sun—dividing the two groupings of clans.[52] Ancient Cahokia in southern Illinois, the only American Indian city north of Mexico, was laid out according to cosmological principles, with orientation of the city and its principle platform mounds to the sacred cardinal directions, and like the Osage village plan, possibly divided into north and south halves by a main east–west axis that bisects the great Monks Mound.[53]

Ceremonial structures and even houses very often served as models for the cosmos, sometimes recapitulating creation itself. The geographer and archaeologist William Gartner showed how the earth lodge of the Great Plains Pawnee incorporated concepts of "sacred" geography, including references to celestial bodies, and was used during certain ceremonies to reenact the creation of the world and the Pawnee people. Peter Nabokov and Robert Easton in their excellent book *Native American Architecture* document wide-ranging examples from throughout North America of this intimate connection between architecture and cosmology.[54]

World renewal seems to have been a major theme in effigy mound ceremonialism—the periodic and cyclical re-creations of both the world and its people in the form of their original animal and spirit ancestors. The mounds of migratory water birds like geese, prominent in the Four Lakes, are obvious symbols of the cyclical death and rebirth of the earth: geese leave in the fall and return in the spring. The existence of the giant Earthmaker symbol mapped by Increase Lapham provides a major link to the concept of world creation itself. The concept of re-creation may help to explain the existence of the most unusual of effigy mound forms—those of human beings with water spirit or buffalo-like horns and bird forms with human characteristics. Although other interpretations are certainly possible, these forms could well have meant to capture or symbolize the transformation of spirits into human clans.[55]

What determined the construction of a particular mound form at a particular time will never be known. Considering the cultural customs of more recent Indian people, it is possible that these involved the directions of religious specialists who were not just invested with certain types of sacred knowledge but were also in touch with the spirit world through visions and dreams. Such specialists are variously referred to as shamans, medicine people, or priests. As mentioned in the preface, the existence of medicine societies in the Upper Midwest could extend back at least nine hundred years, based on combined archaeological and ethnographic information. It is also possible that clan leaders were involved since in more recent times they direct certain clan ceremonies. Whatever the case, a variety of geographical and other factors that had special cultural meaning to the mound builders determined how to make the mounds and where to place them on the natural terrain in relationship to other mounds.

The Effigy Mound Landscape: Cosmology and Geography

A fascinating and extremely important aspect of effigy mound construction is the relationship between effigy mound locations, forms, and arrangements, along with aspects of the natural landscape important in Native American beliefs and worldview. Modern research focuses on these relationships to explain the patterning of effigy mound landscapes.[56]

Distribution of Mound Forms

Most major mound forms can be found throughout the effigy mound region, but there are significant differences in frequencies of certain forms, which reflect broad geographic differences.[57] Bird mounds are most common in central and western Wisconsin, especially in the hill country of the southwestern area and along the bluffs and terraces of the Wisconsin and Mississippi river valleys. The natural association of birds with high places such as cliffs, bluffs, and ridges is obvious. As well, bears (and other earth animals) are concentrated in central and western Wisconsin, while long-tailed water spirits and water birds are most commonly found in mound groups in low-lying eastern Wisconsin where lakes, rivers, and wetlands abound. The great marshes of eastern Wisconsin are today the migration route of millions of ducks, geese, and other waterfowl.

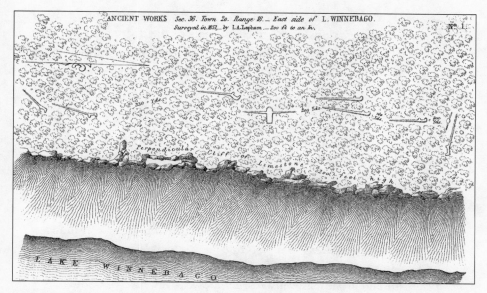

Figure 1.16. This mound group mapped by Lapham occupies a high, west-facing escarpment or cliff top overlooking Lake Winnebago in eastern Wisconsin (now High Cliff State Park) and shows both upper-world and lower-world symbolism in the form of birds and the more numerous water spirits typical of the area.

There are exceptions, but in some cases these associations still relate to changes in local geography. Although birds, with the exception of water birds, are not as common in eastern Wisconsin, they still can be found in important elevated places such as the high glacial moraines (see figure 1.1) and the long Niagara escarpment east of Lake Winnebago (figure 1.16).

Within the eastern and western areas of the effigy mound region, dualism is frequently apparent by the types of mounds present in mound groupings. Birds (often water birds) and water spirits appear many times together in the east, while birds and bears are frequently representatives of the upper and lower worlds in the western part of the effigy mound region.

In between these extremes in south-central Wisconsin and around the Four Lakes, mound groups containing all three forms—birds, mammals (especially bears), and water spirits—are common and are sometimes found together, thus providing the idealized models for effigy mound ceremonialism. Even within this more restricted area, there are differences in the frequencies of mound forms that seem related to the broader natural landscape. Birds, especially the larger ones, are far more common in the generally higher elevations of the northern part of the district, while the southern part with its extensive areas of marsh is dominated by lower-world symbolism that includes many forms interpreted as snakes.

Locations

Although mound groupings are characteristically located at prominent places on bodies of water in areas with obvious access to many food resources, locations also had special cultural meanings to the builders. Many effigy landscapes owe their origins to previously existing mounds; some were built hundreds of years earlier, and subsequent mounds incorporated these into the overall arrangement. Thus, continuity of sanctified places played a major role in the development of effigy mound landscapes.

Effigy mound groups, as well as earlier mounds, are also commonly associated with springs.[58] One example is previously mentioned Nitschke mounds, where springs are the only source of water in the vicinity of the mound areas. Springs are the source of life-giving water, symbolic of life itself, and are therefore held in reverence by ancient people around the world. Fine sands, like those in springs, are occasionally found in mounds of all periods, perhaps placed there as a symbol of the life-and-rebirth concept.

In the Four Lakes mound district, many mound groups are at or near major springs. An unusually dense cluster of effigy mound groups surrounded the spring-fed Lake Wingra, a small, shallow body of water off the main water-transportation route. Some of these springs were considered sacred by the Ho-Chunk residents of the Madison area in the early twentieth century. Like nearby Lake Mendota, deposits of white clay marl cover the lake bottom of Lake Wingra, the dens of water spirits in the traditions of midwestern Indian peoples.[59]

Arrangements and Internal Patterns

The arrangement of effigy mound landscapes differ from area to area, and from grouping to grouping, but there appear to be clearly organized principles consistent with underlying structure and theme (world renewal or re-recreation), as well as other reoccurring factors.

Archaeologist Amy Rosebrough of the Wisconsin Historical Society has indeed identified what she believes to be a "topographically sensitive grammar" to mound construction.[60]

One can easily see many of the following principles and factors illustrated by the mound groupings already shown in this chapter, along with a closer view of the extremely well-organized Nitschke I group (figure 1.17). Other illustrations are provided as we later tour the Four Lakes effigy mound landscape, where some of the best examples still exist. In general, we find:

(1) a tendency for mounds to be built consistent with orientation of the natural feature upon which they were built. Mounds are often parallel or perpendicular to the landform;

(2) a tendency for animal mounds to be built with legs downslope and with heads downstream when located along streams and rivers;

(3) the horizontal and vertical division of the upper and lower worlds following the contours of the natural landscape. Often, mound forms such as conicals and effigy mounds representing air, earth, and water are spatially separated;

(4) orientation and association of some forms to natural features associated with the forms. Notably, water spirit and snake mounds commonly point to or away from water bodies such as lakes, streams, and springs. Mounds are neatly arranged around villages in some cases;

(5) use of natural landscape to animate the mound forms. Birds fly gracefully across ridge tops or up and down slopes. Geese, the harbingers of spring and fall, the death and rebirth of the world, are typically arranged on slopes so as to be arriving or leaving adjacent wetlands and bodies of water. Animals parade across ridges, changing direction, sometimes subtly, with the orientation of the terrain; water spirits and snakes move up and down elevations, crawling to and from water.

Some have noted that the orientations of some mounds in North America appear to match astronomical phenomena such as the winter and summer solstices—the shortest and longest days of the years—and have suggested that the mounds' alignments closely observe the movements of the sun, moon, and stars.[61] Certainly the custom of using ceremonial structures for observing natural seasonal cycles is well demonstrated in other parts of the world. But one of the problems with these sometimes

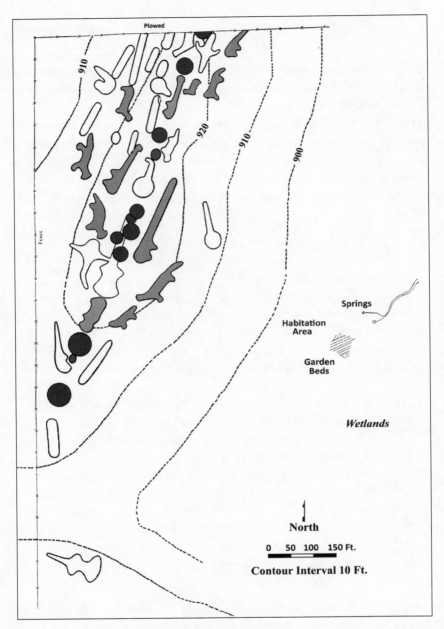

Figure 1.17. The Nitschke I group exemplifies many aspects of effigy mound organization. The mounds are oriented along the top and sides of a drumlin above springs with animals on the sides mainly shown with legs downslope. Conical mounds line the very top, several superimposed on an aerial perspective water spirit. A lone water spirit in front of the drumlin arcs to the spring-fed wetlands. A camp site was recently found at the base of the group near ancient garden beds.

controversial explanations, of course, is that given the myriad of possible sighting points and lines among the thousands of differently oriented mounds and their appendages, almost any alignment that one is looking for could, eventually, be discerned. As we look closely at the Four Lakes mound ceremonial landscape, a few such evocative cases of alignments come to the fore, although purposeful alignments remain obscure.

One thing is clear though: effigy mound arrangements are elegantly patterned, reflecting a number of factors that had great meaning to the builders and thus form ceremonial landscapes such as that of Madison and Four Lakes. These well-organized mound-building rituals in turn reflect a complex ancient society generally not recognized as such. While a product of rapid cultural change, this society and the landscape it created nevertheless had roots in an even more ancient past.

2 | The Ancient Mound Builders

Native Americans first came to the Four Lakes thirteen thousand years ago. Like the lakes themselves, populations subsequently ebbed and flowed, leaving behind many traces of their existence. Archaeologists have outlined this human history based on more than a century of research, and studies by a variety of other specialists have reconstructed broad climatic and environmental changes that many times directly affected the lives of the people.

The landscape sculpted by the effigy mound people is the most visible vestige of pre-Columbian life in this area and certainly the most amazing. The explosion of effigy mound building across the Upper Midwest is unique in North American prehistory and reflected general social, economic, and even climatic changes taking place across the mid-continent during the first millennium A.D. While the making of effigy mounds departed from earlier mound building customs, it had its origins in much earlier customs and beliefs.

Ancient Hunters

Mound building did not begin in the Four Lakes until 2,500 years ago, but the ancestors of the mound builders were here some 11,000 years earlier. Before that time, the land was covered by mountainous glaciers, which would have prevented settlement. One glacial lobe covered

Table 2.1. Cultural and Environmental Chronology of the Four Lakes through Pre-Columbian Abandonment

Tradition/stage	Time	Climate	Environment	Characteristics
Paleo-Indian	11,000–8000 B.C.	Cold and snowy	Glacial Lake Yahara, spruce forest, swamps	Small bands of hunters
Archaic	8000–500 B.C.	Cool early; warm and dry middle; fluctuating wet and dry at end	Hardwood forests and wetlands early; spread of prairies and oak savanna; increasing oak forest late	Hunters and gatherers, long-distance trade, population increase at end, first cemeteries; first mounds at very end
Early Woodland	500 B.C.–A.D. 100	Cooler and wet	Oak forest dominant	Hunters and gatherers, first pottery, long-distance trade, longer warm weather settlements, mound building
Middle Woodland	A.D. 100–500	Cool and wet, sharp drought near end	Oak forest dominant	Hunters and gatherers, long-distance trade, connections to Hopewell culture, large conical mounds, villages
Late Woodland	A.D. 500–1250	Warm, a bit dry, drought after A.D. 1100	Oak savanna, some prairie and forest	Bow and arrow, increasing corn cultivation, population increase, effigy mounds, pit houses, fortified villages toward end

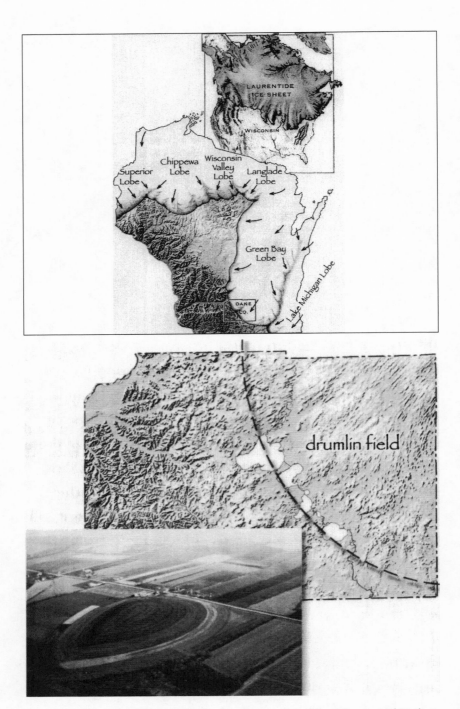

Figure 2.1. *Above*, the natural landscape of the western part of Dane County and Madison was molded by glacial action. The eastern part is an older, dissected landscape. *Below*, a drumlin and map showing glaciated landscape of western part of Dane County.

the Four Lakes, and a high, long ridge, just west of Madison, marks its terminus; a mile-thick sheet of ice covered the present site of Wisconsin's state capitol (figure 2.1).

As the ice age ended and the glaciers slowly melted, small bands of hunters followed game into the area, thus beginning the long Native American occupation of the Four Lakes. The first people, called Paleo-Indians by archaeologists, moved into a cold and wet environment. Torrents of water and dirt from the melting glaciers formed wide river channels, great and frigid lakes, and vast plains of sand, gravel, and rock. The glaciers scraped and gouged the countryside, leaving behind hills and ridges—drumlins, kames, eskers, moraines—as well as deep kettles created by large blocks of detached and wasting ice that would later become small lakes.

Later mound builders gave cultural and spiritual meaning to the natural landscape the glaciers created. Southwest-trending drumlins, large oblong hills of sand and gravel deposited by one glacial lobe, would be especially important to the effigy mound people.

The present lakes of the Four Lakes district are remnants of one huge body of water formed from glacial meltwater named Glacial Lake Yahara by geologists.[1] The vast, cold lake covered much of what is now the Yahara river drainage basin (figure 2.2). Paleo-Indians lived along the shores of this immense lake between 11,000 and 8000 B.C., leaving behind distinctive spear points similar to those found at the time throughout North America. The earliest of these points, called Clovis, Gainey, and Folsom, can be easily identified because of distinctive grooves or flutes for securing these attachment to shafts (figure 2.3).[2] Long, thin, and artistically made spear points later replaced the fluted types.

Paleo-Indians often fashioned spear points from fine and beautifully colored stone originating far from the find locations, which indicates that they covered huge territories or participated in exchange or trade with other small bands of similarly roaming people. The Paleo-Indians obviously gave special meaning to these stones. One type of rock especially important to this early people is called Hixton Silicified Sandstone, which is found only in west-central Wisconsin. The colors of this rock, from off-white to gold to reddish, capture the shades of the sun.

Spruce and fir boreal forest covered the land, much like the environment found today in parts of Canada and Alaska. The climate was harsh and cold with short, cool summers. Humans shared this environment with large and lumbering mammoth and mastodon, giant beaver, and other

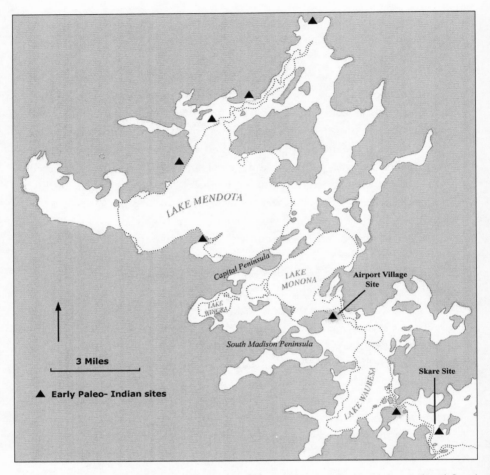

Figure 2.2. Glacial Lake Yahara showing locations of Paleo-Indian sites that have produced fluted points.

animals that disappeared at the end of the ice age. Later Paleo-Indians may have hunted caribou herds migrating through the area, as well as moose, elk, and other more familiar game. Specialized hunters in the western part of the continent focused on now-extinct forms of bison—the ancestors of modern buffalo. These animals inhabited southern Wisconsin at some point as demonstrated by the exciting discovery by a boy in 2005 of a large, horned *bison occidentalus* skull on the banks of the Wisconsin River just north of the Four Lakes (figure 2.4). But studies of the pollen sequence,

Figure 2.3. Paleo-Indian spear or projectile points from the Skare site. The right three are fluted Folsom points; *e* and *f* from honey-colored Hixton Silicified Sandstone from west-central Wisconsin. The left three are later Paleo-Indian points; *b* and *c* from dark blue Moline chert from northwestern Illinois.

trapped and sealed in area bogs, show that the boreal environment of the early Paleo-Indians gave way first to thick conifer and then hardwood forests until about 4500 B.C.—not good habitats for bison herds that need vast grasslands for grazing.[3] Bison or buffalo never seemed to have been present in any great numbers in the Four Lakes because their bones have not been found in the many excavated archaeological sites that span thousands of years.

Judging from the sizes and small number of Paleo-Indian sites, the population was quite small, and the people lived most of the year in tiny family bands moving over large areas in search of food. Occasionally, perhaps on an annual basis, the scattered family bands gathered together for communal hunts and group social activities. One such gathering place is the Skare site on the Yahara River between lakes Waubesa and Kegonsa currently being investigated by archaeologists at the University of Wisconsin–Madison (hereafter UW). Occupied as early as 9000 B.C., artifact collectors and archaeologists discovered large numbers of small Folsom points

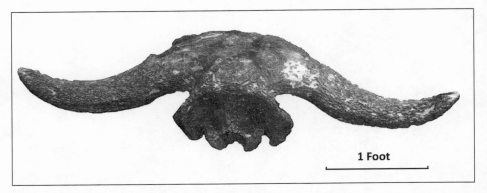

Figure 2.4. Ancient bison horns found on the Wisconsin River.

through the years, as well as many distinctive tools for scraping hides and working bone.[4] Some artifact collectors say that earlier and larger Clovis points have also been found on the same site. In the 1990s, UW archaeologists found remnants of one of the last village sites occupied in the Four Lakes before the area was abandoned ca. A.D. 1250. The researchers unearthed a fluted Paleo-Indian Folsom point beneath the remains of one house in the village, attesting to the long use of that very spot.[5] What game these early people hunted at Skare is yet to be determined.

The Archaic Tradition

Over the next several millennia, the climate continued to alter the environment. As the temperatures warmed, the glacial environment retreated northward. Easily hunted species such as elk and deer proliferated. Expanding forests provided a variety of edible plants and animal life. Streams replaced frigid and rapidly running glacial discharge and offered abundant fish. The many lakes and wetlands left in the wake of the retreating glaciers also provided habitat for fish, waterfowl, and aquatic mammals. Among the new bodies of water are remnants of the once great glacial Lake Yahara: lakes Mendota, Monona, Waubesa, Kegonsa, and Wingra.

People of the area adapted to these changes by inventing new types of tools and weapons, developing food and resource gathering strategies, and eventually growing into larger and more complex societies. The long period of environmental and cultural change is called the Archaic tradition or period by archaeologists and is dated between 8000 and 500 B.C. Archaeologists divide the Archaic into three successive stages, Early (8000–6000 B.C.), Middle (6000–1700 B.C.), and Late (1700–500 B.C.), based on changes in artifact forms, lifestyles, and newly revised dates based on advances in radiocarbon dating.[6]

As with the Paleo-Indian period, the Early Archaic is poorly understood, again due to the very low population density. Much of this period is known only from scattered stone spear points and tools found throughout the area, often times at the same places as the Paleo-Indians before them. It is believed that Early Archaic people lived much like their Paleo-Indian ancestors, ranging widely over the midwestern landscape in search of game. At one rare excavated site in northern Wisconsin, archaeologists found that people lived on small mammals, turtles, birds, and possibly deer.[7] Elsewhere in Wisconsin, evidence of the earliest burial practices appear in the form of a cremated human and burned stone spear points.[8] Cremation continued to be one of the many mortuary customs used by Indians through the time of the mound builders and into the eighteenth century.

As the climate continued to warm, food resources increased and human populations grew, leading to a highly mobile hunting and gathering way of life. Indians used new technologies to take advantage of increased food and other resources that included use of wooden spear throwers, large stone axes, milling stones for grinding plants, and other specialized tools and weapons. Lifestyles differed over time and from region to region depending on the local environment as climate changed the availability of many foods. There were, however, common developments such as long-distance trading networks, efficient use of smaller territories, and the appearance of the first cemeteries.

Climate

For several thousand years during the Middle Archaic the climate became much warmer than today, accompanied by a significant drop in moisture. This resulted in a great, long drought that climatologists call the altithermal or Mid-Holocene Dry Period. The timing and effects of this climatic change varied from region to region across North America and many parts of the world, with some areas not affected at all. In the Four Lakes, the dry period is dated between 4500 and 1500 B.C., based on pollen studies. Climatic models suggest that the warmest and driest periods occurred early during that time.[9]

Vegetation adapted to much warmer and dryer conditions, and expanded as a consequence of this climatic change. Hardwood forests contracted and grasslands spread over the Four Lakes region. Streams dried up, water tables dropped, and lakes shrank. At its most severe, the great drought of the Middle Archaic could have limited many types of foods. Studies of animal remains elsewhere in the Midwest show that deer underwent nutritional stress and that climate affected the populations of other animals.[10] Not surprisingly, both animal and human populations clustered at better-watered areas. We can assume that many habitation sites hugging the shores of the shrinking lakes became submerged as rains returned, hiding them from further discovery. However, some ancient stone tools are occasionally recovered from offshore lake beds.

On the other hand, the great drought established oak savanna as a major vegetation type in southern Wisconsin, one that the first white settlers found in Four Lakes in the 1830s.[11] Oak savannas, frequently called "oak openings," are prairie grasses and forest herbs with scattered oak trees giving them a "parkland" appearance. Such open woodlands, along with prairie, are rich habitats for deer and elk. Oak savannas are maintained by frequent prairie fires that kill off trees except for burr and white oak, which are fire tolerant. These fires can be set by lightning strikes or accidentally by humans during the dry part of the year, but historical evidence suggests that Indian people also intentionally set grass fires to maintain oak savannas as game habitat.[12]

Archaic Life

Until recently, life during the Middle Archaic period in general was not well documented, but discoveries in Four Lakes are changing that situation. Wisconsin Historical Society (hereafter WHS) archaeologists discovered and excavated two sites prior to highway construction that provide important insights into the seasonal mobility and other aspects of Middle Archaic life (figure 2.5).

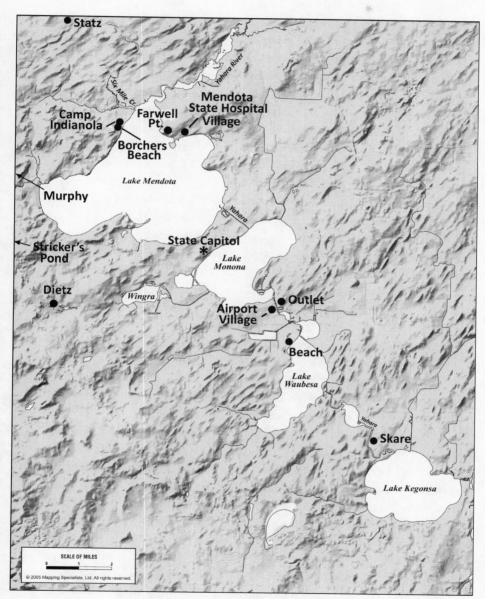

Figure 2.5. Shaded relief map showing sites in the Four Lakes discussed in text.

The Murphy and Statz sites were situated at wetland edges and these same environments remained attractive to the later people who reoccupied the sites during the time of effigy mounds.[13] The Murphy site is a comparatively well preserved Archaic camp located west of Lake Mendota in the present community of Middleton. Organic remains from the camp provided radiocarbon dates between 4000 and 3000 B.C. Fragments of hickory and walnut shells were found in ancient pits, preserved through the ages by charring, and this tells us that the camp was probably near a wooded area and used in the fall when these nuts become available. Protein-rich nuts and acorns would remain an extremely important part of the diet for Four Lakes Native Americans through to historic times.

The Statz site is situated northwest of Lake Mendota on a marsh edge and was used at about the same time as the Murphy site but for an entirely different purpose. Here, WHS archaeologists uncovered a highly specialized activity area—a workshop for the production of stone tools from chert, an easily chipped silica stone similar to flint found in nearby geological deposits. Among these tools were spear points and knives needed for hunting game such as deer. The site essentially functioned as a retooling station prior to or during the hunting seasons.

Rains eventually returned toward the end of the Archaic, punctuated with short, dry periods. The pollen record shows increasing oak forest after 1500 B.C. as a result of the moister conditions. A global climatic shift brought both very wet and cooler weather that lasted for centuries into the next cultural tradition, the Woodland.[14]

The increased availability of food and other resources after the dry period stimulated population growth in the Upper Midwest through the succeeding Late Archaic, laying the basis for the first mound building. Native Americans adapted to resource-rich environments by scheduling food-collecting activities in tune with the maximum availability of food—such as fish, deer, nuts, and other plants. In this way families and bands could efficiently use much smaller territories. By the end of the Archaic, people in the Four Lakes were using all major environmental zones for camps, from the shores of the lakes, streams, and wetlands to upland areas. Artifacts from these camps are commonly found throughout the area.

Trade

One of the most spectacular and famous developments of the Middle Archaic was the copper trade that, like the effigy mounds, centered in the Upper Midwest, especially Wisconsin. Large copper deposits occur in northern Michigan and Isle Royale in Lake Superior, but are also found in the form of "float copper" brought down by the glaciers and deposited on the land as ice melted. Exchanged as raw material or finished items, Archaic people made a diverse array of tools, weapons, and ornaments, heated and hammered into the appropriate shapes. The use of copper continued to be a part of ancient life, but between 5000 and 1000 B.C. copper tools were so common in some parts of Wisconsin and adjacent areas that archaeologists began to call the phenomenon the "Old Copper Culture," although many different groups used and traded the metal.[15] Four Lakes people participated in this custom, but not to the extent as in eastern Wisconsin where tens of thousands of copper artifacts have been found over the years.

As the copper trade waned, other more extensive trade networks developed, moving around exotic and symbolic items that would eventually link much of North America in one vast trade network. Many types of necessities were undoubtedly exchanged, but many remarkable and exotic trade items survive on archaeological sites, especially burial places. Among these items are Atlantic Ocean seashell, blue-gray hornstone chert from Indiana, and obsidian or volcanic glass from the Yellowstone area of Wyoming.

The First Cemeteries

As populations grew and territories became smaller, Archaic peoples selected certain prominent places for cemeteries, and rituals related to the burial of the dead became greatly elaborated. In essence, cemeteries become markers by which these bands of people staked their claim to a place in the world by virtue of links to their ancestors buried at these places. The earliest cemeteries recorded in Wisconsin date to the Middle Archaic between about 4000 and 1500 B.C. These are in the form of large "ossuaries" where the dead were interred as bundles of bones, a form of "secondary burial" or "reburial" that continued to be common practice among the later mound builders and some Native Americans groups up through the time of European contact. After death, the body was either left out on a scaffold or buried in the ground until it decomposed. At an appointed time, people gathered the bones of all those who had died during a certain interval, carefully cleaned the bones, and placed them together in the pits. Beautifully made copper tools, weapons, and ornaments accompanied the mass burial during the Middle Archaic. The communal ritual reinforced the common identity of the living people and would have taken place with great ceremony.

A shift in burial practices occurred during the Late Archaic that signals growing social complexity. Cemeteries now contained "in the flesh" burials made immediately after death, and for the first time in Wisconsin there is clear evidence of status differences.[16] Exotic and beautiful grave offerings obtained through long-distance trade accompanied the burials of certain, perhaps high-ranking people. Among the objects were ceremonial stone knives, seashells, and, in one case, a block of obsidian from Wyoming. The use of copper became largely restricted to the manufacture of ornaments and several types of tools. However, the fact that men, women, and even children were buried with these exotic items means that social status extended to family or kinship groups, not just individuals. A red powdery pigment called red ocher covered burials, a custom that spread from eastern North America.

All of the known Archaic cemeteries are located on prominent knolls or hills that easily functioned as visual territorial markers for the people who created the cemeteries. The same type of location became places where even more visible markers were eventually made in the form of earthen mounds. Visible burial structures marking the bones of honored ancestors would have been particularly important if ancestral territories and resources were being contested. Evidence of violence on some skeletons from this time attests to sporadic conflict as populations grew.[17]

Evolution of Mound Building

Mound building in Wisconsin and the Four Lakes began ca. 500 B.C., a transition time between the Archaic and the next archaeological tradition, the Woodland (ca. A.D. 500–1250).[18] The earliest mounds are fairly large, round (conical), or oval mounds built over grave pits dug into the land surface. Some show a continuity of customs from the Archaic as, for example, in the use of red ocher in the death ritual and grave offerings of special items acquired from other parts of North America.

Early diggers found blades of "blue hornstone," a distinctive bluish gray chert from Indiana, along with burials covered with red ocher at the Indian Hills mound group at the mouth of Yahara River at its confluence with the Rock River.[19] Indian Hills, then, is a candidate for the earliest mound construction in the Four Lakes area.

In the Four Lakes the custom of construction of earthen burial mounds continued for another 1,600 years or so, evolving into the giant effigy mound landscape. Data from throughout the Upper Midwest region, especially the spatial arrangement of different mound forms in large groupings, suggest that this evolution took place in four broad phases. First, beginning ca. 500 B.C., large conical mounds were built at a few prominent locations over burial places for certain segments of the population or kinship groups. Second, short linear and low conical mounds were added to these same places but also expanded to adjacent areas. Some short linear mounds are actually attached to earlier conical mounds. Third, between 700 and 1100 A.D, the great wave of effigy mound construction spread throughout the region and included very long linear and many more conical forms. Finally, the building of small conical mounds continued in some places for a time after the rapid demise of the effigy mound building.

Early Woodland

In some respects, the people during the Early Woodland stage (ca. 500 B.C.–A.D. 100) lived much like their ancestors during the Late Archaic. Long-distance trade networks flourished, and items acquired through this trade accompanied the burials of important people. The climate was wetter and a bit cooler than earlier times and the climate today. Bands of people continued to occupy defined territories, occasionally shifting locations to take full advantage of nature's bounty. But people now stayed longer in warm-weather camps or villages supported by a wide variety of foods and other resources found within short travel distances.

In the Four Lakes, Early Woodland people gathered at the aptly named Beach site on Lake Waubesa, which was discovered by Madison area archaeologist Philip Salkin in conjunction with the development of Lake Farms County Park.[20] Careful excavation unearthed the remains of a wide variety of foods used by the people—fish, mammals, waterfowl, and nuts and other plants. The remains of nuts and acorns found at the site indicate that the people continued to live here through the fall. Elsewhere in the state there is evidence that Early Woodland cultivated small crops of sunflowers and squash. As in the Paleo-Indian and Archaic, no evidence of Early Woodland housing has yet been found, probably because they were small, temporary wigwam-like structures that left little surviving evidence.

Pottery

The manufacture of ceramic containers or pottery for storing and cooking food was one major technological innovation during Early Woodland times. The appearance of pottery reflects decreased mobility that made such breakable containers now practical for storage and cooking. Before that, easily transportable hide, bark, and basket containers served for such purposes. Over the next 1,200 years, Woodland potters used local clays mixed with crushed rock to make vessels; the pots became thinner, better made, and more elaborately decorated through time. Archaeological excavations at the Beach site unearthed many fragments of early pottery made in the Four Lakes, and although fragmentary, this comprises one of the largest assemblages of Early Woodland pottery in the Upper Midwest.

Woodland people first roughened or marked the surfaces of the pots with cords or fabrics. Decorations were then stamped, impressed, incised, or trailed on this surface. Although there is much individual variation, the decorative motifs found on pottery were not based on the fanciful whims of the potters or selected for purely aesthetic reasons. The first pots were plain but soon designs and symbols were added that might have represented the people's belief systems and perhaps even kinship division to which the potter belonged. Chevrons found on Woodland pots are interpreted as bird symbols that denote the upper world in Native American cosmology, while other designs, such as some arrangements of parallel

Figure 2.6. Early Woodland pottery from the Mississippi River Valley.

lines, may represent the earth.[21] Long tail-like designs on the bottoms of some Early Woodland pots seem to symbolize snakes or the tails of water spirits (figures 2.6 and 2.8). Variations on these upper-world/lower-world themes appear in decorations on many types of pottery made in the Midwest through to the time of European contact when imported metal containers eliminated the pottery-making craft.

Mounds

Early Woodland burial mounds occur in small groupings of high (six to eight feet) round mounds built over pit graves, which typically contained several individuals buried as extended, "in the flesh" burials, or as bone-bundle reburials. Remnants of grave preparations and burial rituals suggest, like the later effigy mounds, that the concepts of creation and renewal of the earth were a main theme of the ceremonies. At the Early Woodland Hilgen Springs mounds in eastern Wisconsin, for

Figure 2.7. Conical mound at the Outlet site.

example, pieces of limestone and brightly colored fieldstone were found concentrated alongside the central burial pit in one mound; around it were four other such concentrations. Similar arrangements consisting of sod or mounds of dirt in other mounds in the Midwest have been related to the widespread earth creation stories, the four concentrations of sod or dirt representing the four corners of the earth.[22]

Early mounds in the Four Lakes are primarily concentrated at the Yahara River outlets and inlets of the lakes. One, not far from the Early Woodland camps at the Beach site, is the Outlet site on Lake Monona. The Lake Monona outlet area had long been attractive to Native Americans as revealed by excavations at the nearby Airport Village site, a wetland edge occupied almost continuously from Paleo-Indian times through the time of effigy mound building.[23] Conical mounds form the heart the Outlet site grouping. One of the few mounds left at the Outlet site is a fairly large conical mound measuring sixty feet in diameter and eight feet in height (figure 2.7). It and some of the other larger conical mounds may belong to the following Middle Woodland stage, but Early Woodland pottery has been found in the immediate area indicating use of the knoll at that same time.

Figure 2.8. Early Woodland clay pot from Governor Nelson State park reconstructed by Victoria Dirst.

Another area of activity during the Early Woodland was at the northwest shore of Lake Mendota near the inlet of the Yahara River. Here, the Department of Natural Resources archaeologist Victoria Dirst found characteristic Early Woodland pottery sherds while investigating the area in conjunction with the establishment of Governor Nelson State Park.[24] One partially reconstructed pot shows a decoration made by incised lines and the short impressions of a thick cord (figure 2.8). Large conical mounds occupy a knoll not far from the pottery finds, and like other early mound locations, later effigy mounds were built around these.

Middle Woodland

Mound building during the subsequent Middle Woodland stage shows influence from a distant cultural source. Around 200 B.C., the Early Woodland cultures in the northeastern United States evolved into a phenomenal ceremonial movement with related long-distance trade networks called Hopewell, after a nineteenth-century landowner of a large earthwork site. Hopewell ceremonial centers grew in the Ohio and Illinois river valleys, but Hopewell religious and social influence spread much wider, leading archaeologists to refer to the phenomena as the "Hopewell Interaction Sphere." Hopewell influences on local cultures have been identified at several places in Wisconsin.

During Hopewell times, the construction of earthworks in Ohio reached awe-inspiring dimensions. Huge geometric earthworks—squares, circles, and octagons—covered vast tracts of land, sometimes hundreds of acres. Large, wide "sacred roads" connected some of these ceremonial areas. These spectacular structures required sophisticated engineering, mathematical, and architectural skills, and attest to great social complexity. Although such monuments were not built in the Upper Midwest, unmistakable evidence of Hopewell religious and social influence is seen in the form of Hopewell-style pottery, typical Hopewell trade goods from distant places, and Hopewell-related burial mound building customs.

Middle Woodland and Hopewell period mounds frequently cover the elaborate log-lined or sometimes stone crypts of certain people. The burial chambers appear to have functioned as repositories for the dead for quite some time before being covered by mounds. Some Hopewell mounds covered the remains of wood, bark, and thatch mortuary houses placed over the burial crypts. At some point, the structure was ritually burned or collapsed, and a mound was built over the spot to mark its location.

Offerings of great prestige sometimes accompanied people buried beneath the mounds. Beautifully crafted ornaments and objects of copper, mica, slate, fine chert, obsidian, and silver were placed with these special burials, as were finely crafted pottery vessels with intricate designs. Also included were stone smoking pipes, sometimes carved in the form of elegant animal effigies. Unlike modern habits, tobacco smoking was, and still is, an important part of ritual life for Native Americans. In fact, tobacco, a plant originally domesticated in Mexico, was grown originally only for ceremonial purposes.

The construction of mounds in Middle Woodland and Hopewell times elaborated on the themes of creation. Middle Woodland mounds contained symbolic or metaphorical offerings for rebirth and world renewal in many Native American belief systems. Like earlier mounds, the mortuary pits themselves incorporated earthen representations of world creation.[25]

Middle Woodland Social Complexity

Grave offerings in mounds along the Mississippi River attest to both the status of the people buried in the mounds and their close communication with other Hopewell centers in the Midwest. In the large Nicholls mound, a central burial pit contained several reburials of bone bundles and the remains of seven individuals, one of whom was accompanied by silver-covered wooden beads, copper tools, a copper plate, and freshwater pearls.[26] Offerings found elsewhere in the mound included a Hopewell-style pipe, obsidian, and finely chipped stone blades and ceremonial knives made from fine chert from western North America and Hixton Silicified Sandstone from nearby Wisconsin quarries.

Other offerings and ornaments found in Wisconsin mounds are bear canine pendants and pottery vessels traded up from Hopewell-related communities in Illinois. Bear ceremonialism was especially important to Hopewell ritual and bear imagery is frequently found in Hopewell art and personal ornamentation.[27] Bear symbolism continues through the building of effigy mounds: bear effigy mounds are common in the Four Lakes and western part of the effigy mound region.

If only certain people were interred in tombs beneath the Middle Woodland mounds, where were other people buried? Long a mystery, the UW archaeologist James Stoltman discovered a Middle Woodland mass grave, unmarked by a mound, at the Tillmont site on an island in the Mississippi River. He brought the grave pit to light during excavation of a prehistoric camp. The burial pit remains largely undisturbed due to Wisconsin's burial site protection law.

The large Tillmont grave pit contains the remains of up to thirty individuals and appears to have been long used as a below-ground crypt, probably with some sort of covering.[28] Since most skeletons are extended in natural form and the bones articulated, we can assume that people were placed in the grave pit as they died. Grave goods with prestige value did not accompany these interments, so it is likely that they represent either less important social groups in Middle Woodland society or, considering the low-lying watery location of the site, people associated with a "lower world" social division in Middle Woodland societies.

Dual social divisions have been identified by landscape analysis of the

Figure 2.9. Middle Woodland pottery from Wisconsin. The pot on the left is made in Hopewell style (called Havana ware) and was probably traded up from Illinois. The one on the right is a Middle Woodland style decorated with cord impressions.

great Hopewell earthworks in Ohio and in Middle Woodland burial mound building in Illinois where both bluff top mounds and mounded grave pits low on the landscape occur.[29] It is, then, with the Middle Woodland that we see the first clear evidence for a dual kinship system (moiety), although it is likely that future discoveries will extend this farther back in antiquity. This dual kinship arrangement formed the basis of the later effigy mound landscapes and persists in many Native American societies today.

Elaborate Hopewell and Middle Woodland art also feature themes found in later effigy mounds. These include depictions of sky birds, water birds, bears, long-tailed water spirits, and serpents in the form of small figurines, pipes, and motifs incised within special zones on pottery vessels. In Wisconsin, pottery from this area is also typically zoned and carries forward symbolism found on Early Woodland pots. Some pots from Middle Woodland mounds have decorative elements on the bottom that could be interpreted, as on earlier pottery, as snakes or the tails of the lower-world water spirit (figure 2.9).

Middle Woodland Mounds in the Four Lakes

The Middle Woodland witnessed some mound construction in the Four Lakes, and one site shows Hopewell influence. These are the mounds of the previously mentioned Outlet mound group at the outlet of Lake Monona (figure 2.10). Between the 1930s and early 1950s, Charles Brown of the Wisconsin Historical Society and several University of Wisconsin archaeologists excavated some of the Outlet mounds to save information and burials from destruction by an encroaching subdivision.[30] Pieces of decorated pottery found at the site are similar to Illinois Hopewell pottery. Beneath one mound, radiocarbon dated to the general Middle Woodland time period, UW archaeologists found a large (nine-inch-long) Hopewell-style knife blade made of Hixton Silicified Sandstone in a burial pit, which contained the remains of several individuals (figure 2.11).[31]

In 1948 road builders exposed a classic Hopewell-era tomb immediately south of the largest mound—a large twelve foot by nine foot pit containing the skeletal remains of thirteen people ranging in age from infants to adults.[32] Most of the people lay on their backs in an extended position, and several bundles of bones were also present. Brown's early maps do not show a mound here so it is possible that this was an unmounded crypt of "lower world" moiety people like the Tillmont mass grave. One piece of striking evidence pointing to the latter case is that white clay, probably marl, covered the faces of two of the skeletons. Marl is a calcium deposit composed mainly of shell found on the bottom of some area lakes, and its use has been connected to Native American concepts of rebirth and to the watery and marl-covered dens of the waters spirits.[33]

Middle Woodland mounds appear to have been built elsewhere in Four Lakes, particularly near the outlets and inlets of lakes, and were subsequently surrounded by later effigy mounds and incorporated into the effigy mound landscape. One is on the grounds of the Mendota Mental Health Institute at the inlet of Lake Mendota, where the highest and largest conical mounds in the Four Lakes mound district can still be viewed. Nineteenth-century digging by J. M. De Hart, the hospital superintendent, in one large mound partially exposed a stone burial crypt built on the former surface of the ground, a variation of the in-ground crypts covered by Middle Woodland mounds (figure 2.12). In 1895 Cyrus Thomas of the Smithsonian Institution reported similar above-ground stone crypts

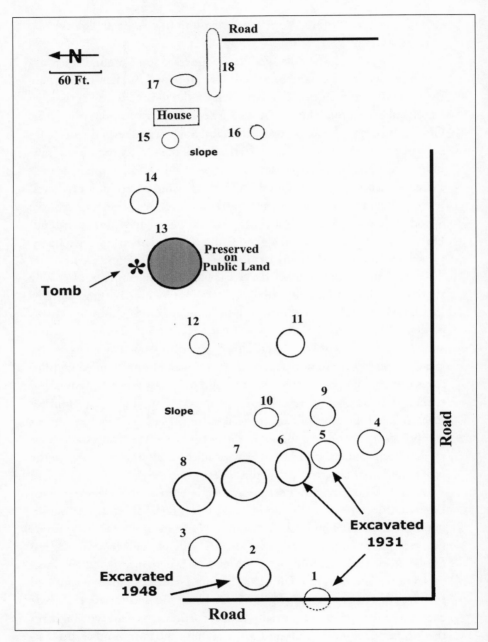

Figure 2.10. The Outlet mound group as originally mapped by Brown, updated by the author.

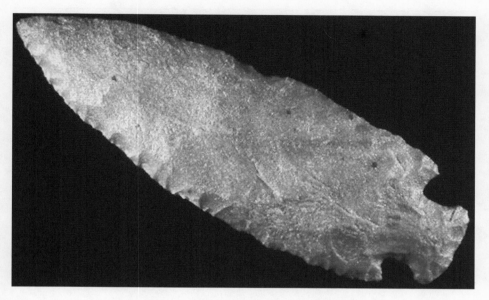

Figure 2.11. A nine-inch-long Hopewell knife of Hixton Silicified Sandstone from a mound at the Outlet site.

covered by mounds along the Mississippi River in areas of Hopewell influence, as indicated by pottery, obsidian blades, and silver beads.[34]

Another possible Middle Woodland stone crypt was at the Fox Bluff mound group on Lake Mendota. In 1908 Charles E. Brown and volunteers excavated a conical mound, surrounded by effigy mounds, as it was about to be destroyed for a subdivision.[35] Brown found the conical mound to be covering a large above-ground stone cairn or enclosure three-and-a-half feet high and seventeen feet in diameter (figure 2.13). Looters had removed artifacts and most of the human remains, so little else is known about it.

The Hopewell interaction sphere, linking many areas of northeastern North America, along with the monumental mound and earthwork construction in Ohio, ended sometime between A.D. 200 and 400. The reasons for Hopewell collapse are unclear, but some researchers have noted that it occurred about the same time as a wide-scale climatic shift that brought drought to many areas. As modeled by climatologists Reid Bryson and Robert Bryson of the University of Wisconsin Climatic Research Center, the Middle Woodland stage in Wisconsin ends with the onset of a

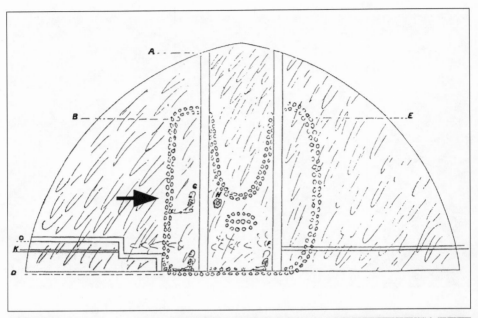

Figure 2.12. *Above*, crude drawing by J. M. De Hart showing central stone enclosure (arrows) with burials at the Farwell Point site. *Below*, the conical mound at the site as it appears today, still showing evidence of De Hart's digging (arrows).

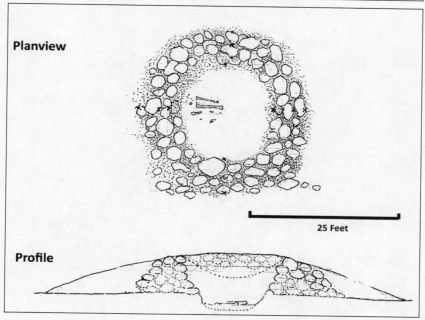

Figure 2.13. *Above*, the Fox Bluff site as mapped by Brown. *Below*, Brown excavated one of the conical mounds prior to its destruction, revealing a stone enclosure.

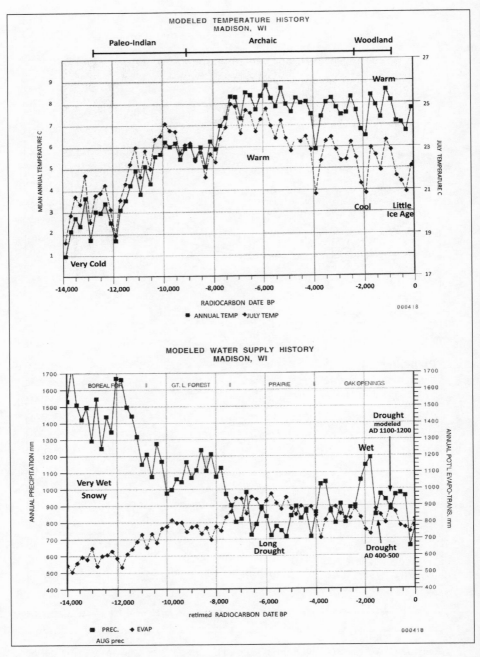

Figure 2.14. Modeled climate charts for Madison, Wisconsin.

sharp drought sometime between A.D. 400 and 500 (figure 2.14). The Brysons suggest that it may have been as intense as the Mid-Holocene Dry Period and comparable to the Dust Bowl years of the 1930s. They add that climatic change seems to have been rapid and "probably catastrophic for the established lifestyle."[36]

This drought may account for the reasons this time is not well represented in the archaeological record of the Four Lakes or other places in Wisconsin. Lack of archaeological evidence for major occupation at the beginning of the Late Woodland in the western part of state caused archaeological experts James Theler and Robert Boszhardt to wonder if the region had been abandoned. At the deep and long-occupied Airport Village site at the outlet of Lake Monona, evidence of human activity is lacking for the centuries immediately before the appearance of pottery of the effigy mound people ca. A.D. 700.[37]

Late Woodland

Woodland societies in North America become much more separated from one another after the Middle Woodland stage, following cultural trajectories unique to various regions. There were, however, some common trends. The tempo of change quickened as new technologies and other food resources were introduced from elsewhere and were rapidly integrated into the existing Woodland cultures. The bow and arrow replaced the spear as a hunting and a fighting weapon sometime after A.D. 500. Different styles of pottery vessels appeared, decorated with elaborate impressions of cords and fabrics made with plant fibers.

Most important, another Mexican domesticated plant, corn, joined squash in the diet and in the economic strategies of people in the Midwest after A.D. 800. The spread of corn northward into Wisconsin would have been facilitated by another climatic fluctuation, a moderately warm and moist period roughly between A.D. 700 and 1000 that provided conditions ideal for plant growth. Some call it the Medieval Warm Period because it is especially well documented for Europe, but like other climatic shifts its effects were highly variable throughout the world. Climatic models show a somewhat drier climate in the Four Lakes than in other places. It is likely that corn cultivation was further promoted by the northward expansion of newly horticultural tribes into the Upper Midwest during this warm and wet period. Much later, around A.D. 1300, yet another Mexican domesticate, beans, joined the economy. Corn, beans, and squash, "the three sisters," formed the basis of Indian farming at the time of European contact.

With the incorporation of corn ca. A.D. 900, Native Americans began a shift to village-based farming as a way of life. By A.D. 1000, virtually all people living in areas of the Midwest where agriculture could be successful were growing corn and other crops. Some of these people established large permanent agricultural settlements. The great Indian city of Cahokia and the Mississippian civilization sprang from the Mississippi River floodplain and was based on corn agriculture. The shift from a hunting and gathering economy to one centered on growing corn brought about enormous cultural change that affected not only economy and types of settlements but social patterns and religion as well. It is perhaps one of the most revolutionary developments to have occurred in the pre-Columbian cultural history of North America.

Archaeologists define four different lifeways in the Wisconsin area that overlap in time and which derive from all these changes. The earliest to emerge is the Late Woodland stage of the Woodland tradition (ca. A.D. 500–1250 in Wisconsin). A complex and intensely agricultural Mississippian tradition arose in southern Illinois from local Woodland populations after A.D 1000. Shortly thereafter, the Mississippians expanded north into Wisconsin and then disappeared off the midwestern cultural landscape within the space of two centuries or less. A third cultural tradition called Oneota, consisting of farmers, hunters, and gatherers, emerged after A.D. 1050 and lasted into the time of European contact. The Langford tradition (A.D. 1200–1500) shares some similarities with Oneota but represents farming and hunting adaptation to the prairies of northern Illinois and southern Wisconsin. Only the Late Woodland is well represented in the Four Lakes, but its nature and fate is inextricably linked to the other cultures in various and complex ways that are still being researched.

Late Woodland of the Four Lakes

As the term implies, Late Woodland cultures are regarded as direct descendants of the Middle Woodland cultures. It was the Late

Woodland people who constructed the effigy mound landscapes, but effigy mounds were not built throughout the Late Woodland stage and, according to some, not by all Late Woodland people living at the same time in Wisconsin.

The very beginnings of Late Woodland are murky, possibly due to the effects of the long drought, but like earlier populations, Late Woodland people relied on hunting and gathering wild food resources. Small seasonal villages along the lakes and rivers were occupied during warm weather; other more specialized camps were established in different parts of the territories to hunt and gather foods, extract other necessary materials, or in some cases to perform rituals in sacred caves. No doubt the people of the Late Woodland supplemented their diet with produce from gardens of indigenous plants, which had been domesticated in former times, as well as squash, previously introduced into Wisconsin from the south. Corn, too, became increasingly important to the diet of the Late Woodland people after its introduction.[38]

Archaeologists also document another dramatic period of population growth in the Midwest throughout the Late Woodland stage, as reflected in the large number of Late Woodland habitation and mound sites as compared with earlier times. In the Four Lakes, many of the habitation places are located on the lakes or associated wetlands where people had gathered for thousands of years in warmer months. One of these is, again, the Airport Village site at the outlet of Lake Monona. But throughout the Midwest, Late Woodland people pushed out of the main river valleys and lake regions, settling in remoter upland regions. Examples in the Madison area are the Dietz site in Madison and the Stricker's Pond site in the adjacent community of Middleton.[39] Both settlements were located on pond and marsh areas in the uplands well away from the lake shores.

At the Dietz site in the early 1950s, UW archaeologist David Baerreis uncovered a substantial Late Woodland camp with elaborately decorated pottery he had earlier named Madison Ware. The pottery is now viewed as the hallmark of the effigy mound tradition. Mound groups were once located nearby, one that contained two long linear mounds that, oddly, crossed each other. Late Woodland people grew substantial amounts of corn sometime between A.D. 1016 and 1233 at a warm-weather village on Sticker's Pond, well away from the shores of the lakes or major streams. In this case, though, no mounds are recorded for the vicinity.

Climatic models for the Four Lakes show much rainfall during this time but also much evaporation because of warm weather causing drier soil conditions. Bryson and Bryson observe that this would have again caused the spread of oak savanna throughout the Four Lakes.[40] The combination of oak savanna, prairies, woodlands, and wetlands provided a variety of wild foods such as deer, elk, small mammals, fish and other aquatic life, as well as nuts and many other edible plants. The presence of so much savanna and prairie would have facilitated construction of expansive mound groupings unhindered by dense forest growth. Indeed, large heavy axes for chopping trees are not found at Late Woodland and effigy mound period habitation sites and do not appear to be a part of the tool assemblage. Instead, smaller and lighter woodworking tools, called celts, are common.

But good conditions for hunting, gathering, and gardening could have been interrupted about A.D. 1100 because of a sudden decrease in precipitation, which may have lasted a century. Bryson and Bryson characterize this period as sharp drought. The effects have not been studied for southern Wisconsin, but a similar time of drought, apparently more intense, has been suggested as the most likely cause for the demise of the city of Cahokia and Mississippian civilization in the Midwest.[41] Whether this climatic fluctuation was a direct factor involved in the demise of effigy mound building is yet to be documented, but the correlation in time is certainly interesting. Milder conditions returned after A.D. 1200, followed by a cooler period known as the "Little Ice Age," which lasted into the early nineteenth century.

Villages and Houses

Late Woodland habitation sites in other areas include small villages and camps of various types. As in earlier times, there was a great deal of variation in lifestyles from region to region, reflecting adjustments to local environmental conditions and food resources. At least in the later part of the Middle Woodland, people in Wisconsin congregated in small seasonal villages with wigwam-like structures, but a more sedentary village life did not become widespread until the shift to farming.

In the rugged southwestern part of Wisconsin, small groups broke off from summer settlements to gather clams and to hunt deer during the winter and early spring in the sheltered valleys, temporarily occupying caves and rock overhangs. The people of the Four Lakes seem to have followed a similar pattern of congregating during warm weather, then dispersing into smaller groups. Population estimates are difficult to make, but settlers found about six hundred Indian people living along the lakes in the early nineteenth century, and this may indeed be the low end of an educated guess for the ancient population. A large number of camps and villages found throughout the Four Lakes support the crowded landscape findings of Theler and Boszhardt in southwestern Wisconsin.

The general population growth in the Midwest has led some to propose that other Late Woodland people from the south expanded into areas already occupied by indigenous peoples. The evidence is arguable, but the end of the Late Woodland is certainly marked by increased warfare, as is evident by the sudden appearance of fortified villages throughout southern Wisconsin. As has so often happened, the shift to agriculture and more permanent settlements is predictably accompanied by great friction as people competed for land and resources. In the 1980s Victoria Dirst made the dramatic discovery of a village at Governor Nelson State Park on Lake Mendota fortified by a circular wall of wooden posts (figure 2.15). Limited excavations at the village (the Camp Indianola site) produced fragmentary Late Woodland pottery and a large number of stone arrow points.[42] Extrapolating from the arc of posts, the village would have been 360 feet in diameter, covering a little over two acres of land.

The houses found at Late Woodland camps and villages were small, accommodating not more than a single family. Some temporary wigwam-like structures, oval or rectangular in form, have been directly associated with the effigy mound builders. But a new house type appeared in many places in the northeastern United States during the later centuries of Late Woodland stage. Called a "pit house," the structure was partially dug into the earth and covered with bark attached to wooden poles. The living space was circular or rectangular, and there often was a long narrow entranceway, giving the pit house a keyhole-shaped appearance (figure 2.16). Some modern-day Indian people suggest that these structures with their small entranceways were actually sweat lodges, specially built for purification rituals.

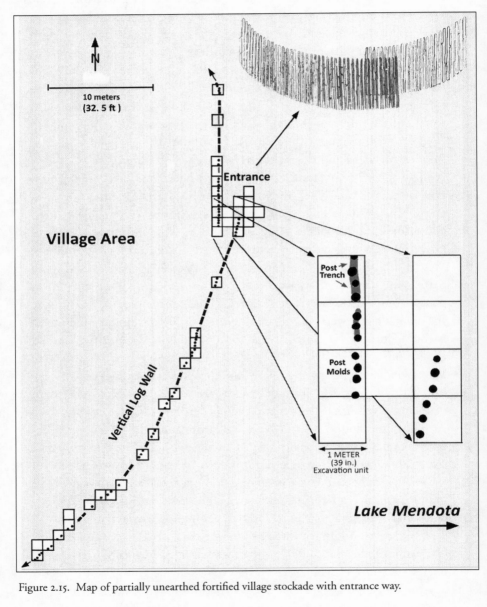

Figure 2.15. Map of partially unearthed fortified village stockade with entrance way.

Figure 2.16. *Above*, aerial photo of the Statz site showing keyhole-shaped houses excavated by the Museum Archaeology Program of the Wisconsin Historical Society. *Below*, reconstructed keyhole pit house with low entrance at the Hoard museum, Fort Atkinson, Wisconsin. The modern window is for public viewing of the interior.

Late Woodland pit houses occur in settlements throughout southeastern and south-central Wisconsin, including two small sites in the Four Lakes region, Statz and Murphy, first occupied in Archaic times.[43] Radiocarbon dating places the use of these structures at the two sites sometime between A.D. 900 and 1200, making it probable that the people who lived there were the effigy mound builders themselves.

Consisting of three pairs of pit houses, the Statz site was reoccupied several times, perhaps by a single family. Some charred corn was found here, but WHS archaeologists conclude that people lived at Statz in the autumn and winter. Significantly, Statz was situated at the headwaters of the Six Mile Creek that drains to the Yahara River just above the former inlet with Lake Mendota, quite near the fortified Indianola village and several major effigy mound groups. It seems likely that Statz functioned as the winter quarters for some of the people who lived in the fortified Indianola site during warm weather. The Murphy site, located west of Lake Mendota, also appears to be a small, seasonally occupied family hamlet where the people lived in keyhole-shaped pit houses.

Late Woodland Pottery

The main pottery of the effigy mound people was a variety of styles originally defined from Four Lakes' archeological sites and known collectively to archaeologists as Madison Ware (figure 2.17). This

Figure 2.17. Madison cord impressed pottery from the collection of the University of Wisconsin.

pottery begins to appear ca. A.D. 700 and is among the most exquisitely decorated pottery made in the midwestern United States; it is also the pottery most often found in effigy mounds. Intricate decorations were made by impressing woven fabrics or single cords made from plant fibers into the wet clay surface before firing. The complexity of the fabrics and decorations attest to much care and time spent in pottery making at this time.

Unlike earlier wares, symbolic decorations on Madison pottery are restricted to the upper part or neck of the pot where they occur in three zones. In the major central zone, the potters made a wide variety of abstract decorations, many of which appear on earlier Woodland pottery, such as parallel lines (earth?) and chevrons (birds). These appear to be the dominant symbolic or cosmological theme of the pot and may even identify the kinship group, perhaps even the clan, of the potter. This major zone is bordered most often on the bottom of the pot with short, curved knots, reminiscent of the possible tails of water spirits or snakes on earlier Woodland ceramic vessels.

Images of birds, made by cord impressions, appear on some Wisconsin Late Woodland pottery styles related to Madison Ware after ca. A.D. 1000, and they mirror the clear iconography of the effigy mounds themselves. Outside of the effigy mound region in Illinois, Late Woodland corded pottery images from the same time period include depictions of bird-men and panther-like water spirits, both of which suggest that a trend from abstract to more explicit imagery on some special pottery types extended over a large region (figure 2.18).

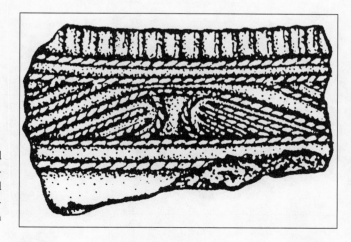

Figure 2.18. Cord impressed bird, probably a thunderbird, on Late Woodland pottery, from the Fred Edwards site in southwestern Wisconsin.

Other more common pottery styles appear after A.D. 900 that coincide with the expansion of corn horticulture among the Late Woodland people. These also have corded designs similar to Madison pottery but added is a distinctive collar or thickening around square- or five-sided rims (figure 2.19). Before the disappearance of the Late Woodland from the archaeological record, this distinctive collared ware is the predominant form of pottery found at Late Woodland sites in southern Wisconsin. For some archaeologists the appearance of collared pottery signals the appearance of new Late Woodland culture entering the area, eventually replacing the effigy mound builders. Others see it as ceramic changes within the same society.[44] It is more likely that the collared pottery simply becomes more popular and utilitarian as the Late Woodland people turn increasingly to farming—the braced rim logically needed for lifting pots in and out of food storage pits.

At the Statz site, both Madison Ware and collared style pottery were found mixed together in the pit houses, but with the collared styles increasing in frequency through time at the long-occupied site. Direct evidence that effigy mound people also made the new collared pots comes from several effigy mounds in which some people were interred with the collared pots, as at the Nitschke I site mentioned in chapter 1.[45]

There is also direct physical association between effigy mounds and the camps and villages that produced the new collared wares. On the grounds of the Mendota Health Institute on Lake Mendota, Salkin also excavated a

Figure 2.19. Late Woodland collared pottery.

small part of what appears to be a substantial village with rather narrow calibrated radiocarbon dates between A.D. 960 and 1030.[46] This would be before the postulated end of construction of the effigy mounds at A.D. 1100 and before the modeled twelfth-century drought. The excavations yielded numerous pottery sherds from collared Late Woodland vessels in addition to some Madison Ware pottery linked to the effigy mound builders. Significantly, the habitation area is surrounded on three sides by huge effigy mounds (see chapter 4).

The remains of food at the site suggest that this village was occupied much of the year. The people here gathered wild plums, available in spring, and acorns and other nuts, available to fall, and grew corn in summer. They captured turtles and hunted waterfowl and deer. The presence of juvenile deer bone indicates an early summer kill. The village is notable in one other regard—the presence of many deer bones, juvenile and adult, demonstrates that deer was still plentiful at this late date in Four Lakes despite the postulated collapse of the herds about the same time in western Wisconsin.

Effigy Mound Building

No Late Woodland mounds have been directly dated in the Four Lakes district and only a few have been excavated by professional archaeologists in modern times. But examination of the mound groups and the overall landscape suggests that mound construction followed a pattern found elsewhere. Groups of short linear mounds accompanied by low conical mounds seem to immediately predate the construction of the effigy mounds themselves and are built in many more places than the higher Early and Middle Woodland mounds. These may represent the upper (conical) and lower (linear) worlds and the presence of a two-part moiety. Later mound building spread over vast areas. Effigy, conical, and much longer linear and tapering linear mounds were built around former mound groups. Then, mound construction, like settlements themselves, expanded to more remote areas including drumlins farther away from the lakes and upland ponds not used by previous people for ceremonial purposes. Incorporating earlier mounds, the Four Lakes mound district of one thousand years ago became one giant and spectacular ceremonial landscape.

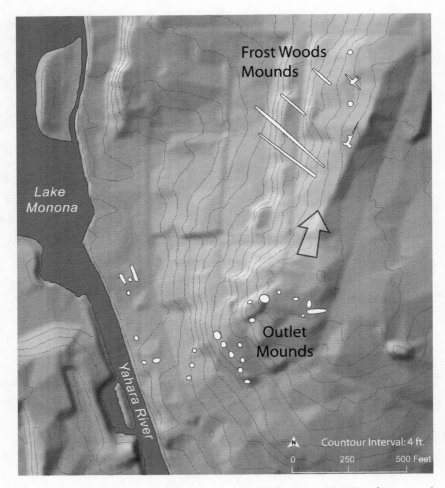

Figure 2.20. Shaded relief map showing expansion of effigy mound building from around the earlier Outlet site.

This progression is best viewed around the Outlet site. Here, a cluster of fairly large conical mounds occupied the top and sides of a high hill overlooking the Yahara River outlet of Lake Monona (figure 2.20). Archaeological work on portions of the site prior to development of a subdivision generally dated the site to around two thousand years ago, during the Early and Middle Woodland times. On lower slopes and the periphery of these early mounds are smaller conical mounds and short linear mounds. Farther to the northeast along the same glacial ridge was the Frost Woods site, a complex of classic zoomorphic effigy mounds and very long linear mounds that occupied another prominent elevation on the same general ridge as the Outlet site. Other effigy mounds were known to have existed near the lakeshore to the west of Frost Woods. These different locations trace the evolution of mound landscape for the Four Lakes over at least that thousand-year period. Other examples of this evolution are provided as we later tour the Four Lakes mound district.

The End of the Effigy Mound Culture

Precisely how long effigy mound building continued in the Four Lakes is unknown, but archaeologists record the complete end of the Late Woodland in southern Wisconsin, now represented by small communities of farmers, as between A.D. 1200 and 1300, perhaps earlier in some places. After those dates much of southern Wisconsin, including the Four Lakes, appears to be abandoned of major settlements for several centuries. During this time there was a major shift in population as people nucleated into large farming villages in several areas of the state, including nearby Lake Koshkonong. Like many of the earlier Late Woodland communities, these larger villages are sometimes fortified. The customs and material culture of these people, including pottery made with crushed clam shell, are so different from the earlier Late Woodland that archaeologists have given them a new name—Oneota.

The end of the Woodland and emergence of the Oneota coincides with the intrusion of a new and powerful cultural force. Perhaps even as the effigy mound landscapes in the Four Lakes were being constructed, a new and even more complex culture took root nearby. Called Mississippians by archaeologists, a colony of the newcomers—farmers and fierce warriors— migrated from southern Illinois between A.D. 1050 and 1100 and moved in with a group of Late Woodland people, presumably allies and kin. The Mississippians built one of their characteristic towns, complete with large earthen temple mounds and heavy fortifications, on the Crawfish River, thirty miles east of the Four Lakes, now called Aztalan (figure 2.21).[47] Like the Yahara, the Crawfish is a tributary of the Rock River. Descending down the Rock River, and then down the Mississippi to present-day East

Figure 2.21. Platform mound and reconstructed stockade at Aztalan State Park.

St. Louis, Illinois, one would come to Cahokia, the capital city of the Mississippian civilization.

Cahokia is the largest Native American settlement that existed in North America. Archaeologists trace the evolution of the city, beginning ca. A.D. 900, from a concentration of villages and ceremonial centers based on corn agriculture. At its greatest power ca. A.D. 1100, Cahokia covered five square miles and accommodated a population of ten thousand to fifteen thousand people.[48] At one end of a large public plaza loomed Monks Mound, a flat-topped platform mound one hundred feet high and covering fourteen acres at its base. On top of the mound lived the paramount chief of Mississippian society. Although much more complex than the local Late Woodland populations from which they evolved, many of the age-old cosmological and dualistic social themes are present in Mississippian society and iconography, although expressed in somewhat different ways. One Mississippian theme, for example, relates to fertility and is famously represented by the Birger figurine—that of women hoeing the back of a snake-like serpent representing the watery, and therefore fertile, underworld. Falcons and hawks represent the aggressiveness of the new culture, and are often associated with warriors. Here, sun symbolism is especially important and seems associated with the upper or ruling clans of Mississippian society.

Movements or influence from southern Illinois is evident from many places throughout southern Wisconsin where Mississippian ceramics and other distinctive artifacts have been found, including many Late Woodland village sites. Human figures on the walls of the famous Gottschall Rockshelter, a ritual cave site in southwestern Wisconsin, were painted in an unmistakable Mississippian art style, and on a low bluff knoll in Trempealeau along the Mississippi River the Mississippians built ceremonial platform mounds ca. A.D. 1050.[49]

Within the heavily fortified town of Aztalan, Late Woodland allies lived side by side with Mississippians, no doubt interconnected by intermarriage. Aztalan flourished until sometime between A.D. 1200 and 1300, at which time it was abandoned. At about the same time, Cahokia itself was in decline and it, too, was eventually abandoned. The great Mississippian civilization disappeared from the Midwest altogether but persisted in southeastern North America until the time of European contact.

There are a number of hypotheses as to what brought these new people and their ideas north and why they disappeared. Explanations for expansion include population growth, political or religious factors, or trade and the need to acquire resources for the rapidly expanding new society. Perhaps all are true. Among the explanations for the demise of Cahokia and the Midwest Mississippian society are environmental degradation and overexploitation of resources, warfare, disease, and climatic change that brought a series of long droughts.

Relationships between the Mississippians and at least some of the indigenous Late Woodland people seem to have been close. The Mississippians either lived among Late Woodland people in many communities, as in the case of Aztalan, or maintained such close trading ties that Mississippian artifacts are common at Late Woodland villages. The Mississippians introduced new ceramic forms and technologies, including ways of making thin-walled pots tempered with crushed mussel shell—as did the subsequent Oneota—and new religious ideas drawn from old and familiar themes. Being intensive corn agriculturists, the Mississippians almost certainly accelerated adoption of corn farming among the Late Woodland people.

Because of these close relationships, many archaeologists believe that the indigenous Late Woodland people gathered at locations of Mississippian activity and trading centers, abandoning large areas of the state and many of their former customs, such as effigy mound building. Under Mississippian influence, the Late Woodland became Oneota. James Stoltman, for example, proposes abandonment of southwestern Wisconsin as people moved to centers of Mississippian activity.[50] In this view, the new Oneota culture evolved at these places where there was major Mississippian and Late Woodland contact.

Whether all Late Woodland people in Wisconsin shared a friendly relationship with the Mississippians is debatable, since the Mississippian era in Wisconsin was a time of intense warfare as indicated by many fortified villages throughout southern Wisconsin and the presence of the massively fortified town of Aztalan itself. Moreover, there is tantalizing evidence that Late Woodland culture persisted in some areas, notably the Four Lakes, through this time without much contact with the Mississippians.

There is as yet no solid evidence that the Mississippians themselves occupied the Four Lakes or had a major influence. Nor did the Four Lakes subsequently become a major habitation center for the subsequent Oneota. Occasional pottery tempered with crushed shell characteristic of both Mississippian and Oneota has been found, but this could as well reflect short-time use of the area by Oneota later on. Instead, a large Oneota population grew up at nearby Lake Koshkonong on the Rock River, not far from Aztalan. Lake Koshkonong had been another center for the effigy mound builders and one where archaeologists found an apparently well-fortified village of early Oneota people making pottery similar to Mississippian styles and living in Mississippian-style houses.[51]

In the view of some, Oneota began developing on Lake Koshkonong prior to the formal establishment of Aztalan and eventually came into conflict with the intruders as they competed for local resources and land. Others argue that Oneota itself emerged as a separate cultural entity only after the Mississippians left. Whatever the case, Lake Koshkonong becomes *the* major population center in southern Wisconsin with its cluster of large fortified Oneota farming villages, lasting perhaps to the dawn of European contact.[52]

Although firm evidence of Mississippian contacts with the Four Lakes Late Woodland people is still lacking, professional excavations of the fortified Indianola village and the early destruction of a nearby mound provide some clues to the relationship between the two groups. Among the many arrow points found along the former wooden walls at Camp Indianola, Victoria Dirst identified several of a notched style used by both the Mississippians and Late Woodland people but made of a white chert called Burlington.[53] Burlington chert occurs in geological deposits near the Mississippi River in Missouri, southeast Iowa, and Illinois not far from Cahokia. Arrow points of the same type and material have also been found at Aztalan and the Fred Edwards site, a Mississippian and Woodland fortified village in southwestern Wisconsin. Dirst speculates that the arrow points might have been a result of a Mississippian attack on the village, perhaps launched from Aztalan itself. But this proposal is based on evidence from only a small part of the fortified village that was excavated.

Not far from the village, the contents of a burial mound near Borchers Beach suggests an entirely different type of relationship. The mound, one of a series of conical mounds, was leveled in 1907 and 1908 by a landowner to acquire dirt for property improvements (figure 2.22). The landowner contacted Charles E. Brown at the WHS several times to examine the finds, which included artifacts and human bone.[54] In addition, the landowner uncovered one rock-lined burial at the edge of the mound that may be intrusive—that is, dug into the mound sometime after it was built. He reported finding a glass trade bead in the mound dating to the historic period, feasibly dislodged from this burial. Toward the center of the mound, Brown himself documented a flexed burial with a broken pot, which we now recognize as Late Woodland Madison Ware.

This find is not surprising, considering the history of the area. What is perplexing is the description of two tightly flexed burials found facing each other, evidently buried in a pit *below* the center of the mound and the other burials. As documented by Brown, one of the skeletons had some sort of garment around the waist or a belt made of numerous beads made from a small marine shell called Marginella. A stone celt had been placed in the hand of this same burial and several notched arrow points similar to those found at the Camp Indianola village were recovered near the feet. Elsewhere in the mound, the landowner reported finding a columella or the inside pillar cut from a large whelk seashell.

Celts and the arrow-point styles were used by Late Woodland people, but marine shell was not. Such foreign objects have not been reported for any other of the hundreds of excavated Late Woodland and effigy mound burials. Marine shell was used and traded in Middle Woodland times and

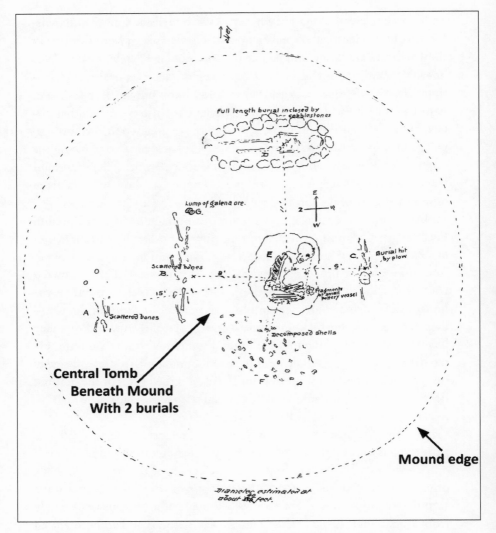

Figure 2.22. Map of Borchers Beach mound by Brown with additions by the author.

by the Mississippians, who commonly traded for Atlantic Ocean seashell and wore both Marginella shell beads and whelk-shell columella pendants as indicators of high social ranking. Both whelk columella pendants and marine shell beads similar to Marginella have been found in some quantities at Aztalan.[55]

Taken at face value, this unique burial indicates close contact with Mississippians and perhaps even the presence of Mississippians themselves in the Four Lakes Late Woodland community. If the burials are of Late Woodland people, as the nearby pottery would imply, the presence of marine shell would at least argue for the presence of high-ranking people in Four Lakes Late Woodland society whose status was reinforced by the display of exotic objects acquired through trade (or war) with the Mississippians. This is a particularly attractive interpretation since the northwest shore of Lake Mendota seemed especially important to the effigy mound people of the Four Lakes, as demonstrated by the presence of major settlements and the unusual scale of mound building.

Unfortunately, the intriguing and potentially important evidence from the mound was hastily salvaged, and much of the information derives from landowner accounts after material had already been removed or dislocated. As a result, we have to view the information with a critical eye. It is possible that the artifacts are from several different periods. Perhaps corroborating evidence will one day be found. More clues to the Mississippian–Late Woodland connection and the fate of the Late Woodland people are certain to emerge in the future as more archaeological discoveries are inevitably made in the Four Lakes mound district, and especially from a newly discovered habitation on the Yahara River where Native Americans first began gathering eleven thousand years earlier.

Abandonment of the Four Lakes

Around A.D. 1250, the Four Lakes region was abandoned after nearly thirteen thousand years of human occupation. What precisely happened to the Four Lakes Late Woodland people is a question that will surely be solved by additional archaeological work at many of the well-preserved settlements in the area. As it stands at present, there are several possibilities.

First, the people may have been dispersed or decimated by warfare. Evidence that conflict was occurring *with somebody* comes from the fortified Indianola site. If Dirst's idea is correct, it would have been the Mississippians. Other Late Woodland people could have been involved as well in sporadic raids. It is quite likely that the shift to corn agriculture with its land commitment and population growth, as well as the intrusion of the Mississippians, created a tense and unstable environment where alliances and enemies changed quickly and frequently.

Second, and as is proposed for elsewhere in the Upper Midwest, at least some people of the Four Lakes may have been drawn to the vicinity of Mississippian centers, like nearby Aztalan, perhaps even comprising some of the Late Woodland population at Aztalan. These people might have been absorbed into Mississippian society, suffering whatever fate befell the Aztalan Mississippians or moving from there to Lake Koshkonong or another Oneota center after the Mississippians left. Except possibly for the puzzling Borchers Beach burial, there is as yet no evidence that the Four Lakes Late Woodland people had extensive relationships with the Mississippians.

Last, the Late Woodland people of the Fours Lakes may have moved *directly,* but perhaps gradually, to nearby Lake Koshkonong or other Oneota centers, becoming absorbed in the growing Oneota settlements. However, very little of the collared styles of pottery, like those used by Four Lakes Woodland people, have been found at the extensively researched Lake Koshkonong Oneota settlements. If Late Woodland people did move directly to Koshkonong, cultural assimilation must have been rapid.

Another important area that may help answer the question of what happened to the Four Lakes people is the Skare site located on the Yahara River between Lake Waubesa and Lake Kegonsa—the same place where Paleo-Indians gathered eleven thousand years earlier, leaving behind numerous fluted points. Here excavations by Sissel Schroeder of the University of Wisconsin found yet another pit house, apparently a part of a larger Late Woodland village that existed at the site some time between A.D. 900 and 1250.[56] The house seems to be rectangular in form and had been burned. The charred remains included a mass of burned corn cobs attesting to a farming way of life (figure 2.23). Careful detective work leads the UW archaeologists to believe the house was deliberately burned by the people living there.

As yet, no pottery has been found that would reveal the identity of the occupants. The researchers did find a few pottery pieces of effigy mound Madison Ware, but these could have been mixed into the house from an earlier occupation of the site. That these people may have built mounds at some point in the village's existence is suggested by two linear mounds directly across the narrow Yahara River. Elsewhere on the site, pottery sherds similar to Oneota styles have also been found. The dates of the apparently

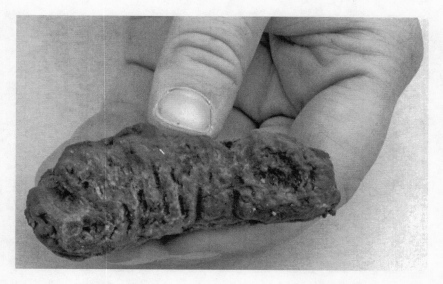

Figure 2.23. A burned corn cob from the Skare site. Midwestern corn cobs of the time were much smaller than present-day corn cobs.

small Oneota presence at the site have not been determined, but it could mean that the Late Woodland people of the Four Lakes had continuing contact with Oneota people (their relatives?) before they left.

A number of calibrated radiocarbon dates for the burned remains of pit house produced another surprising discovery. The dates extend to A.D. 1250, later than one would expect for Late Woodland in the area and overlapping in time with Mississippian occupation at Aztalan as well as the emergence of Oneota settlements of Lake Koshkonong. It is, for now, the last dated pre-Columbian site in the Four Lakes. The Skare site could indeed represent the last of the Four Lakes Woodland people and, as such, may hold the key as to why the area was abandoned and what cultural changes were taking place at the time.

The Descendents of the Effigy Mound Builders Return?

Native Americans did not return to the Four Lakes until after European contact. Although the Sauk and Fox—tribes that migrated into Wisconsin from the east—maintained villages in the region in

Figure 2.24. A nineteenth-century Ho-Chunk camp in southwestern Wisconsin as painted by Seth Eastman.

seventeenth and eighteenth centuries, it is the Ho-Chunk that historic documents mention as living here along the shores of the lakes when the first white settlers arrived.

Oral tradition and historic documents describe the Ho-Chunk as a large and populous tribe that had occupied much of what is now eastern and southern Wisconsin, and perhaps parts of northern Illinois. Warfare and European disease greatly decimated the tribe, leaving only small remnants living in northeastern Wisconsin by the late seventeenth century. Populations eventually rebounded, and the Ho-Chunk expanded to south-central Wisconsin in the late eighteenth century. By the early nineteenth century the Four Lakes had become a major hub of Ho-Chunk activity (figure 2.24). An 1829 Indian-agent census for the Four Lakes lists a total of 598 Ho-Chunk people with villages on all five lakes.[57] Ho-Chunk is almost certainly among those tribes descended from the pre-Columbian Oneota. If the Oneota are in turn derived from the ancient effigy mound builders, as many believe, the expansion of the Ho-Chunk into the Four Lakes could be considered a return to the home of their ancestors.

It is not recorded if making of effigy mounds was a part of Ho-Chunk oral history of that time, but certainly they would not have been surprised coming across the ancient mounds. The effigy mounds had been part of the landscape of their territory elsewhere and doubtless figured importantly in their beliefs. The arrangement and symbolism of the mounds would have reaffirmed their beliefs and links to the land, since it mirrored the Ho-Chunk kinship structure and cosmology. The principal settlements of the Four Lakes Ho-Chunk on Lake Mendota were near earlier major settlements and ceremonial areas of the Late Woodland people, perhaps for the same practical reasons but perhaps because the Ho-Chunk would have recognized the huge effigy mounds as their own principal spirit beings.

Ho-Chunk occupation of the Four Lakes did not last long. Friction with white settlers in southwestern Wisconsin led to the sale of part of Ho-Chunk territory immediately west of the Four Lakes in 1829.[58] In 1832 a defiant Black Hawk and his band of Sauk and Fox attempted to resist the consequences of white settlement, sparking a conflict called the Black Hawk War. Federal troops and militia chased Black Hawk and his band up the Rock River from Illinois and through what is now the city of Madison, past the ancient mounds, and finally to the mouth of the Bad Axe River on the Mississippi, where troops massacred many of the Indian people.

The conflict resulted in an immediate call for removal of all Indian people in southern Wisconsin. In 1833 and 1837 the Ho-Chunk were forced to cede their remaining lands to the federal government, and most were relocated west of the Mississippi River, ultimately to a reservation in Nebraska where many live today as the Winnebago Nation. Some Ho-Chunk either refused to relocate or came back from the reservations and lived as refugees on their former lands, being harassed by authorities until 1884 when some acquired homesteads under the Indian Homestead Act.[59] Many Ho-Chunk families continued to use traditional hunting, gathering, and fishing grounds into the twentieth century. Some buried their dead in the ancient mounds, a pattern that developed among many tribes as they lost traditional villages and cemeteries to white settlement, apparently in the hope that this would protect the graves of their loved ones.[60]

The descendants of the people who refused to leave are now the Ho-Chunk Nation, with government headquarters in Black River Falls, Wisconsin. Still without much land, the Nation purchased property near Madison for a bingo hall and casino that brings in much-needed revenue for medical care, homes, jobs, and buying back land lost to treaties. They call it Dejope, short for *Taychopera*—"The Four Lakes."

3 | The Effigy Mound Landscape of Madison and the Four Lakes

THE MOUNDS OF THE FOUR LAKES are among the best documented in the effigy mound region. This is a result of more than 150 years of attention stimulated by the unusually dense concentration of spectacular mounds as well as the early establishment of Madison as a political center and one of learning and history. The Wisconsin Historical Society (WHS) was established in 1846, two years before statehood and the founding of the University of Wisconsin on the shores of Lake Mendota in 1848. Both institutions have contributed heavily to our knowledge of ancient people of the Four Lakes.

Largely through the early efforts of Charles E. Brown of the WHS and the active membership of the Wisconsin Archeological Society (est. 1901), more than two hundred individual mounds are preserved on or near the lakes (figure 3.1). Among these are stunning examples of effigy mounds and the largest remaining in the effigy mound region. In the city of Madison alone, visitors can see a dozen mound sites, including whole groups in parks and other public places, preserved largely at Brown's instigation. In contrast, not one effigy mound exists today in the nearby city of Milwaukee, once another large effigy mound center. Long gone are the very effigy mounds that first captured the interest of a young land surveyor from Ohio by the name of Increase Lapham, leading him to start a landmark documentation of Wisconsin mounds and putting him on the road to becoming a famed natural scientist.

Figure 3.1. Charles E. Brown taking a mound measurement.

Reconstructing the Landscape

Documentation of mounds in the vicinity of the Four Lakes began in the early nineteenth century. Richard C. Taylor, a visitor to the area, wrote about the puzzling earthworks in an 1838 article titled "Notes Respecting Certain Indian Mounds and Earthworks in the Form of Animal Effigies, Chiefly in Wisconsin Territory," which was accompanied by the first fairly accurate maps. Taylor had apparently read a widely published newspaper account of effigy mounds written by Lapham in 1836 and had heard of a concentration of such mounds in the area of the Four Lakes. He characterized the curious mounds he found here as "forming a species of *alto relievo* of gigantic proportions."[1]

Shortly thereafter, the mounds of Madison and the Four Lakes gained a bit of fleeting national fame. John Locke, a physician, natural scientist, inventor, and earthwork researcher from Cincinnati, Ohio, traveled to the area to see the mound landscape for himself. He was so struck by the mounds that he published descriptions in the *Congressional Record* in 1844 under the title "Earthwork Antiquities in Wiskonsin Territory."[2]

Increase Lapham, destined to be recognized as Wisconsin's first natural scientist, continued his interest in mounds with the book *Antiquities of*

Wisconsin in 1855, a landmark in North American archaeology published by the Smithsonian Society and dealing mainly with the subject of effigy mounds of southern Wisconsin (figures 3.2 and 3.3). He visited the mounds of the Four Lakes in the 1850s, where "the mound-builders have left unusually numerous traces of their former occupancy and industry" and later engaged in some informal mound excavation at the Dividing Ridge mound group, apparently to help settle the question of who built the mounds.[3]

The numerous mounds attracted many more mound researchers throughout the late nineteenth and early twentieth centuries, researchers who, like Lapham, published or otherwise provided descriptions and maps of many mounds and mound arrangements now no longer extant. Among the most valuable studies of this period are those of Theodore H. Lewis, A. B. Stout, Charles E. Brown, and Dr. W. G. McLachlan, a physician from McFarland on Lake Waubesa. Stephen Peet, a minister from Beloit, Wisconsin, also took an interest in the effigy mounds of the Four Lakes and other places, writing articles and books on the topic in the late nineteenth century. He founded *American Antiquarian,* a national archaeology journal, and published many maps of mounds he saw in Four Lakes. Despite his enthusiasm, however, the maps are often impressionistic and incorrect, making them difficult to reconcile with later information. Errors can also be found in the later works of Stout and Brown, who no doubt mapped with only a hand compass and measuring tape, but on the whole their work has been found to be far more trustworthy.

Theodore H. Lewis came to the Four Lakes several times in the 1880s and 1890s as part of his extensive midwestern mound-mapping project, the Northwestern Archaeological Survey, funded by Alfred Hill, a Minnesota businessman (figure 3.4). Hill and Lewis sought evidence about the inception of the mounds, producing the best source of accurate maps of mounds throughout Wisconsin and other states.[4] As a trained land surveyor using a transit and accurate measurement techniques, Lewis made maps and compiled data that are still used, as they were for this book, to reconstruct ancient mound groups now destroyed. He mapped many effigy mounds in the Four Lakes, but usually only those that were, to him, noteworthy. Nevertheless, he added short notes about the nature of unmapped mounds.

As a student at the University of Wisconsin and as a member of the Wisconsin Archeological Society, A. B. Stout mapped mounds in the Four

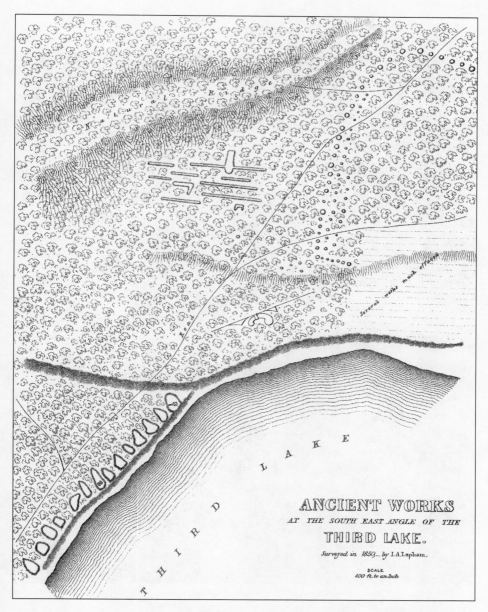

ANCIENT WORKS
AT THE SOUTH EAST ANGLE OF THE
THIRD LAKE.

Surveyed in 1850 by I.A.Lapham.

SCALE
400 ft. to an inch

Figure 3.2. Lapham map showing a part of the Four Lakes mound district. "Third Lake" refers to Lake Monona.

Figure 3.3. Increase Lapham.

Figure 3.4. Theodore H. Lewis.

Lakes and also of nearby areas on Lake Koshkonong in 1906.[5] His work in the Four Lakes was taken up by Charles E. Brown a few years later.

Charles Brown and "Mound City"

No single person did more to document and preserve the mounds of Madison and the Four Lakes than Charles E. Brown.[6] Brown served as museum director at the WHS between 1908 and 1944 and was founding father, editor, and guiding spirit of the Wisconsin Archeological Society, the organized vanguard of mound documentation and preservation in the early twentieth century. Arriving in Madison in 1908, he was so impressed with the mound landscape that it led him on a lifelong crusade to preserve or at least document every mound he found there. In speeches and presentations, he touted Madison as "Mound City." Brown worked tirelessly for mound preservation until his death in 1946, two years after he retired from the WHS.

In many respects Brown came to Madison at the best possible time to launch a preservation campaign (figure 3.5). Under the direction of Reuben Thwaites, the WHS had already begun a new era of public education and outreach in the area of Wisconsin history. At the state capitol, less than a mile away down State Street, sat progressive governor Robert M. La-Follette and a state legislature sympathetic to cultural and educational concerns. At the city level, land-use conflicts in rapidly growing Madison stimulated long-term landscape and land-use planning to enhance the city's natural and cultural strengths. The progressive landscape architect John Nolen came to Madison in 1908, the same year that Brown did, to create a city plan.

Brown's efforts to preserve Indian mounds began earlier with the organization of the Wisconsin Archeological Society (WAS) in 1901. Alarmed by the statewide destruction of mounds, the WAS established mound preservation as one of its first priorities. In 1911 a WAS delegation under Brown's leadership successfully lobbied the legislature for enactment of a law protecting archaeological sites on public lands from vandalism and looting. This was the state's first historic preservation law. At the same time, the legislature made an annual appropriation of $1500 to the WHS to have the WAS locate and map ancient places in the state, particularly mounds. To

Figure 3.5. Charles E. Brown (*right*) along with mound survey volunteers, noted University of Wisconsin poet Professor William Ellery Leonard (*center*) and Rev. P. M. Gilmore (*left*) of the Unitarian Church, at the Fox Bluff mound group on Lake Mendota in 1908.

do this, the WAS organized a special section, called the Wisconsin Archeological Survey, consisting of volunteers who fanned out across the state. The funding, used for travel expenses, lasted only two years, but during this time hundreds of new mound groups were recorded and mapped. It would be another half century before state funding for this type of preservation work would again become available.

From his base at the WHS, Brown mapped mounds and recorded ancient village and camp sites in and around Madison (figure 3.6). He

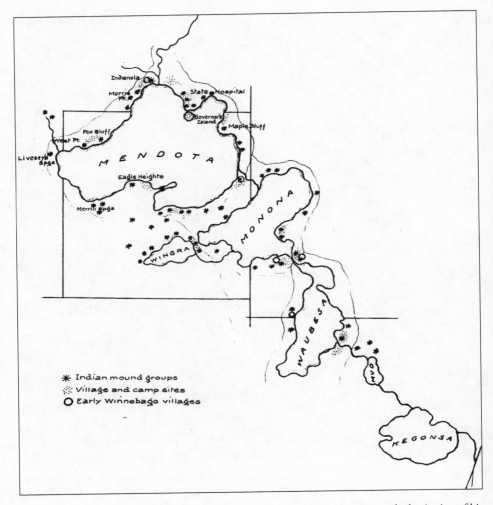

Figure 3.6. Map made by Brown of Four Lakes mound groups and other sites at the beginning of his research.

expanded the survey to the other lakes by enlisting the help of talented and energetic volunteers such as Dr. W. G. McLachlan (figure 3.7), who mapped and described a considerable number of mound groups (many now gone) during his vacations. The *Wisconsin Archeologist* published lengthy reports on the mounds of lakes Mendota, Monona, Wingra, Waubesa, and Kegonsa between the years 1912 and 1922, showing maps of many ancient earthworks for the first time.[7] Like maps made by earlier researchers, the

Figure 3.7. W. G. McLachlan.

only evidence we have now of the existence of long-destroyed mounds are those that Stout, Brown, and McLachlan published during this time.

In 1912 the WAS established a permanent committee that worked to save mounds, primarily by public and WAS acquisition. Collaborating with a variety of philanthropic and public service organizations, as well as local governments, the WAS placed historic markers and plaques at mounds on public lands as a means of calling attention to the importance of these ancient earthworks. Many of these are still in place. By the early 1920s the WAS could boast that five hundred mounds had been preserved in the state largely by its efforts, eighty-two of which are in the Madison area.

Brown's strategy is one still used by modern-day preservations—systematic surveys, protective legislation, public acquisition and education, partnerships with influential individuals and organizations, landmark designations, fund-raising, and relentless promotion. Brown worked vigorously to encourage public acquisition, the only tool at the time that provided a way of permanent preservation. He cajoled and badgered public officials into taking better care of mounds in their jurisdictions and convinced Madison officials to incorporate mounds into city parks as city planning progressed. Brown later worked with the university when it acquired land for a large arboretum where he had previously identified and mapped effigy mound groups. He served on the University of Wisconsin Arboretum's first advisory committee and personally supervised the restoration of mounds damaged by vandals and burrowing animals. In the late 1930s Brown led Works Progress Administration projects to restore mounds on campus and elsewhere in the Madison area.

When mounds were carelessly destroyed, Brown was there to take responsible parties to task. He was especially furious when the university itself allowed mounds to be destroyed as it expanded in the late 1930s, allowing him only a short time to retrieve human bones from the mounds. He even characterized the destruction as "criminal." His much-publicized complaints drew a response from the university promising to preserve the mounds and inviting Brown to advise it as it acquired a mound group on Picnic Point.[8]

Brown recognized the need for public education regarding the uniqueness and importance of the mounds. He wrote articles, pamphlets, and brochures, and became a popular lecturer. He organized public and university tours of ancient sites on the lakes. He consulted widely with Indian people, particularly the Ho-Chunk, on mounds and other traditions, and solicited their help in educational and preservation work.

But as an archaeologist and student of ancient Indian culture, Brown was naturally curious about the physical structure of the mounds themselves and how they fit into the archaeological scheme of things. Brown and his volunteers excavated several mounds and accompanying burials in the Four Lakes, although most often immediately before they were to be destroyed by development (figure 3.8). Neither his training nor the state of knowledge at the time allowed Brown to gain great insights, but his descriptions continue to inform present studies. At the very least, the bones

Figure 3.8. Volunteers working under the direction of Charles Brown dig a Madison area mound in 1931 before it was destroyed by development.

of some of the ancient people of the Four Lakes have been rescued and preserved for anticipated reburial.

The Preservation Movement

After Brown, a gap in coordinated mound documentation and preservation occurred, resulting in the loss of many mounds to urban expansion and farming. Some of the slack in documentation was taken up by archaeologists from the University of Wisconsin. From the late 1940s through the 1960s, faculty and students of the university's Department of Anthropology conducted emergency excavations of those mounds about to be destroyed by housing developments.

A new wave of mound research and preservation began in the late 1970s, fueled by increasing recognition and respect for Native American history and culture that accompanied the national bicentennial in 1976, the passage of the National Historic Preservation Act of 1966 (NHPA) that stimulated a preservation ethic throughout the nation, and the passage of a special Wisconsin burial sites preservation law in 1985 that eventually applied to mounds.

Central to the new preservation movement was Brown's institution, the Wisconsin Historical Society, which under the auspices of the NHPA had been given funding and the responsibility, through a historic preservation office, for inventorying the state for historic buildings, historic sites, and archaeological sites worthy of protection. These are listed on the National Register of Historic Places and therefore need to be considered by federal officials during the course of federally funded or permitted projects such as road building. Over the years, the WHS in turn passed on millions of dollars of this federal funding to communities, universities, and private institutions and organizations to locate and document such places. One early project conducted in the late 1970s by Luther College of Decorah, Iowa, was a review of early records and an on-ground search for effigy mounds in Dane County and in three other counties in southern Wisconsin. This marked the first attempt to systematically relocate previously recorded effigy mounds and assess their current condition over a large area. Although the study concluded that as much as 80 percent of the mounds in the Four Lakes had been destroyed, many mounds listed as missing and destroyed have since been found intact through more intensive research.[9] More than thirty of the state's mound sites, sometimes encompassing large areas with many mounds, are now listed the National Register of Historic Places, eleven of them in Madison. New mound sites are still being listed on the National Register but only as the Wisconsin Historical Society's slim and decreasing archaeological site-preservation budget allows.

As directed by state law, the WHS historic preservation office added a burial sites preservation program in the late 1980s. The first mound it catalogued under the law, and put under state protection, was a long-tailed mound on the shores of Lake Monona (see figure 6.9). This particular area became a center of controversy because of a proposed housing development on the mound site. Since passage of the law, purposeful mound destruction has virtually ceased (there are few notable exceptions) and documentation needed for formal cataloguing has led to the creation of many up-to-date maps.

In the late 1980s, the city of Madison, through its own historic preservation office, initiated a program of designating the community's many mounds as city landmarks, offering added protections. Dane County joined preservation efforts in the 1990s with a countywide mound identification and inventory project though its Parks Department.[10] This study was funded by federal grants administered by the WHS and manned by Larry Johns, a mound researcher of Oneida Indian ancestry who had become a passionate advocate of mound preservation. He was assisted by many community volunteers. This project also added accurate and up-to-date maps of mounds, and updates on mound conditions. Mound sites were then catalogued as burial sites under Wisconsin state law.

Private groups also stimulated public interest in mound preservation. James Scherz, a University of Wisconsin civil engineering professor, along with the Ancient Earthworks Society, produced the first truly accurate maps of mounds in the Four Lakes since the time of T. H. Lewis.[11] Scherz has been pursuing the controversial ideas that mound groupings are mathematical and astronomical expressions, and that there are connections between the mounds and ancient Old World societies that, he believes, frequently visited North America.

In the late 1990s, cutbacks in federal and state funding slowed the ability of the WHS to focus its attention on preservation on archaeological sites, but by that time a great momentum had been already achieved. Other state agencies and local communities acquired mound sites for permanent protection and to enhance public history. For example, the city of Monona, bordering Lake Monona, created the new Woodland Park around several mounds. In 2004 the University of Wisconsin's planning division obtained funding from the Getty Campus Heritage Fund to inventory its many mounds and ancient sites and develop master plans that maximize protection during continuous university expansion.[12] This certainly would have pleased Charles Brown, who harshly criticized the university for the destruction of mounds for a dormitory earlier in the twentieth century.

Today, the state archaeology office at the WHS serves as a central repository for mound site information as well as for other archaeological sites. This also began with Brown, who compiled an inventory of Wisconsin archaeological sites called the "Record of Antiquities," published in the *Wisconsin Archeologist*. The inventory is now a state-of-the-art electronic database with information on more than thirty thousand sites.[13] This database has been used to estimate the number of mounds and mound groups once found in Wisconsin. The office continuously updates old records with more accurate information. Remarkably, new mounds are still recorded nearly every year through reviews of old literature and on-ground surveys. The manuscript of this book had to be revised several times with new information, and likely some mound numbers will have changed slightly by the time of its publication.

Still, much has been lost over the years. Hundreds of individual mounds had been destroyed in the Four Lakes prior to Brown's efforts and the later institution of federal, state, and local protections. Further, while preservation attention has been focused on individuals mounds, the landscape that framed their construction and helps explain their meaning continues to disappear. However, surviving effigy mounds and mounds groups, along with the many maps and descriptions of those that did not survive, allow for the reconstruction of much of the remarkable effigy mound landscape of Madison and the Four Lakes.

The Effigy Mound Landscape of Four Lakes

More than 1,200 individual mounds were built on or near the shores of the lakes in at least 160 different groups or locations (figure 3.9). In many cases, the groups merged into one another, creating a larger landscape. It is difficult, in fact, to find any elevation along the shores of the lakes that were not covered by mounds. Most of these date to the effigy mound era ca. A.D. 700–1100, but there are also locations that include large conical mounds typical of the earlier mound construction, particularly at inlets and outlets of lakes.

Most effigy mounds are part of small and large groupings. The largest single concentration of mounds recorded is the Fuller's Woods group

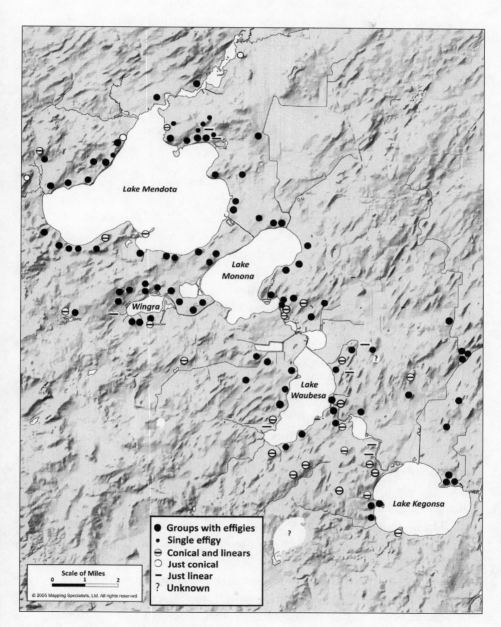

Figure 3.9. Map of Four Lakes mound sites.

Legend:
- ● Groups with effigies
- • Single effigy
- ⊖ Conical and linears
- ○ Just conical
- − Just linear
- ? Unknown

Lake Mendota
Lake Monona
Wingra
Lake Waubesa
Lake Kegonsa

Scale of Miles
0   1   2
© 2005 Mapping Specialists, Ltd. All rights reserved

overlooking the east shore of Lake Mendota with more than fifty mounds, including many small conical mounds consistent with the mound building during the effigy mound era. Individual mounds away from groupings do occur but are part of the overall landscape. It is argued here that separation of mounds into individual groups or sites is artificial. At one time, mounds were so densely arranged around the lakes and beyond that they formed one giant ceremonial landscape.

Mound Forms

The landscape of the Four Lakes mound district may be the best example of the of effigy mound ceremonial activity, since most types of mound built during the effigy mound period could be found here. While conical and linear forms account for most mounds, at least two hundred of the recorded mounds are clearly recognizable as birds, mammals, and spirit animals (table 3.1 and figure 3.10). Some forms cannot be easily interpreted; sometimes effigy mounds were built so low and blend so well into the natural landscape that exact forms cannot be discerned. This has led to different depictions being made by different people of the very same mounds. Farming often mutilated mounds, leaving behind obscured and easily misinterpreted shapes.

The ubiquity of conical and long and short linear mounds is due in part to the fact that these forms were made over a longer period of time than were the animal effigies. Conical or round mounds spanned 1,700 years of construction through the effigy mound era and beyond, although earlier mounds tended to be much larger. In many cases the smaller conical mounds believed to have been constructed during the effigy mound era occupy high, prominent positions, suggesting that they are associated with the sky or upper world.

The first construction of linear mounds also starts sometime before the appearance of the classic and realistic zoomorphic mounds, and may be the harbingers of the explosive effigy phenomena, generally representing the lower part of the cosmos. Many long mounds associated with the zoomorphic mounds are straight and tapering, curved, bent, and distinctly serpentine. A case has been made here that these represent snakes—an animal associated with the watery lower world or underworld in many Native American worldviews. Four Lakes mounds also include several crossed linear mounds as well as combined conical and linear forms called compound

Table 3.1. Four Lakes Mound Forms

Lake	Goose	Other Bird	Bear	Canine	Deer	Water Spirit	Water Mammal	Compound and Club	Snake-like	Linear	Conical / Oval	Other	Total
Mendota	4	44	14	4	1	29	0	1	8	96	152	17	370
Wingra	3	12	10	2	1	16	2	1	7	56	105	7	222
Monona	1	10	3	0	0	10	1?	3	9	72	96	29	234
Waubesa	1	11	3	3	0	3	1	4	17	73	44	23	183
Kegonsa	1	4	2	0	0	4	2	4	4	75	92	6	194
Total	10	81	32	9	2	62	6	13	45	372	489	82	1,203

Note: "Snake-like" includes tapering linear, bent, curved, and serpentine mounds; "Linear" includes short and long straight mounds (many of these may predate the construction of effigy mounds); "Other" includes unknown, uncertain identification, and unique forms; in some cases records indicate that more mounds were present but no number is specified so cannot be included in counts.

Figure 3.10. A representative sample of mound forms of the Four Lakes Mound District.

mounds. Among the latter are conical mounds with straight tails, often called "club mounds."

Clear animal effigy forms of the Four Lakes include substantial representations of all three natural realms—sky, earth, and water—as do other mound concentrations in south-central Wisconsin. This contrasts with the mound landscapes of some eastern mound centers of the effigy mound region that are heavily oriented to water symbolism (especially long-tailed water spirits) and southwestern areas where there is a marked dominance of sky or bird symbolism along with that of bears.[14]

Birds in the Four Lakes mound district include straight-winged, eagle-like forms, and bent-wing birds that often look exactly like hawks. Some of these may be meant to represent the invisible thunderbirds, historically depicted with straight or bent wings, and sometimes with a split tail. Although not common as compared to some other mound forms, goose effigies are found in greater frequency in the Four Lakes than in some other areas of the effigy mound regions. No geese, for example, are reported in the western part of the effigy mound region in Wisconsin. Examples of geese occurred at ten locations on or near lakes or large wetlands, mainly flying to and from bodies of water (figure 3.11). The bent-wing form of the goose is distinctive to the Four Lakes according to a study by Amy Rosebrough of the Office of the State Archaeologist. It is, therefore, the signature Four Lakes effigy mound.

Four Lakes earthly forms include canines (fox, wolf), deer, and especially bears, which particularly represent the earth plane in the traditions of Native Americans. Representatives of the lowest watery realm are long-tailed water spirits, a few long-bodied water mammals, and snakes. The vast majority of the sixty-two recorded water spirit mounds in the Four Lakes are of the panther type, showing the creature in profile. At least four were made with curved tails. Only three are flattened or built in an aerial perspective, incorrectly identified in the past as "turtle" mounds. In contrast, nearly 40 percent of the many long-tailed water spirits recorded for Waukesha County in the eastern part of the effigy mound region are aerial perspective or as comprehended from above.[15] This difference seems again to be a product of topography, with the aerial perspective mounds reflecting the generally flatter natural landscape of eastern Wisconsin. On the grounds of the Mendota Mental Health Institute on Lake Mendota, a large curve-tailed water spirit was sculpted in profile on a hillside so steep that

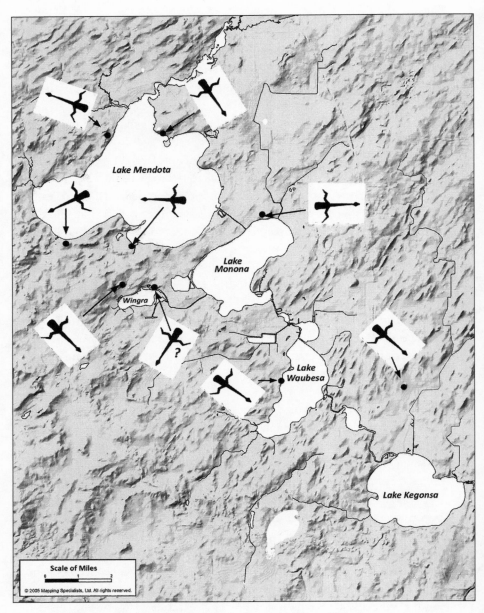

Figure 3.11. Distribution of Goose mounds in the Four Lakes Mound District.

the spirit animal seems to be emerging sideways from the slope (see figure 4.8).

If effigy mounds do indeed represent clan animals as well as cosmological maps or creation landscapes, at least ten clans occupied the Four Lakes, judging from reoccurring mound forms. These include thunderbird, eagle, hawk, goose, bear, wolf or fox, deer, water mammal, water spirit, and snake. Some effigies may represent other types of birds. Missing are effigy forms identified elsewhere as buffalo. Extremely long-necked, crane-like forms occasionally found elsewhere also do not seem to have been present, although one eroded form on Lake Mendota mapped by Lewis could be interpreted as such.

Some of the largest, as well as some of the most unusual effigy mounds representing both the upper and lower worlds are found in the Four Lakes area. The wingspan of one huge straight-wing bird on Lake Mendota is 624 feet in length. In the form of an eagle, it is perhaps a thunderbird, the powerful and mainly invisible spirit being that, in some native traditions, is envisioned as an eagle-like form. Some linear and tapering mounds in effigy mound groups on or near Lake Monona in the Madison area reached lengths of seven hundred feet and more.

Rare forms include two deer presented with all four legs, a two-tailed water spirit, several spectacular water spirits with curved tails, two crossed sets of long linear mounds, a canine form with two conical mounds attached to the legs, and mounds that have been referred to as "swan" and "rabbit" effigies. One type of mammal form, a fox-like animal with prominent ears and an arched back, seems to be unique to the Lake Waubesa area.

Distribution of Mound Forms

The distribution of mound forms reveals substantial differences between the upper or northern part of the Four Lakes mound district and the lower or southern part. Lake Mendota, the largest lake, and the nearby tiny "fifth" lake, Wingra, witnessed the heaviest use by the effigy mound people (see table 3.1). Of the zoomorphic forms, bird effigy mounds are most common on Mendota, Wingra, and Monona, and proportionally much less so in the lower lakes, Waubesa and Kegonsa. The largest lake, Mendota, has the largest number of bird forms. Long narrow mounds are common on the south part of Lake Monona, on or near Lake

Kegonsa, and especially on Lake Waubesa. Among these are several clear serpentine or snake forms. Water mammals occur more frequently in the lower lakes, although still not in great numbers.

This pattern may reflect geography rather than social divisions since it is probable that the Four Lakes were occupied by a single group living in several nearby communities. Given the close connection of mound symbolism to landscape, it is easy to see that proportionally more birds would be found on the generally higher landscapes of the upper lakes, while lower-world symbolism would dominate the lower lakes, where larger areas of wetlands are found. However, one area of the effigy mound ceremonial landscape may reflect a social difference—the principal habitations of Four Lakes leaders. The huge birds arranged around the village near the inlet of the Yahara River on Lake Mendota suggest a settlement of great importance. Here, it is interesting to note that traditional chiefs of the Ho-Chunk Nation come from the Thunderbird Clan.

A Tour of the Lakes

The following chapters take the reader on a tour of the Four Lakes effigy mound ceremonial landscape, beginning with Lake Mendota and the Yahara River headwaters and continuing south to the mouth of the Yahara River with its confluence with the Rock River. The places described are by no means all of the effigy mound sites. Highlighted are mounds and groups that illustrate the concepts discussed in this book, those that make the Four Lakes distinctive, and those that are associated with interesting recent histories. Effigy and other mound sites located on park or other public lands are highlighted with visitor information in an appendix. A few key mound sites described are on private property and are not accessible to the public. In these cases, precise locations are not provided.

4 | Yahara Inlet and Mendota
Lake of Spirits

THE YAHARA RIVER has its headwaters several miles north of Lake Mendota. It flows through the Cherokee Marsh and widens into Lake Mendota at a point near where Late Woodland people built some of largest and most spectacular mounds in the Four Lakes. Late Woodland people used the marshy headwater areas for small seasonal hamlets or other special purposes, constructing keyhole-shaped pit houses (see chapter 2). One such place, the Statz site, is located on the marshy west end of Six Mile Creek that once flowed to the Yahara River at its original inlet at Lake Mendota. Prior to the construction of a dam and lock at the lake outlet, the water levels were about five feet lower and the mouth of the inlet well south of where it is today.

The largest of the Four Lakes, Lake Mendota now covers nearly ten thousand acres. The Wisconsin state capitol overlooks this body of water from an isthmus dividing it from Lake Monona. Lake Mendota was originally referred to as the "Fourth Lake" by early settlers. The Ho-Chunk also called it *Wonk-sheek-ho-mik-la* ("where the man lies"), derived from a legend concerning the love of a young a man for a female spirit that lived in the lake.[1] The legend recounts how the man obtained a vision from the spirit and magically turned himself into a catfish to pursue her. Traveling from lake to lake, he arrived at Lake Mendota where he found his spirit love and lives with her today beneath its waters.

Mounds occupied virtually every elevation and piece of dry land around Lake Mendota. Current state records count at least 370 individual

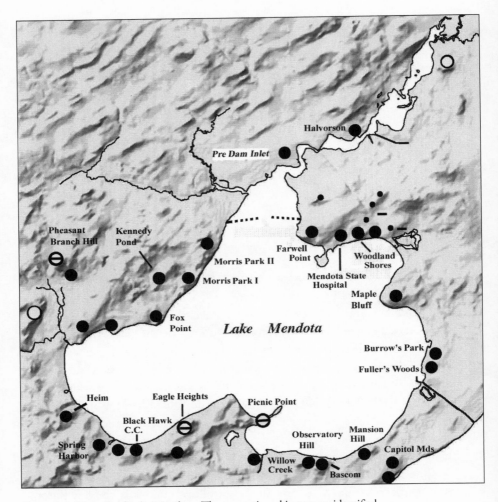

Figure 4.1. Mounds of Lake Mendota. Those mentioned in text are identified.

mounds at more than fifty locations, most of which appear to date to the effigy mound era between A.D. 700 and 1100 (figure 4.1).[2]

Particularly dense concentrations were at the Yahara River inlet and on a large, high rock-bluff area overlooking the northeast shore, north of the formerly marshy outlet of the lake. Mounds on the lake include some the of best and largest examples of effigy mound forms, and in several instances provide models for the ideological structure of effigy mound landscapes.

Most major types of effigy mounds can be found in the vicinity of Lake Mendota although, as elsewhere in the Four Lakes, conical and linear mounds dominated the landscape. Of the zoomorphic mounds, birds, long-tailed water spirits, and bears were the most common. Snake forms were plentiful, if we can include tapering linear mounds in that category, as proposed here.

Here too are major Late Woodland lakeshore settlements, including the fortified Camp Indianola village and the probable village partly encircled by effigy mounds on the other side of the inlet at the Mendota Mental Health Institute. Everything about this large lake suggests it was the center of the Four Lakes effigy mound society and its most important ceremonial area. Given the number, size, diversity of mound forms, and degree of modern preservation, one could rightly consider Lake Mendota the symbolic capital of the whole effigy mound region.

Other Lake Mendota Legends

The Ho-Chunk lived on Lake Mendota during the early nineteenth century and had their principal village on the western shores, perhaps because of major Indian trails that skirted the lake and ran from the Mississippi River to the Fox River, the main transportation route to eastern Wisconsin and Lake Michigan. Some Ho-Chunk people continued to use the lake long after their formal removal west in the 1830s. These landless people passed down stories about the lake's supernatural inhabitants, possibly inspired by the visible presence of these very beings in the form of ancient effigy mounds. The long-tailed water spirits dwelled in deep water off Governor's Island on the north shore. Here, the legend says, one must exercise caution should the water spirits rise, capsizing canoes and drowning people.[3] The Indians made tobacco offerings to gain the goodwill of the water spirits. Marl deposits, the dens of the water spirits, cover some of the bottom of Lake Mendota.

According to one Ho-Chunk story, the thunderbirds once roosted on the west shore at Fox Bluff, presently occupied by a Middleton subdivision. According to this account, the thunderbirds could be seen flying high in the air during stormy weather, thunder rolling from their wings and lightning flashing from their eyes. This bluff was also the focus of longtime mound ceremonialism with one mound enclosing a circular and nest-like stone tomb.

A spirit horse, which could be seen on the hill on misty days and heard neighing and stamping, inhabits Eagle Heights, now a part of the University of Wisconsin on the south shore. The Indians went to the heights, called *Sho-hetka-ka* (Horse Hill) to gain power from the spirit horse through fasting and dreaming. Since a horse is featured, the legend must necessarily postdate the appearance of Europeans who brought the animal to the New World. But the story reinforces the sacred nature of this natural feature. It too was used by the ancient mound builders who built linear and conical mounds on the hill, one linear with a curious bend (figure 4.2).

Yahara River and North Shore Mounds

A large water spirit mound and a bear mound can be found in Yahara Heights County Park, just north of the present Yahara River inlet, and these serve as an appropriate introduction to the mound landscape of the Four Lakes. Measuring 208 feet in length and shown in profile (panther shape), the water spirit mound is a part of a larger grouping of effigy mounds called the Halvorson group that once contained two water spirits, the bear, an oval mound, and a linear mound (figure 4.3). The water spirit is oriented toward the river and marsh. Only the bear and water spirit mounds survived early cultivation. Another effigy mound grouping of large birds had been on higher ground to the southwest, but this mound disappeared before the area could be mapped.

Farther down both sides of the former inlet are mounds and habitation sites that span a millennium and establish Lake Mendota as a long-standing and very important ceremonial center. Construction of a dam and lock raised the level of the lake, flooding formerly marshy ground and moving the inlet north. In what is now Governor Nelson State Park on the northwest shore, a group of relatively large conical mounds are found on a high ridge, part of the Morris II group (figure 4.4). Pottery found by archaeologists near the mounds include Early and Middle Woodland types consistent with the types of mounds on the ridge.[4] Effigy mounds, including large water spirits headed toward the lake, were later built. One

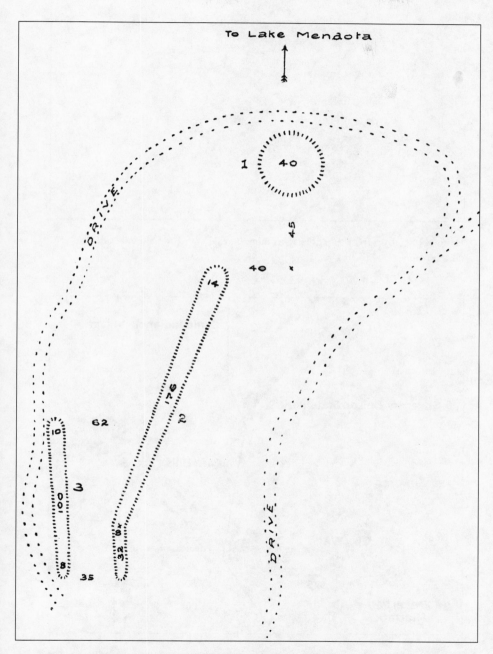

Figure 4.2. The Eagle Heights mound group is situated on a high hill on the University of Wisconsin campus overlooking Lake Mendota.

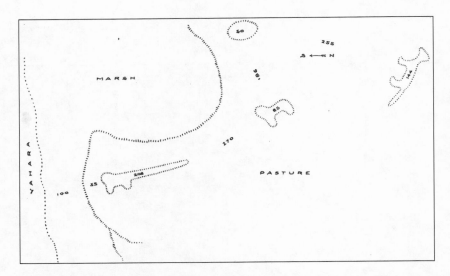

Figure 4.3. Halvorson or Yahara Heights mound group above the old inlet of Lake Mendota as mapped by Brown.

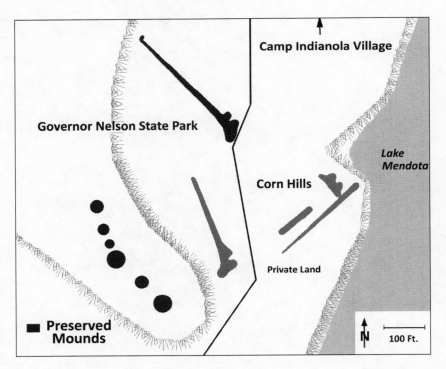

Figure 4.4. Morris Park II mound group. The huge water spirit or water panther and the conical mounds on the ridge are preserved in Governor Nelson State Park.

Figure 4.5. Early-twentieth-century photo of a large mound at Morris Park.

measuring three hundred feet in length can be viewed at the park. Immediately north is the Late Woodland fortified Camp Indianola, almost certainly home to the people that made this impressive mound. Ho-Chunk people continued use of this important spot in the nineteenth century and cultivated the agricultural fields called "corn hills" recorded among the effigy mounds. The Borchers Beach conical mounds (see figure 2.22) lay along the lakeshore near the village and the Morris II mounds, one with the possible evidence for Mississippian contacts in the form of marine shell beads (figure 4.5).

Across a small bay and former Yahara River inlet, the most spectacular part of the effigy mound landscape of the Four Lakes originally spread along the north shore of Lake Mendota to the marshy outlet of the Yahara River. Lone mounds in the form of bear, birds, and linears also occupied elevations to the north of the lake.

Several large conical mounds and a massive effigy mound still occupy a high elevation called Farwell Point, now a part of Mendota Mental Health Institute grounds (figure 4.6). Like the Governor Nelson mounds on the other side of the inlet, the conical mounds undoubtedly represent the earlier period of mound building. Nineteenth-century digging revealed

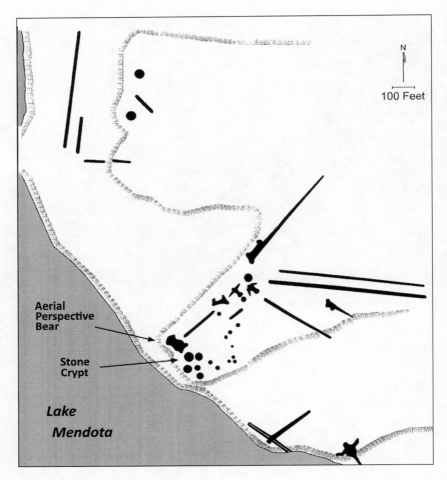

Figure 4.6. Map of Farwell Point mounds.

that one of these conicals covered a stone burial vault built on the former surface of the ground; the marks of this excavation are still visible.

An unusually massive tailless effigy mound shares the same knoll as this large conical (figure 4.7). It is probably a bear with a flattened or aerial perspective. It is eighty-five feet long and stands over five feet, higher than other effigy mounds in the Four Lakes mound district. Although referred as a "turtle," it is most likely a bear. Aerial-perspective bears occur elsewhere in the Four Lakes and in the effigy mound region. The proximity of

Figure 4.7. Photo of massive tailless effigy, probably an aerial perspective bear, at Farwell Point.

the large effigy to the earlier conical mounds suggests that it may have been among the first effigies built on Farwell Point.

Bears are a common effigy form in the Four Lakes but earlier Middle Woodland Hopewell people also venerated the bear as indicated by much surviving art and the common use of bear-tooth necklaces. Given this, and the massive nature of the mound—more similar in height to Middle Woodland mounds than to later Late Woodland earthworks—one has to wonder if it was actually built during the later part of the Middle Woodland period. If so, this would offer a physical earthwork link between Middle Woodland beliefs and later effigy mounds. Generally dated after Hopewell, a few effigy mounds have been recorded among the Hopewell earthworks of Ohio, including birds, an "alligator" (probably a version of a water spirit), and the great serpent mound (see figure 1.15). This is the only other place in North America where effigy mounds have been recorded in some number. Whatever the case, the presence of this massive effigy further identifies the Lake Mendota and Yahara River outlet area as a very important part of the Four Lakes effigy mound landscape.

Linear mounds, smaller conical mounds, and zoomorphic effigy mounds surround these early mounds at Farwell Point. A water spirit, now gone, extended for a length of more than five hundred feet, the largest such form recorded in the Four Lakes. Three very long linear mounds, one tapered like a body of a snake, radiate downslope from conical mounds and

Figure 4.8. Aerial photo of curve-tailed effigy mound on the grounds of the Mendota Mental Health Institute.

bird effigies, a characteristic pattern for these mounds. The longest of these reached more than six hundred feet. A linear mound of similar length was once part of grouping lower on the landscape near the Yahara River inlet.

At the south end of the Farwell Point, a bent-wing goose mound, the Four Lakes symbol, once flew downslope to the lake. This is one of a dozen geese recorded in the Four Lakes mound district, each of which was found on or near all of the lakes. Nearby, Lewis surveyed another possible long-necked bird eroding into the lake with wings that had a strange depression down the middle. Both are now gone, but farther to the west remains what is perhaps the most beautiful mound of its type found in the effigy mound region—a huge, curve-tailed water spirit shown in profile on a steep slope above a wetland (figure 4.8). It is one of three such forms documented in the Four Lakes and the only one that survives.

The curve-tailed form is part of an extraordinary and comparatively well-preserved arrangement of effigy mounds located on a low terrace above the lakeshore. The Mendota State Hospital group (figures 4.9 and 4.10)

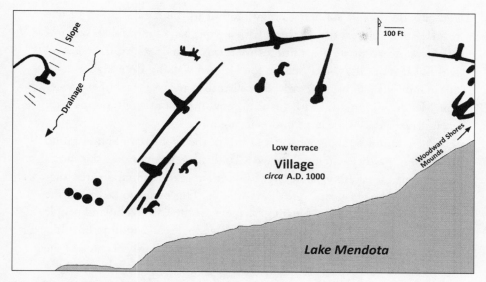

Figure 4.9. Mendota State Hospital mound group.

Figure 4.10. Aerial photo of large eagle mounds on the grounds of the Mendota Mental Health Institute.

contains the largest surviving effigy mound in the region, an eagle-like form, perhaps a great thunderbird, with a wingspan of more than six hundred feet. Adjacent are other impressive forms: bears, water spirits, conical and linear mounds, and a unique four-legged walking deer (figure 4.11). Some mounds had been destroyed or disturbed in the past, but the state-run Mendota Mental Health Institute now maintains the mounds with great pride and uses the large bird as its logo.

These mounds, along with large birds of the Woodward Shores group to the west, partly encircle a Late Woodland village of unknown size found lower along the lakeshore. The large birds orient to the habitation area, suggesting that the village had great importance. This seems to be one of the main settlements, if not *the* main settlement, of the Late Woodland people of the Four Lakes. It is possible that the large eagles and thunderbird-like mounds and their arrangement identifies the village of the civil chiefs of the Four Lakes effigy mound builders. In his excavations, archaeologist Philip Salkin found some Madison Ware pottery here, attributed to the effigy mound builders, along with a larger amount of later collared pottery.[5] Madison pottery has also been reported for nearby Governor's Island, a point of land that extends into the lake from the north shore.

The Model of Effigy Mound Symbolism

Effigy mounds extend continuously along the north shore and include the Woodward Shores mound group. This grouping is one that best illustrates the principles of effigy mound landscapes, and it has been rendered artistically as a symbol of the ancient people in the Madison area by L. Brower Hatcher in his public installation *Forum of Origins* (figure 4.12).

Unfortunately, most of the mounds have been destroyed by residential expansion. But maps made by T. H. Lewis in 1888 show a classic effigy mound group neatly segregated into birds, mammals, and water spirits, with water spirit and linear mounds radiating from a large, and probably earlier, conical mound (figure 4.13). The bird and mammal mounds follow a slight ridge, but the water spirits and snake-like linear mounds are oriented downslope to the water. The bird effigies, several of which still survive on private land, show both straight- and bent-winged birds, the former bearing clear resemblance to modern Native American depictions

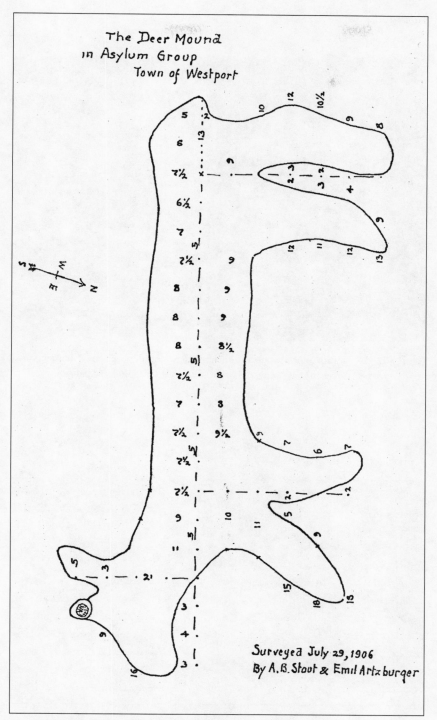

Figure 4.11. Drawing of deer effigy by A. B. Stout.

Figure 4.12. Woodward Shores group and ancient effigy mound people are commemorated in *Forum of Origins* by artist L. Brower Hatcher near the state capitol in Madison.

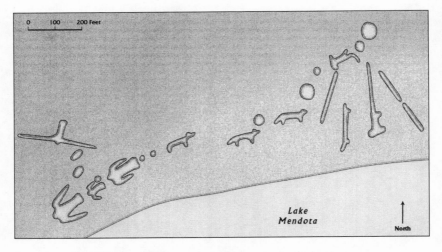

0 100 200 Feet

Lake
Mendota

North

Figure 4.13. The Woodward Shores group based on mapping by Lewis.

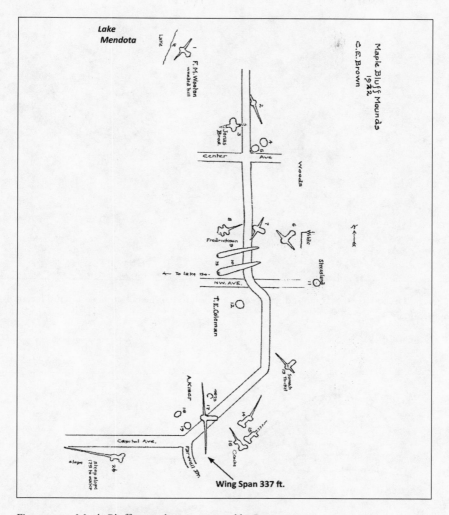

Figure 4.14. Maple Bluff mound group mapped by Brown.

of thunderbirds. The straight-winged bird also appears to be a part of the arrangement of similar mounds partly encircling the Late Woodland village to the west.

The largest single concentration of mounds in the Four Lakes, which spread across the high limestone cliffs of Lake Mendota's northeast shore close to the outlet, were mostly destroyed by residential construction. The Maple Bluff mound group once comprised more than fifty mounds, including linear and zoomorphic effigies of birds and water spirits (figure 4.14).

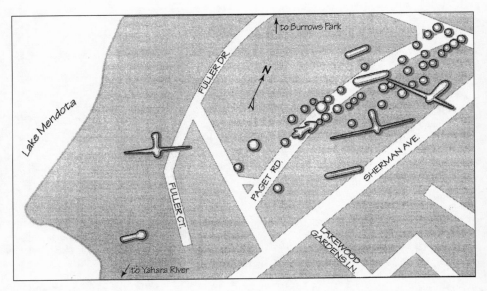

Figure 4.15. Fullers Woods mound group overlaid on modern neighborhood. Mound locations are approximate.

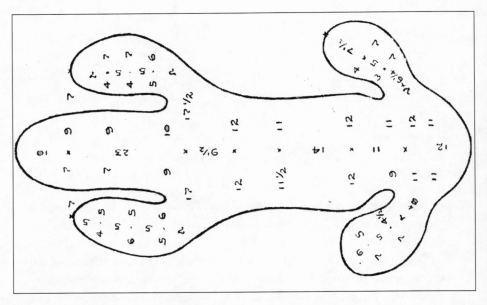

Figure 4.16. Drawing of an effigy that Brown called a frog but is probably an aerial perspective bear.

Figure 4.17. *Above*, photo of Burrows Park bird flying upslope to Lake Mendota, looking east. *Below*, drawing of Burrows Park bird.

Conical mounds by far dominate the Fullers Woods grouping and suggest that the area maintained an identity or history slightly different from other parts of the Four Lakes (figure 4.15). One mound in Fullers Woods was an unusual four-legged animal constructed in a flattened, aerial perspective (figure 4.16). Brown called it a frog, but more likely it is a bear with its legs extended forward. T. H. Lewis recorded an almost identical form in Minnesota, attesting to a wide distribution of the concept.[6] In between these groups, Burrows Park preserves a single bird mound, reconstructed by Brown with a WPA crew (figure 4.17). Another mound, referred to as a fox, was once located nearby.

South Shores

Moving over the once-swampy isthmus that divides Lake Mendota from Lake Monona, a water spirit and other mounds formerly adorned the sides of the high hill now occupied by the present state capitol. Many more mounds were to be found on an adjacent elevation called Mansion Hill, so-named because of the stately residences built here. Unfortunately, the desirability of the Mansion Hill location led to destruction of the mound landscape there before accurate descriptions and maps could be made.

The campus of the University of the Wisconsin occupies a large part of the south shore of Lake Mendota. At least one water spirit mound form lived on Bascom Hill, a drumlin that is now the administrative center of the university. Many surviving examples of mounds are found on the large, sprawling campus, most recently described by George Christiansen of the Great Lakes Archaeological Research Center in a report made for campus landscape planning.[7]

The Picnic Point mound group extended along a prominent Lake Mendota peninsula and might have started as an early Late Woodland mound site consisting of low conical mounds and short linear mounds (figure 4.18). However, archaeological excavation by Charles Brown during reconstruction of one conical mound recovered a collared Woodland pottery rim in the mound fill. Such collared pottery was made late in the sequence of Late Woodland cultural activity after ca. A.D. 1000. Maps made by Charles Brown show Indian garden beds around the mounds, indicating that this was a good place to grow corn. It is not possible today to determine the age of the beds as they have disappeared.

The most unusual of the Lake Mendota mounds is the two-tailed flattened or aerial perspective water spirit mound on Observatory Hill, named for the university's Washburn Observatory located there (figures 4.19 and 4.20). This is a part of an effigy mound group that spread down the hill. Next to the water spirit is a small southward-flying bird, but a panther-shape, long-tailed water spirit and a linear mound once lay low on the landscape near the lake.[8] Before this was university land, modern farming had already obliterated surface features of the mounds.

The two-tailed effigy mound is the only one recorded in the entire effigy mound region, perhaps lending greater significance to Observatory Hill, the highest hill on a lake that was viewed as the residence of the

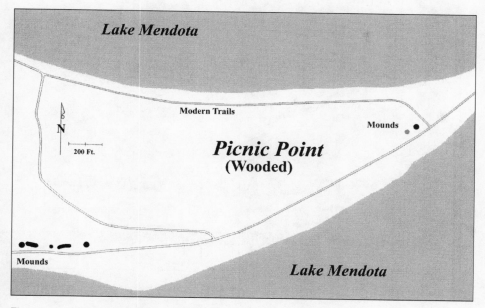

Figure 4.18. Map of Picnic Point mounds based on a drawing by Brown.

water spirits by more recent Indian people in historic times. Its form remains enigmatic, but it might represent not one spirit but two shown in profile and joined at the back. Paired or twin mounds of the different types, sometimes joined, have been recorded at other places in the effigy mound region.

The unusual mound had been marred by sidewalks serving the campus community, but the university is now removing these intrusions. This adds another less dramatic possibility for the two tails that may occur to some alert readers who are closely examining the map of the mound: sometime early in the history of the university, well-meaning groundskeepers moved the tail of a single-tailed mound, as campus pedestrian traffic began to obliterate the first. This would not be the only case where land stewards reformed mounds to accommodate modern land use. In some mound groups, extra dirt seems to have been added to make the features of the characteristically low effigy mounds more apparent to viewers. Since Lewis mapped two tails in 1888, this modification would have to have taken place before that date. The adjacent observatory and necessary land alterations were completed a few years earlier in 1884. An examination of university records may shed light on this possibility.

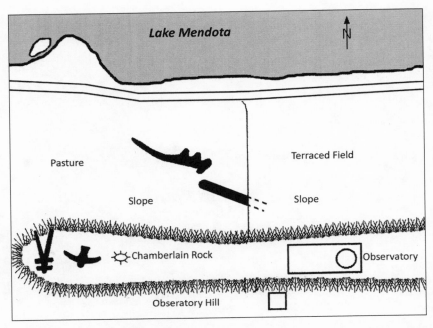

Figure 4.19. Map of Observatory Hill group as it appeared in the late nineteenth century.

Figure 4.20. Early-twentieth-century photo of the two-tailed mound on Observatory Hill outlined by snow.

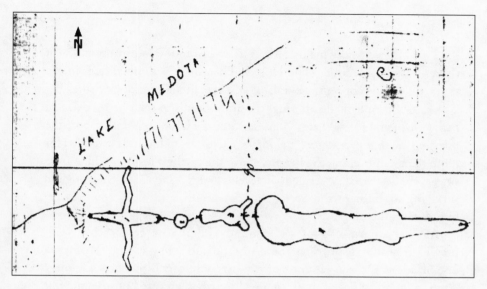

Figure 4.21. Lewis map of Willow Creek mound group.

Some published information attaches additional significance to Observatory Hill, suggesting that the ancient Native Americans used the Chamberlin Rock, a huge, upright boulder on top of the hill, for astronomical sightings or as part of a geometric pattern connecting other ancient places.[9] The rock bears a 1926 plaque honoring pioneer geologist and university president Thomas Chamberlin. University records reveal, however, that the rock, deposited by a glacier, is not at its original place or even standing in its original position. Instead, it was found lying flat farther down the slope of the hill and was hauled to the present spot using cables and pulleys solely for the purpose of the Chamberlin dedication.[10]

To the north of the University of Wisconsin Natatorium and along a small creek are three low-lying mounds of the Willow Creek group that appropriately seem to feature water symbolism. A map made by T. H. Lewis in 1888 shows that the mounds were originally located on an east–west trending ridge near the lake shore (figure 4.21). Already marred by early cultivation, Lewis mapped a goose, headed west to the lakeshore, and several odd forms, one that may have been a long-tailed water spirit or water mammal, mutilated by later land use. Charles Brown later reconstructed the goose but in the opposite direction shown by Lewis, since Brown seemed unaware of Lewis's work.

Springs

Many major springs flowed from the southwest and west shores of Lake Mendota. The Ho-Chunk, who still camped here in the 1850s, called one concentration *Mauelohanah*, literally "group of springs." The Indian people made offerings of various kinds to the waters of *Ma ka ma i* ("medicine spring") at present day Spring Harbor.[11] Another bore the puzzling name *E woo sanau* ("he thirsts"). Clusters of mounds extended for more than a mile along the heights above the springs, most of which have since been destroyed by residential development. A large bear is among the surviving mounds of the Spring Harbor group, and other mounds are found in residential yards.

At the eastern end of the mound complex, a remarkably well-preserved grouping provides more insight into effigy mound landscape organization. On the grounds of the privately run Blackhawk Country Club, different types of mounds are all neatly segregated on the hill and adjacent landscape: conical mounds on top; birds, including a third Lake Mendota goose; lake-oriented linear and tapering linear mounds; and bears. A water spirit once paralleled to the bank of the lake (figures 4.22 and 4.23).

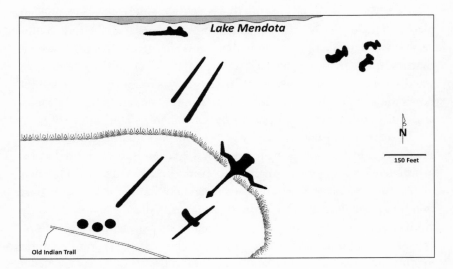

Figure 4.22. Blackhawk Country Club mounds.

Figure 4.23. *Above*, early photo of goose at the Blackhawk Country Club. *Below*, as it appears today.

As is often the case for effigy mounds, the two birds fly perpendicular to the hill slope. In his *The Eagle's Voice: Tales Told by Indian Effigy Mounds*, Dr. Gary Maier of the Mendota Mental Health Institute suggests that the direction of the birds may be explained in terms of the seasons, based in part on mapping and observations by James Scherz.[12] The upward-flying goose of the Blackhawk Country Club group points in the direction of the winter solstice sunset (238 degrees azimuth) while the bird in front of the goose wings its way downhill in the approximate direction of the sunrise on the same day (122 degrees azimuth). Unfortunately, the latter bird is now gone, and whether it actually aligned to the sunrise over hills to the east is unknown.[13]

Whether these are purposeful alignments or coincidence of topography are unclear, but both concepts—solar orientations and topography—could have been artfully merged as the mound builders were no doubt capable of doing such, given the close relationship of effigy mound symbolism and geography. One logical question emerges as to symbolism, however, in that the goose is flying up and away from the lake at a time when life would have been perceived as returning to the land after the winter solstice.

At the southeastern end of the lake, Pheasant Branch Creek flows from a large spring, appropriately called *Mau e pinah* ("beautiful spring") by the Ho-Chunk and now referred to as Belle Fontaine, through wetlands to Lake Mendota (figure 4.24). Above the spring is a plateau and a large, isolated hill that provides a stunning view of the wetlands and the lake some distance to the east. As would be expected, mounds were and still are a feature of this marvelous natural landscape and are now a part of the Pheasant Branch Conservancy (figure 4.25). The Pheasant Branch Hill mound group on top of the high hill is another example of mound construction just prior to zoomorphic mounds in that it consists only of low conical and short linear mounds. A later group—two birds, a linear, and two conical mounds—was once found on the plateau below, adjacent to the springs (figure 4.26). Here, too, farming obliterated all traces of the mounds. However, a solitary conical mound of uncertain dating continues to reign over Lake Mendota on the highest elevation in the area, a large ridge to the west of Pheasant Branch Conservancy. To whom the honor of this probable burial location was accorded will never be known, but it may be one of the most important individuals or families of the time. The mound now shares this natural landmark with a housing development.

Figure 4.24. View to south from top of hill showing the Belle Fontaine spring and the Pheasant Branch creek flowing through wetlands to Lake Mendota.

Figure 4.25. The Pheasant Branch mound group is preserved on a high, isolated hill in an oak savanna overlooking a large spring in the beautiful Dane County Pheasant Branch Conservancy. Pheasant Branch Grove lay on the plateau below the hill but was lost to farming.

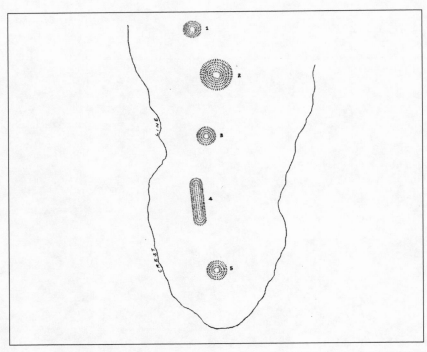

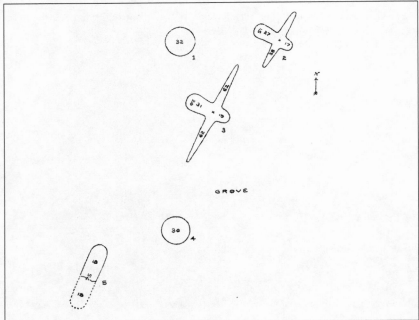

Figure 4.26. Pheasant Branch Hill (*top*) and Pheasant Branch Grove (*bottom*) groups mapped by Brown.

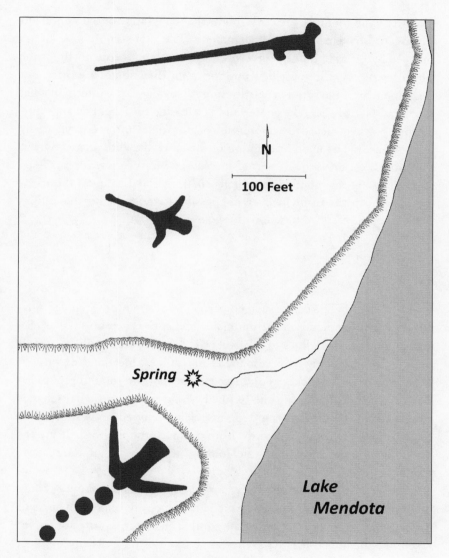

Figure 4.27. Morris Park I mound group.

Mound groupings extended up the west shore of Lake Mendota, one of which is the Morris Park I group mapped by T. H. Lewis. His maps show an impressive water spirit, a goose, a hawk, and four conical mounds, all arranged around a spring (figure 4.27). The water spirit heads to the lake while both birds fly upslope in opposite directions. Like the Blackhawk

Country Club mounds, the birds follow the topography of the slopes, but a case can also be made for solar alignments. The goose is now gone, but as mapped by Lewis (a trained surveyor) and adjusting for true north for the time of mapping, the goose flew upslope in the direction of a solstice, but this time that of the summer solstice sunset (304 degrees azimuth on a flat horizon).[14] In this case, the goose would be leaving the lake at an appropriate time—when the earth symbolically begins to die and geese eventually leave the area. The main orientation of the hawk-like bird seems to be in the same direction as the winter solstice sunset, but this view appears to be blocked by arching mounds immediately in front of it that follow the orientation of the ridge. Again, here it is not possible to state whether these alignments are purposeful, a function of topography, or both.

Upland Ponds

The ceremonial construction of mounds expanded during the Late Woodland away from major bodies of water, up small creeks and rivers, and sometimes to relatively small spring-fed ponds in upland areas. Late Woodland people also used some of these locations for villages, as we have seen at Stricker's Pond (see chapter 2). Two mound groups located on upland ponds are the Kennedy Pond group and what Charles Brown called the Big Cross group, also called referred to as Bacchus or Hammersly Pond in state records. Both of these groups also share an unusual mound configuration—the joining and crossing of long linear mounds.

The Kennedy Pond group once composed a spectacular array of effigy mounds: birds, water spirits, and paired linear mounds built at an angle to one another (figure 4.28). One of the panther-like water spirits was curve-tailed like the one at Farwell Point. Some mounds have disappeared, including the wonderful curve-tailed water spirit, but others are preserved on private land and what are now the grounds of the peaceful Holy Wisdom Monastery, appropriately devoted to spiritual renewal.

The odd angling of the mounds of Kennedy Pond brings to mind possible celestial orientations, as do the two other crossed mounds elsewhere in the Four Lakes district. The matter here is again ambiguous. As mapped by modern surveyors, the southernmost mound comes somewhat close

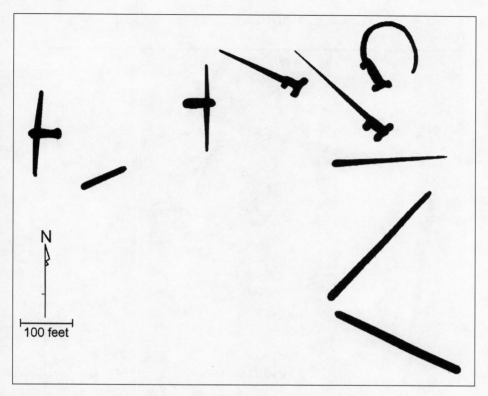

Figure 4.28. Drawing of Kennedy Pond mound group.

(within 10 degrees) to a line that describes the winter solstice sunrise and summer solstice sunset, but the other mound has no obvious directional significance.[15] Another linear mound at Kennedy Pond aligns almost precisely east–west, the directions of the equinox, but this as well could be coincidence since single linear mounds in the Fours Lakes are oriented in all directions.

The Big Cross mound group was located in what is now a residential area of Madison, and all the mounds are now gone (figure 4.29). It was located on high ground at the edge of a large marsh and pond, which are now part of Odana Hills Golf Course. Early maps show only long linear mounds, but a bird effigy mound was reported to have been in another grouping nearby.[16] The site derives its original name from the two long linear mounds that crossed each other. The cross is not oriented near cardinal

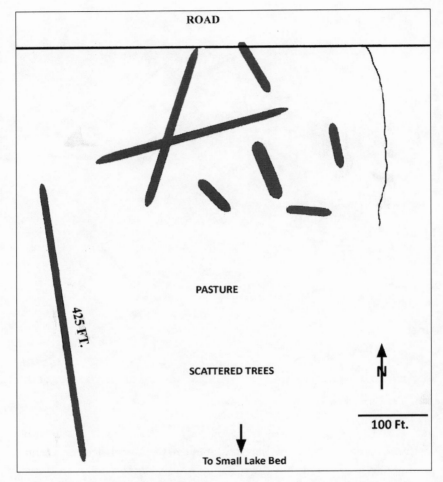

Figure 4.29. The Big Cross (Bachus, Hammersley) mound group as drawn by Brown is another example of an upland mound group near a pond and wetlands. A group with animal effigy mounds was recorded nearby.

directions, as with Lapham's cross, nor is it close to the directions of solar events, as is possibly another set of cross mounds on Lake Waubesa. The repeated pattern of crossed linear mounds in various directions in the effigy mound region suggests it was an important part of effigy mound cosmology even if the overall significance is not as yet understood. The pattern seems related to the pairing of other types of mounds also found throughout the region.

Figure 4.30. Drawing of the Heim Fox mound.

Brown and the Heim Mound

During his career, Charles Brown tried to save every threatened Indian mound in the Madison area that came to his attention. Sometimes it took decades for his efforts to come to fruition. In 1915 he examined and described a large running fox or wolf effigy on the property of Ferdinand Heim near the south shore of Lake Mendota (figure 4.30). Brown wrote the landowner a cordial letter extolling the uniqueness of the mound and urging Heim to preserve the mound and prevent others from digging into it. He predicted that the land would someday be subdivided into tracts for vacation homes and suggested that either the mound be preserved on a small public oval or that the landowner insert a preservation clause in the deed for the property. Two decades later—in 1937—Heim deeded the mound to the Wisconsin Archeological Society.

In a letter to Brown, Heim wrote: "It gives me a feeling of satisfaction to give this mound to your society and to know it will be preserved for the future. I want to thank you personally for the suggestion contained in your letter of more than twenty years ago. I still have your letter and a clipping from the *Milwaukee Sunday Sentinel* of August 29, 1915, which describes the mound in detail and published your tracing of it. Undoubtedly when you wrote the letter you thought you were looking a long way ahead in predicting that 'summer homes' would be located on the above property. Little did we then think that in about twenty years permanent homes would be built in this area."[17]

Yahara Inlet and Mendota

Although some limited archaeological explorations took place to find out more about the mound, the Heim mound remains today on an undeveloped lot in a residential neighborhood in Middleton and is the only canine effigy mound form left near the shores of Lake Mendota.[18]

5 | Wingra

Lake of Sacred Springs

THE FIFTH LAKE in the Four Lakes district is today barely more than a large, shallow pond, yet surrounding its shores there are among the densest and most impressive effigy mound groupings found anywhere (figure 5.1). The Ho-Chunk called it *Ki-chunk-och-hep-er-rah* ("where the turtle rises up") and maintained a village on the west side along a major Four Lakes trail.[1] The Ho-Chunk name *Wingra* was also used in the early nineteenth century, a reference to ducks. Ho-Chunk families camped here to fish, trap muskrat, and capture large turtles until about 1910.

Lake Wingra covers a little over three hundred acres and is surrounded by large wetlands, although at times increased moisture probably expanded the lake water to more than twice the present size. This body of water differs from other lakes in that it is not an expansion of the Yahara River but one of its sources. Several large springs feed the lake and a small creek brings the water to Lake Monona and the Yahara River. Water from one of the springs, called Silver Spring, was sold in Madison for some years and several small soft drink plants operated here.[2]

Some early settlers also called Wingra "Dead Lake," evidently because it didn't have the river flow like the others. But with the presence of so many springs, ancient Native Americans no doubt perceived it quite differently—as the source of life itself. The Ho-Chunk considered one particular spring, called White Clay Spring by others, a "medicine" spring, contributing to health and well being.[3] They left offerings in its waters. The white clay in the name of the medicine spring no doubt refers to another

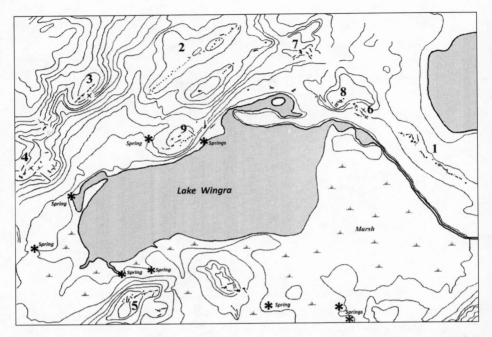

Figure 5.1. Topographic map showing recorded Lake Wingra mounds. Mound sites mentioned in text are (1) Dividing Ridge, (2) Monroe Street, (3) Forest Hill Cemetery, (4) Wingra, (5) Lake Forest No. 1, (6) Greenbush, (7) Vilas Circle/Curtis, (8) Vilas, and (9) Edgewood.

physical characteristic of the lake important in Native American beliefs: like Lake Mendota, the shallow waters cover a thick deposit of white marl important in the beliefs of the Ho-Chunk and other Indian people.

Perhaps because of the spiritual and symbolic importance of springs and marl, the small lake attracted much ceremonial activity. There are few other places in the effigy mound region that had such a density of mounds in such a small area, an impression that Charles E. Brown also had from his early documentation.[4] Native Americans sculpted at least 233 mounds on the elevations around the small lake, creating a vast part of the Four Lakes ceremonial landscape and covering several square miles. Urban expansion destroyed many of the mounds, but the University of Wisconsin Arboretum preserves several whole groups, and remnants of others are found at the Forest Hill Cemetery, the Edgewood College campus, Vilas Circle Park, and Vilas Park.

Documented mounds of Lake Wingra include zoomorphic mounds—birds, geese, bears, canine forms, and water spirits—as well as the snake-like

Figure 5.2. Unusual Lake Wingra mound forms.

tapering linear mounds and conical mounds. Among the effigy mounds are unusual forms (figure 5.2). In the 1880s T. H. Lewis mapped a possible antlerless deer effigy, now gone, which is similar to the preserved deer mound at Mendota Mental Health Institute in that it shows all four legs. It appears to be running or walking. Other unusual mounds are a long-bodied water mammal (mink or otter?) and a mammal with two conical mounds built over or joining the legs, giving the mound a wheeled appearance.[5] The superposition of conical mounds on effigy mounds is documented elsewhere in the effigy mound region, as for example in the Nitschke I mound group, reflecting the continuing construction of conical forms during the final years of Late Woodland and/or the symbolic superposition of celestial upper-world forms over those of more earthly association. None of these unusual forms on Lake Wingra survived modern development.

Lake Wingra Groups: "Conspicuous and Beautiful"

Some of the most spectacular and interesting mound groups of Lake Wingra also no longer exist but fortunately drew the attention of early mound researchers and cartographers. The Dividing Ridge group lined the top of a seventy-foot-high glacial ridge separating Lake Wingra from Lake Monona, a Madison landmark until quarried away for gravel in the early twentieth century, much to the regret of many Madison people (figure 5.3). The mounds extended along the ridge, merging into adjacent mound groups. Increase Lapham, who had investigated the mounds in the 1850s, described the scene: "Their sharp outline, projected against the sky for background, with the scattered trees and shrubs, all reflecting in the clear still water of the lake, render this spot conspicuous and beautiful."[6]

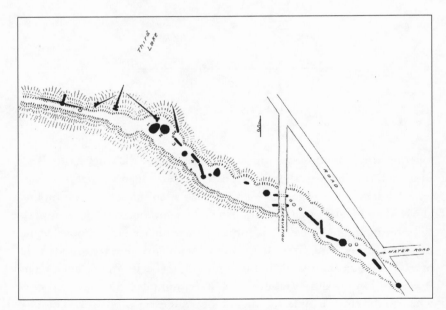

Figure 5.3. Dividing Ridge mound group mapped by Brown in 1915.

Figure 5.4. Photo of Dividing Ridge mound before its destruction.

Ancient people also found this ridge conspicuous and beautiful, beginning ceremonial and burial activity more than two thousand years ago.
Two main conical or oval mounds are of a large size (nine feet high and up
to sixty feet in diameter) consistent with Middle Woodland mound construction. Excavation of one mound by Lapham revealed an extended "in
the flesh" skeleton, also typical of mound burials in the earlier part of the
Woodland.[7] Around them and to the northwest were effigy mounds in the
form of a straight-wing eagle, panther-shape water spirits, and a tapering
linear mound. The eagle-like bird dramatically swooped upslope with its
wings parallel to the ridge top. The water spirit and snake-like mound extend up the slope from Lake Monona. Linear mounds and smaller conical
mounds line the ridge top to the southeast. Wholesale destruction of the
Dividing Ridge mounds began in the late nineteenth century as the city of
Madison grew and new residents of the area dug up the mounds out of cu-
riosity or to develop their properties (figure 5.4). Sand and gravel operations then leveled the ridge and the remaining mounds. Brown's notes
record the destruction of the last remaining linear mound in 1915 where

several wagon loads of dirt were removed, littering the ground with broken human bones and skull fragments. In characteristic bluntness, he called destruction of the Madison landmark "a crime which should never have been perpetrated."[8]

Another long line of conical mounds, the Monroe Street group, once followed a high, long ridge overlooking the lake basin to the southeast. The area is now a commercial district that includes the offices of the publisher of this book. Linear and effigy mounds were found mainly at the two ends of the area. The conical mounds seem to be smaller than some of the Dividing Ridge mounds, and the overall lack of large conical mounds throughout the rest of Lake Wingra basin suggests that, despite seasonal use of its shores by people for thousands of years, most ceremonial mound building took place during the Late Woodland, climaxing with the giant effigy mound landscape.

The Lake Wingra part of the Four Lakes mound landscape incorporated at least two and possibly four goose mounds. One can still be viewed at Forest Hill Cemetery flying down a steep slope in the direction of the lake (figure 5.5). Above are linear and water spirit mounds in a straight line, following the main orientation of a ridge. Several were destroyed to make space for the newly dead. In an 1890 map, Rev. Steven Peet shows another goose at the end of this line but oriented toward Lake Wingra like the other goose. Since Peet's maps and descriptions have been shown to be inaccurate in many cases, we cannot say much about this goose mound except that it would not be out of place.

Other water symbolism was expressed by a large number of water spirit mounds and linear mounds. One of the water spirit mounds near Lake Wingra is a flattened aerial perspective form while the remaining fifteen are of the panther shape. Some of the linear mounds, like at the now destroyed Wingra effigy mound group, assumed a tapering, snake-like form.

The Wingra grouping illustrates the close connection between springs and effigy mound groups, and major principles of effigy mound arrangements. This group once spread across a high elevation, now home to a large, former school building on Monroe Street, directly overlooking a prominent spring that still bubbles up near the shore of the lake in the University of Wisconsin Arboretum (figure 5.6). The famed landscape architect Jens Jenson created a "council ring" near this spring in 1938 for intimate and reflective gatherings. A straight-winged bird flew on the highest

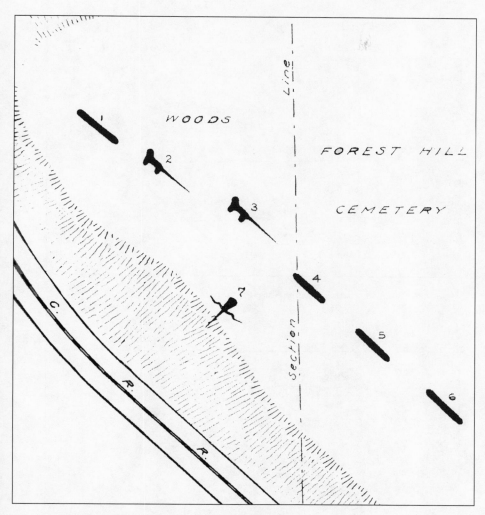

Figure 5.5. Forest Hill Cemetery group mapped by Brown in 1915.

and most prominent elevation along with a large goose, which flew down to the lake. Some of the tapering linear (snake) mounds, one measuring 291 feet, ran downslope toward the lake and springs. A map based on a 1908 survey by Arlow B. Stout, then a University of Wisconsin student, implies that other mounds had been destroyed by plowing and other land use.

Another intimate connection between mounds and springs is at the Lake Forest group situated above two springs on the south shore, which

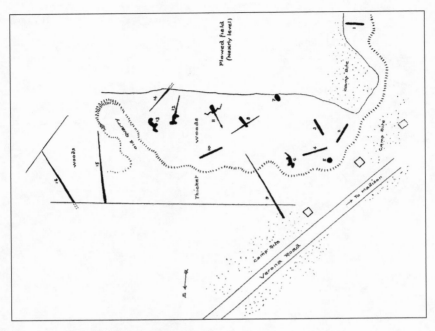

Figure 5.6. Wingra group based on 1908 survey by Stout.

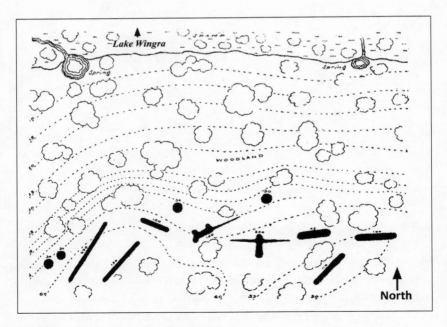

Figure 5.7. Lake Forest group mapped by Brown.

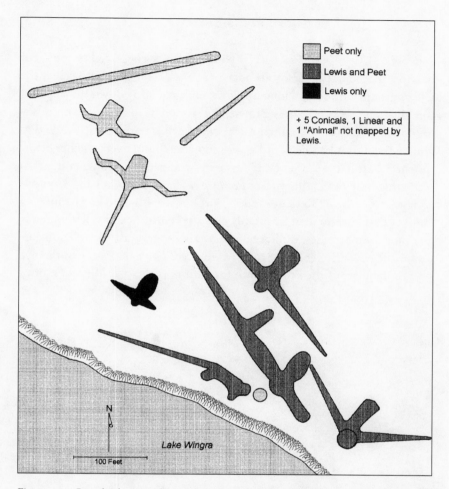

Figure 5.8. Greenbush mounds as mapped by Rosebrough from the records of Lewis, Brown, and Peet. Precisely what the original group looked like is unclear.

were held in reverence by the early twentieth-century Ho-Chunk who camped here (figure 5.7). Brown excavated a portion of the panther-style water spirit form here when the mounds were being restored, finding that the earthwork covered a single "bone bundle" burial along with ash and charcoal. Peet published a map of the Greenbush mound group on the northeast shore in 1890 that shows yet another goose and, appropriately, a duck. These are not shown on a similar map of the group by T. H. Lewis, so the overall composition of the group remains uncertain (figure 5.8).

The Sword in the Bear

Vilas Circle, a city park, preserves a large eighty-four-foot bear on the side of large knoll, once part of a larger grouping called the Curtis group, with several long linear mounds radiating down the slopes of the hill (figure 5.9). Charles Brown reported that, in 1905, a young boy found a short, twenty-six-inch metal sword with a broken tip while digging in the mound.[9] The sword was supposedly found twelve inches below the surface. It had a leather and brass wire-wrapped hilt, iron guard, and a blade that bore the Latin phrases *Pro Deo et Patria* (For God and County) and *Soli Deo Gloria* (To God Alone, Glory) on opposite sides. The first is a familiar Latin motto used frequently over the centuries and still used today as a motto for families, military and fraternal organizations, religious orders, colleges, and even Boy Scout awards. *Soli Deo Gloria,* one of the five scriptural pillars of the Protestant reformation, is also an old Latin motto,

Figure 5.9. Photo and drawing of the Vilas Circle bear effigy.

an admonishment to return to God in all aspects of life. The motto is still used by some religious organizations, churches, and institutions such as Luther College of Iowa, which was established in 1846.

How the sword got into the top of the mound remains a mystery. It might have accompanied a very shallow burial in the mound, reflecting a nineteenth-century pattern of reuse of mounds as burial places as Indian people lost their lands.[10] The sword could have feasibly been acquired as a gift or in trade. However, given its reported shallow depth, the broken sword more likely would have a been a discarded relic of some more recent religious-oriented organization or even placed there by an earnest believer in symbolic counteraction to the "'pagan" symbolism of the mound. Of course, lacking archaeological documentation, we have no way of knowing if the sword was really found in the mound.

Charles Brown and Lake Wingra

Lake Wingra is known for its mounds, but the locale also played a significant role in life and death of Charles E. Brown.[11] After relocating from Milwaukee in 1908, Brown moved to his first home on Monroe Street, which was then on the outskirts of Madison. It is near the north shore of Lake Wingra and is today just a short distance from the University of Wisconsin's Camp Randall football stadium. One winter day in 1909 an old Ho-Chunk man, whom Brown only identifies as White, came to his door asking for food for his family camped on the other side of the lake, now the University of Wisconsin Arboretum. Brown befriended the family and frequently visited the seasonal camp, spending hours in the smoky wigwam listening to stories about the area and learning about traditional Ho-Chunk culture.

Brown's ties to Native American communities expanded over time. Visitors to a later home in the area, now itself on the National Register of Historic Places, included Oliver Lamere, who traced his ancestry through both the Ho-Chunk and an early Four Lake's fur trader, and John Blackhawk, a descendant of famous Ho-Chunk chief Winneshiek. Brown also befriended Albert Yellow Thunder from Wisconsin Dells, grandson of Yellow Thunder, a noted war chief and a leader of those who resisted removal from Wisconsin to the western Indian Territory (figure 5.10). Albert

Wingra

Figure 5.10. Charles Brown and Albert Yellow Thunder, who is a wearing a Great Plains style headdress.

participated in educational tours of area Indian sites, led by Brown, providing a Ho-Chunk cultural and historical perspective.

From all of these Indian people, Brown collected place names, stories, and traditions regarding the Madison area. He learned Ho-Chunk names and identifications for some of the effigy mounds and collected stories about the spirit beings the mounds represented to the Ho-Chunk. He learned of the prevalent belief that effigy mounds represented clan totems. Although it cannot yet be demonstrated that the effigy mounds were built by ancestors of the Ho-Chunk, the perspectives that Brown obtained added immeasurably to our understanding of the underlying belief systems of ancient Native American societies.

As with other places, the preservation of many mounds on Lake Wingra are the result of various devices used by Charles Brown to ensure protection. For example, he served on the committee that planned the Arboretum to ensure preservation of the three remarkably intact groupings still found

Figure 5.11. Forest Hill mounds today. *Above*, a long-tailed water spirit. *Below*, a goose swoops downslope to the Lake Wingra wetlands.

there. When the Society of Native Americans held their annual conference in Madison in 1914, he seized the opportunity to draw public attention to his efforts to preserve what are now the Vilas Park mounds, at that time threatened by new city plans. He arranged a well-publicized dedication ceremony attended by representatives of thirteen tribes from throughout the United States.[12]

Brown is also responsible for saving the surviving mounds in the Forest Hill Cemetery (figure 5.11). He appealed directly to the Madison city mayor to save the surviving mounds from cemetery development. They were indeed preserved and fittingly Charles Brown himself was interred at the Forest Hill Cemetery not far away. His grave can be found in Lot 1 beneath a large granite monolith bearing a single word: Archaeologist.

6 | Lake Monona
Let the Great Spirit Soar

From Lake Mendota, the Yahara River flows through a formerly swampy isthmus to Lake Monona, called Third Lake by early settlers and Great Teepee Lake or *Tchee-ho-bo-kee-xa kay-te-la* by the Ho-Chunk who maintained camps here through the early twentieth century.[1] The Wisconsin Historical Society documents that at least 234 mounds once existed at twenty-seven locations on the shores of the lake or the surrounding area (figure 6.1), not including the Dividing Ridge group that also overlooks Lake Wingra. Many of the Lake Monona records derive from the published work and files of Charles Brown.

Lake Monona Geography and Symbolism

The air, earth, and water effigy mound symbolism around Lake Monona was similar to that of Lake Mendota and Lake Wingra, except for the larger number of linear mounds near marshlands on the southern reaches of the lake. The latter pattern continues on to Lake Kegonsa where linear mounds, some obviously snakes, are by far the most numerous mound form.

One Lake Monona mound concentration that underscores the principles of effigy mound landscape organization extended along the northeast shore, adjacent to modern Olbrich Park, filled land that was once a

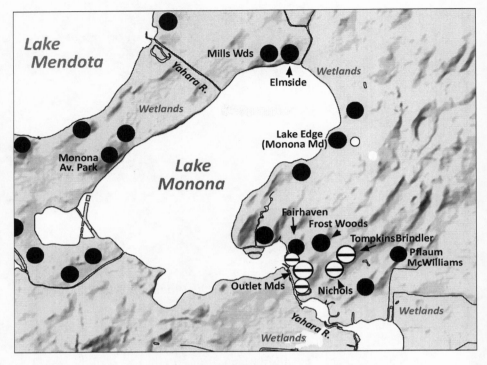

Figure 6.1. Mounds of Lake Monona. Those discussed in the text are identified.

swampy bay in Lake Monona (figure 6.2). At least twenty mounds covered two hills divided by a deep, wide valley and drainage. Most of the earthworks were destroyed by later home building in the twentieth century, but T. H. Lewis had mapped a number of mounds in 1888 and Charles Brown later added maps and locations of others.[2] The three that survive in two small city parks once again owe their survival to the preservation efforts of Brown.

The eastern grouping, called Elmside, included four large, straight-winged birds—eagles or thunderbirds—similar in form to the giant birds on the grounds of the Mendota Mental Health Institute on Lake Mendota. One huge bird here had a wing span of 563 feet. Many additional birds are depicted on an impressionistic map rendered by Rev. Stephen Peet in 1890. This would have been the largest concentration of bird effigies in the Four Lakes. The many errors found generally in Peet's drawings and mound descriptions, however, leaves one with some skepticism. On the other hand,

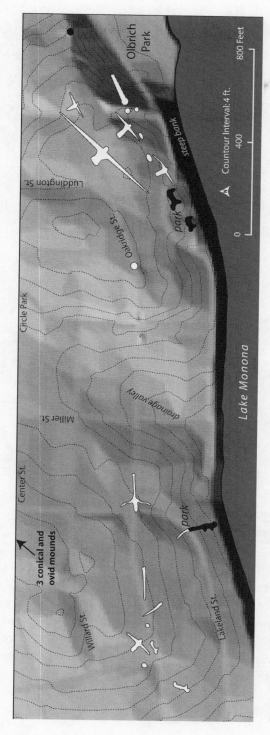

Figure 6.2. Shaded relief map showing Mills Woods and Elmside mounds.

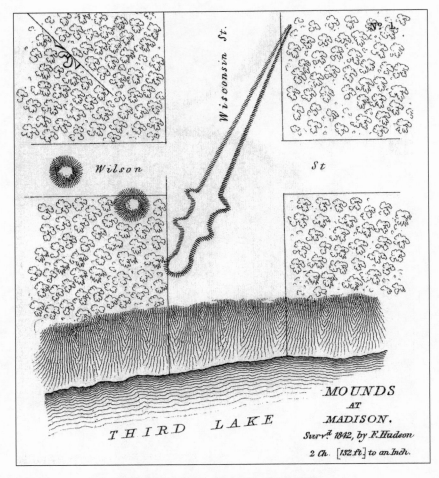

Figure 6.3. Monona Avenue Park mounds mapped by Frank Hudson.

Lewis did note the presence of other mounds in the area that he did not map.

Peet's inaccuracies also led to some confusion about other mounds in the area. He published a map that has been called the Shooting Park mound group in older records, but research by the state archaeologist's office at the Wisconsin Historical Society concludes that the map is merely a wildly imaginative rendition of the Mills Woods grouping, located on the western side of the valley.

Like several other mound groups in the Four Lakes, the many classic effigy mound forms in these related Elmside and Mills Woods groupings are spatially and geographically segregated, conforming to topography and cultural symbolism. Conical mounds once occupied the highest elevations, with the birds also on prominent high places. Lower along the lake and bluff edge, earth mammals can still be viewed, along with a bear and another tailless mammal, legs oriented downslope. On one side of the large birds, a tapering linear mound extended up a steep slope from the former marsh, a pattern repeated many times for these snake-like forms throughout the Four Lakes. Finally, low on the landscape in the western Mills Woods group, a panther-type water spirit with a slightly curved tail still crawls to the to the lake in Hudson Park. A goose in the Mills Woods group, the only one recorded for Lake Monona, once flew east down toward a valley and drainage.

The Wisconsin state capitol overlooks lakes Mendota and Monona from a high hill on the isthmus that divides the two lakes. As mentioned in chapter 5, mounds were recorded for Capitol Hill. In 1842, near the base of this hill and on a bluff overlooking Lake Monona, Frank Hudson, a notable early Madison settler, mapped a long-tailed effigy constructed in a flattened or aerial perspective along with two conical mounds. This map was subsequently published in Lapham's *Antiquities of Wisconsin* (figure 6.3). Hudson's rendition shows an effigy with a rather long neck. It may have been either a water spirit or a water mammal. As noted by Lapham, "Like most mounds of this general character, it has its head directed towards the water."[3] The earthworks, which were later called the Monona Avenue Park mounds, were destroyed in the nineteenth century by urban development, and the location is now the entranceway of Madison's lakefront community center, Monona Terrace Community and Convention Center.

The Outlet

Like the Yahara River inlet on Lake Mendota, the Monona outlet was long an important ceremonial and living area for Native Americans. Here was the earliest dated mound group in the Four Lakes, the Outlet mound group. Established as a ceremonial and burial

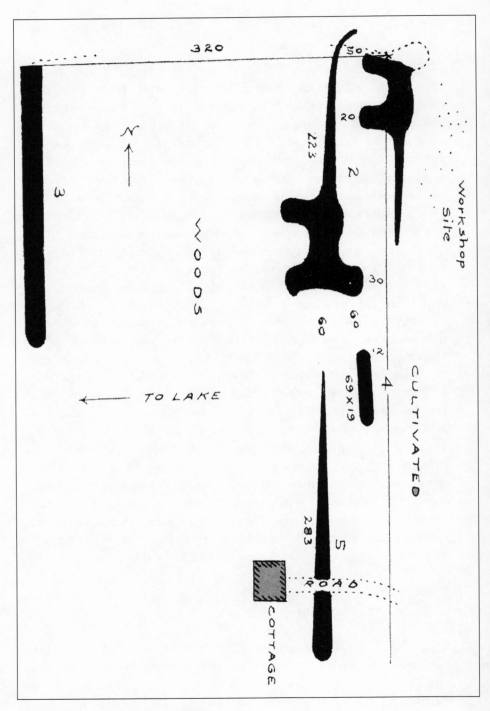

Figure 6.4. Fairhaven group mapped by Brown.

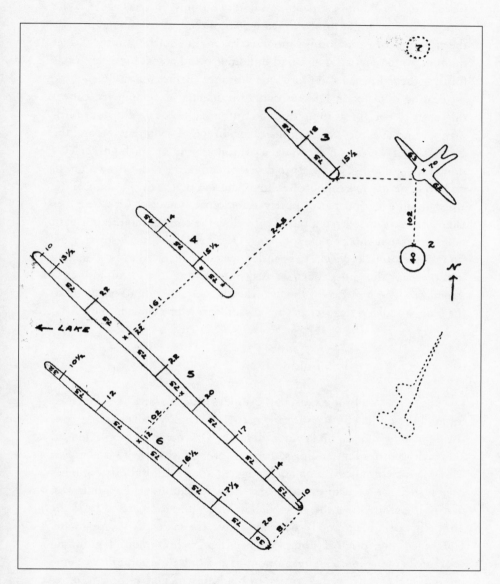

Figure 6.5. Frost Woods group mapped by Brown.

place by earlier Woodland people around two thousand years ago, the site continued to be used through the early part of the Late Woodland prior to the appearance of zoomorphic mounds. Extending north from the Outlet mound group, later effigy mound building spread across high elevations forming the Fairhaven and Frost Woods groups (figures 6.4 and 6.5).

Fearing destruction by encroaching residential development, Brown dug parts of two linear mounds and an unusual fork-tailed bird or bird-man mound at Frost Woods in the 1920s. In 1947 David Baerreis and the University of Wisconsin excavated a conical mound on the highest elevation of the grouping, just prior to development of the area.[4] Brown found no burials or artifacts supporting the conclusion that many mounds of the effigy mound period had a purely ceremonial function. On the other hand, Baerreis uncovered a burial pit below the conical mound but with only a few fragments of bone surviving. He also found a small, stone arrow tip in the mound and a cut deer antler, which he believed to be a digging tool (perhaps the antler tool was used in loosening dirt for mound construction). The presence of the arrowhead dates the mound generally to the Late Woodland stage when the bow and arrow first came into use.

Drumlin Mounds

Drumlins east of the outlet seemed to have been first used for mound building during the early part of the Late Woodland stage, consisting mainly of linear and conical mounds. One notable group extended along a huge drumlin trending southwest through what is now downtown Monona for a distance of a half mile (figure 6.6). A part of the drumlin has been leveled for road construction and other development. The southwest part of the group was called the Nichols group and is separated from the Tompkins-Brindler group by Monona Drive, the main city thoroughfare. Combined, the original Tompkins-Brindler/Nichols mound grouping contained at least fourteen linear mounds and one conical mound.[5] Some mounds had already been destroyed by road construction at the time of recording by Charles Brown in 1913, and the Nichols part was lost entirely to subdivision development after that time.

The Monona municipal water tower rises from one end of the Tompkins-Brindler group location. New water tower construction disturbed

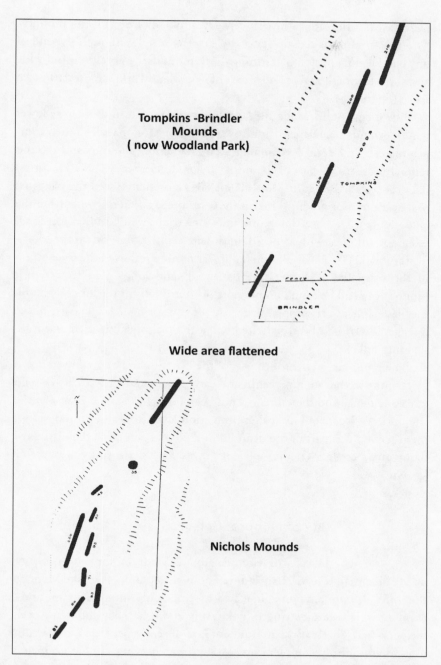

Figure 6.6. The combined Tompkins-Brindler/Nichols groups mapped by McLachlan.

two graves in the late twentieth century, probably from former mounds. Two linear mounds remain (200 and 210 feet long), although the end of one had been truncated by farming; both mounds are about ten feet wide and three feet high and are now part of Woodland Park, a protected green space (figure 6.7).

The theme of linear mounds, undoubtedly related to the watery lower world, extends to another drumlin east of Lake Monona, also much compromised by modern development. The remaining mounds and mound remnants are now a part of the Edna Taylor Conservancy Park. The original group, called Pflaum-McWilliams, also closely followed the contours of a drumlin overlooking a marsh (now restored) about one mile from the lake (figure 6.8). Three linear mounds, one over seven hundred feet long, ran along the crest with a curved linear and a conical mound on the southwestern end. The snake-like curved linear mound followed the orientation of the ridge. Four shorter linear mounds and long-tailed water spirit mounds can still be found on the northwestern slope of the long, high hill, the water spirit in its proper place just above a spring. Middle parts of the linear mounds had been flattened when the drumlin was used as winter sledding hill.

The grouping on the south part of the drumlin had been plowed down by farming in the late nineteenth and early twentieth centuries, leaving no visible evidence and therefore had not been formally catalogued as a burial site under Wisconsin burial sites protection law. Condominium development leveled this part of the drumlin in the 1990s, much to the distress of many area people. Whether ancient graves were destroyed will never be known.

City of Monona: Celebrating the Mounds

The city of Monona adjoins Madison, forming a continuous residential, commercial, and recreational area along the Lake Monona shoreline. Monona at one time had a remarkable number of mounds, many of which were destroyed by farming and urban development. Even the persistent Charles Brown could not save the entirety of the Frost Woods mound group from summer-cottage development when the land came up for sale in 1928. In an effort to save the woods and the mounds, Brown and

Figure 6.7. *Above,* linear mounds follow the top of a glacial ridge at Woodland Park. The park is being restored to an oak savanna. *Below,* a linear mound.

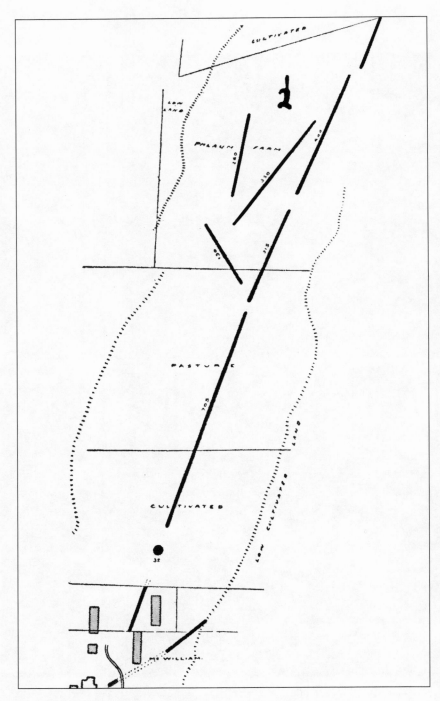

Figure 6.8. Pflaum-McWilliams mounds mapped by McLachlan.

Figure 6.9. The Monona Mound was wedged in between two buildings. One building, the historic Reindahl house, burned down and that property awaits development.

others formed the Lake Monona Wildlife Sanctuary Association. Their vision was a culture and nature center consisting of a wildlife sanctuary and education center, an outdoor museum, an Indian mound preserve, and a recreational area for youth organizations. Despite several years of clever fund-raising that included a traditional Ho-Chunk camp organized by Brown's Ho-Chunk friend Oliver Lamere, the association came up short of money.[6] Several mounds, including an unusual fork-tailed or bird-man mound, survived subdivision development on private property where they are treasured by current land owners.

During the 1990s, the city of Monona, led by an active landmarks commission, began a campaign to honor the mounds and the people who made them by designating any surviving mounds as city landmarks. The movement was stimulated by the threat to the locally famous "Monona Mound" by new housing construction (figure 6.9). The mound, wedged between two developed lots, was originally mapped as a "club form"—a conical with a long, tapering tail. Protests by many area people, Indian and non-Indian,

Figure 6.10. The Whitehorse family at the Outlet Mound dedication. Artist Harry White-horse is at far left.

led to its being catalogued as a burial site, the first mound so designated by the Wisconsin's burial site preservation law (157.70 of Wisconsin Statutes).

The Monona Landmarks Commission re-dedicated the Outlet Mound in a 1998 ceremony. Native American community leaders spoke to large crowd of the importance of such places, and afterwards Art Shegonee (Menominee/Potawatomi) led a powwow dance. The mound, the largest of the Outlet group, had been purchased by the Wisconsin Archeological Society decades earlier under the leadership of Charles Brown and deeded to the city of Monona. Also in attendance was the Ho-Chunk Whitehorse family, prominent residents with deep roots in the Four Lakes (figure 6.10). The celebrated wood-carver Harry Whitehorse created the tree-stump sculpture *Let the Great Spirit Soar* that adorned Madison's Hudson Park until deterioration forced its removal in 2007. Thanks to efforts by neighborhood people, the Madison Arts Commission, the Ho-Chunk Nation, and many others, a bronze replacement was installed in 2009 (see figure P.3).

Monona created Woodland Park around the two remaining linear mounds of Tompkins-Brindler, and a ceremony was held dedicating a new

Figure 6.11. Ada Deer (Menominee), Art Shegonee (Menominee/Potawatomi), and Dallas White Wing (Ho-Chunk) at 2002 dedication of historic marker at the Woodland Park mounds.

historical marker in 2002 and was well-attended by city and state officials as well as representatives from several Indian nations (figure 6.11). Among those at the dedication ceremony was Ada E. Deer, a Madison resident and famous Menominee leader whose distinguished career included serving as assistant secretary for Indian affairs in the U.S. Department of the Interior and as director of the American Indian Studies Program at the University of Wisconsin–Madison.

7 | Waubesa

Lake of Reeds and Snakes

THE HO-CHUNK called Waubesa *Sa-hoo cha-te-la* or "lake of reeds" because of its extensive marshlands. Much of what is known of Lake Waubesa mounds comes from the early works of T. H. Lewis, Charles Brown, and especially Dr. W. G. McLachlan of McFarland, all of whom mapped mounds when much of the shoreline was undeveloped. At least 183 mounds in thirty locations existed here, arranged along hills, drumlins, and high banks (figure 7.1). Like the southern end of Lake Monona, both Lake Waubesa and Lake Kegonsa differ from the northern part of the Four Lakes mound district and other areas of the effigy mound region in having a proportionally large number of linear mounds. Thirty-eight percent of the mounds on Lake Kegonsa, for instance, are straight or linear embankments, some of extraordinary length. Groups of linear mounds with a few small and low conical mounds were common. One example is the Bram mound group, now a part of Goodland County Park (figure 7.2).

Snake-like mounds are especially evident on Lake Waubesa. Some assume a curved or bent shape, and several serpentine mounds are quite definitely snake effigies. This lower-world symbolic pattern reflects the environment much dominated by marshes, especially on the south end and around an adjacent body of water called Mud Lake on the north end. Oddly, though, there are few water spirit mounds. The Uphoff Ridge group, mapped by Brown in 1935, followed the top of a ridge one mile west

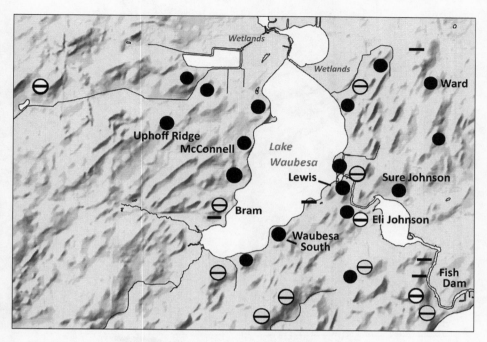

Figure 7.1. Mounds of Lake Waubesa. Those discussed in the text are identified.

of the lake and is surrounded by marsh and open water.[1] A snake, 333 feet in length, runs along the ridgetop and is joined by an animal that Brown called a lynx and a short, teardrop-shaped mound (figure 7.3).

Twenty-five bird and mammal effigy mounds are known to have existed on or near Lake Waubesa. The most spectacular clustering of animal effigy mounds was the McConnell group where remnants of fourteen of the original seventeen mounds survive among residential lots on the west shore. Fortunately, the mounds drew the attention of early mound researchers, and their maps, along with modern mapping, allows for a nearly complete reconstruction (figure 7.4).[2]

Most of the mounds at McConnell run parallel and perpendicular to a long ridge above the lakeshore. The arrangement included two sky birds, rare for the lake and now gone, and a large goose, also destroyed by property development. Mammals in the McConnell group are tailed canine forms (wolf or fox) as well as one that Brown later referred to as a rabbit

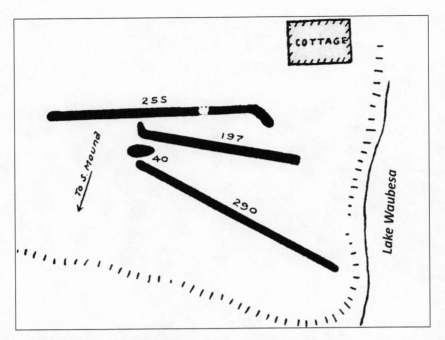

Figure 7.2. Bram mound group, Goodland Park, mapped by McLachlan.

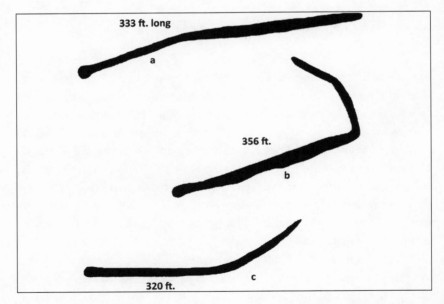

Figure 7.3. Lake Waubesa snake or serpent mounds: (*a*) from the Uphoff Ridge group; (*b*) from the Lewis group; and (*c*) from the Voges group.

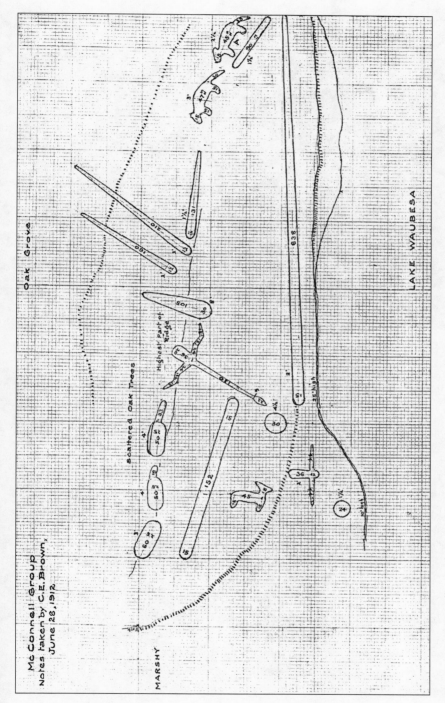

Figure 7.4. McConnell mound group with notes by Brown.

Figure 7.5. Photo (ca. 1914) of deer or rabbit from the McConnell group.

(figure 7.5). The short-tailed canines have a distinctive arched back found among other Waubesa mounds illustrated by McLachlan. A large teardrop-shaped mound of unknown symbolism occupied the center of the group along with several large amorphous shapes following the ridge to the southwest. Three tapering linear mounds extend up the back or western part of the ridge from a wetland. Another linear mound runs parallel to the lake for an extraordinary distance of 638 feet.

Both Lewis and McLachlan mapped tapering linear mounds extending up a high hill overlooking the east shore of Lake Waubesa.[3] These were part of Morris Park group, recently renamed Lake Waubesa South by the Wisconsin Historical Society. Here, as with many groups in the Four Lakes, these snake-like mounds ran upslope from the water's edge, in this case a very steep hill (figure 7.6). Significantly, a large spring flowed from the base of the hill on the opposite or eastern side. Lewis mapped a lone hawk, representing the upper world, flying across the west slope of the hill. A conical mound on top of the hill and short tapering linear mound completed the grouping. None of the mounds of this interesting and informative group survives.

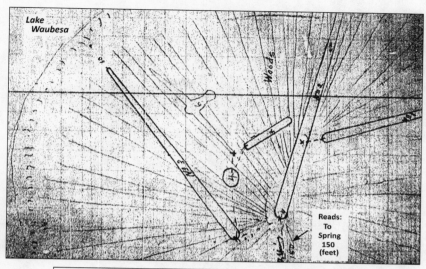

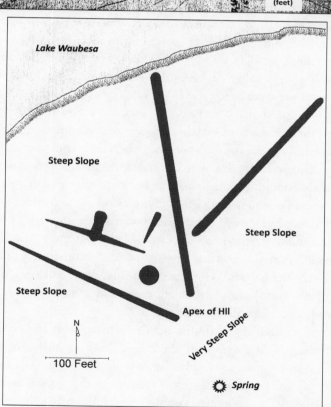

Figure 7.6. Lake Waubesa South mound group. *Above*, sketch by Lewis. *Below*, map by Rosebrough from Lewis notes.

Outlet Mounds

As with the other lakes, notable mound building took place near the confluence with the Yahara River. McLachlan reported a mound complex just north of the outlet, already nonextant by the time of his research, with a conical mound reportedly of "exceptional elevation."[4] This was probably an earlier Middle Woodland mound characteristically found near inlets and outlets of the lakes. A mile down the Yahara River from the outlet adjacent to large wetlands is the linearly arranged Sure Johnson group that probably also had its origins in earlier mound building (figure 7.7). Short and long linear mounds extend north from the Yahara River from an odd, partly enclosed earthwork. Bear and bird effigy mounds were positioned near the north end and were among the last to be built.

The earthen ridged structure lies closest to the river on the south. It measures about 150 feet by 137 feet with a twelve-foot gap, and what McLachlan simply called "a heap of dirt" extending to the west.[5] The earthen walls stand about five feet high. The structure has been interpreted by some as a type of sacred enclosure occasionally found at mound groups. However, the uneven banks enclose an area that is concave and dug out. Given its location near the outlet, a place where early conical mounds were built elsewhere in the Four Lakes, and the pattern of later mound building that extends from it, it is likely that the banks and depression are the remnants and spoil piles of a large Middle Woodland mound, which had been massively looted by people looking for bones and antiquities. This was a common Sunday-afternoon pastime in the late nineteenth century. W. G. McLachlan reported that when he visited the site sometime around 1914, the enclosure had been used for farm refuse and cattle carcasses, no doubt adding to the disturbance. Fortunately, the surviving Sure Johnson mounds are now a part of a private conservancy.

Situated along a high drumlin, the Lewis mound group overlooks the modern village of McFarland and the Yahara River outlet (figure 7.8). The mound group is now a part of Indian Mound Conservation Park maintained by the village and volunteers. The name of the group derives from a previous landowner and not the famous mound surveyor who mapped the site. Conical and short linear mounds occupy the top, a common pattern. As with those mounds on the high drumlin at Woodland Park in Monona, some mounds were damaged by the construction of a water tower. Moving

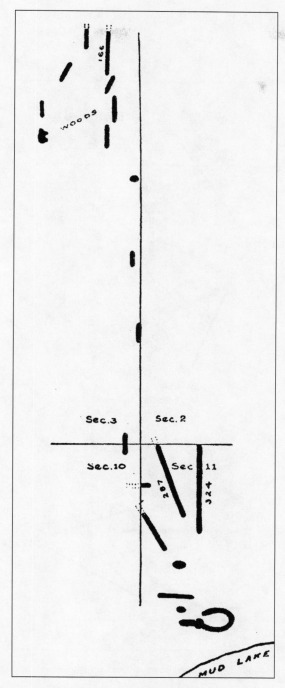

Figure 7.7. Sure Johnson mound group mapped by McLachlan.

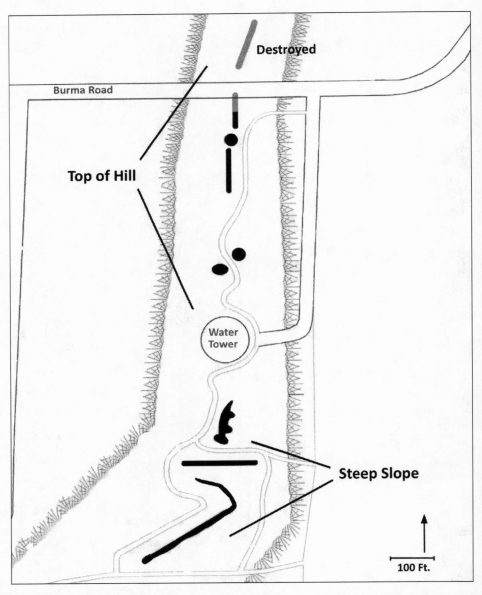

Figure 7.8. The Lewis mound group overlaid on modern features, based on maps of McLachlan and Lewis.

downslope, one encounters a short-tailed fox or wolf (mistakenly mapped by McLachlan as a bear), a linear mound, and then a curved, 325-foot-long earthwork. First mapped by T. H. Lewis, it can be seen clearly today as a snake effigy with a slightly bulbous head and tapering tail. It appropriately "snakes" it way down the lower part of the drumlin to a wetland.

Monitored by a professional archaeologist, installation of a new water pipe to the water tower in the 1990s revealed that there had been burials made outside of the recorded mounds. Workmen uncovered a burial with a large, unusual bone pendant made with two deer mandibles (lower jaws) joined together. Holes in the upper part of the jaws had been drilled for a cord attachment. The burial is undated, but it is quite likely these are the remains of one of the Late Woodland people who used the hill for mound building.

Linear mounds make up most of the Eli Johnson group arranged along the slope of a high hill overlooking the Yahara River (figure 7.9). Here, too, a tapering linear mound runs up the slope, but farther up is the other of the two crossed mound arrangements in Four Lakes mound district. Three oval and conical mounds top the hill and seemingly provide an upper-world complement to the linear mounds.

The directions of the crossed mounds here differ from Big Cross near Lake Mendota and may be the most compelling case in the Four Lakes for solar orientations as sketched (perhaps not precisely) by McLachlan in the early twentieth century. The axes of the two long mounds seem to describe the general directions of both summer and winter solstice sunrises and sunsets. The earthwork still exists in a wooded lot (on private land), so precise mapping and analysis of its positioning on the slope of hill should tell whether there is good evidence that at least some ancient mounds were used to make celestial observations.

The Ward Group, a Preservation Problem

Several groupings such as the Uphoff Ridge mound group illustrate the expansion of effigy mound building to more remote areas away from the lakes. Sadly, another one of these more distant groupings has become symbolic of previous destruction and continuing threats. The seven original mounds of the Ward group consisted of a straight-winged

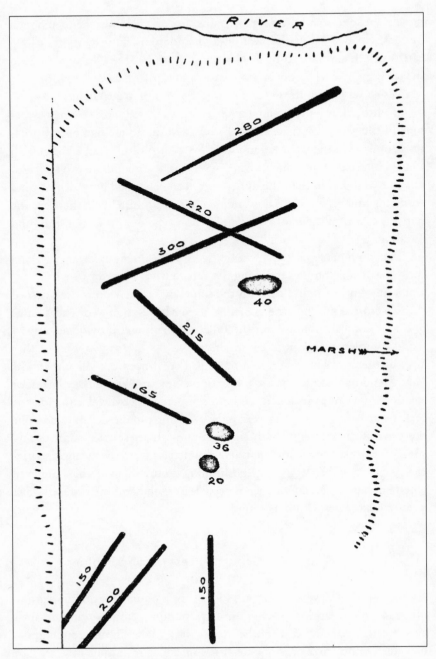

Figure 7.9. The Eli Johnson mound group mapped by McLachlan.

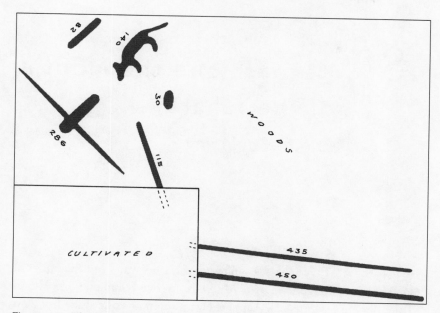

Figure 7.10. The Ward mound group mapped by McLachlan.

bird, a fox or wolf mound, and linear mounds in excess of 450 feet in length arranged on a drumlin about one and a half miles east from the lake (figure 7.10). Over the decades, most of the land around the mounds has been quarried away for sand and gravel, destroying some mounds and their original landscape and leaving only three mounds on a high earthen pedestal. These surviving mounds are now protected by state law (157.70 Wisconsin Statutes), but provisions of this law also allow landowners to apply to have any burials removed. Whatever the ultimate legal fate of the Ward mounds, erosion will continue to eat away at what is left of the land around them.

8 | Kegonsa and the Mouth of the Yahara

End to Beginning

THE YAHARA RIVER winds its way from the outlet of Lake Waubesa through the Lower Mud Lake wetlands and on to the shores of Lake Kegonsa (figure 8.1). Along the way, remnants of a stone fish dam can still be viewed in a narrow part of the river, used by Indian people into the twentieth century to trap great quantities of fish. It is situated right below the Skare site, a place used continuously by Native Americans for camps and villages from between 9000 B.C. and A.D. 1250. Several linear mounds on the opposite side of the river attest to the presence of the Late Woodland mound builders.

This stretch of the Yahara River provided a natural ford and was an important trail crossing where a short iron bridge was later built. Early white settlers took advantage of this narrow and shallow stretch to build one of the first water-driven sawmills in the Four Lakes region. Remnants of the wooden mill dam can also be glimpsed during low water between the bridge and the Indian fish dam. The unique complex of historic and archaeological sites represents nearly the entire span of human occupation of the Fours Lakes through early white settlement. It has been placed on the National Register of Historic Places as the Lower Mud Lake Archaeological District.

Kegonsa was called First Lake by early settlers because it is closest to the confluence of the Yahara and Rock rivers. The Ho-Chunk maintained camps or villages at several places on the lake. One camp on Williams Point is where Ho-Chunk people made maple sugar and near where garden beds

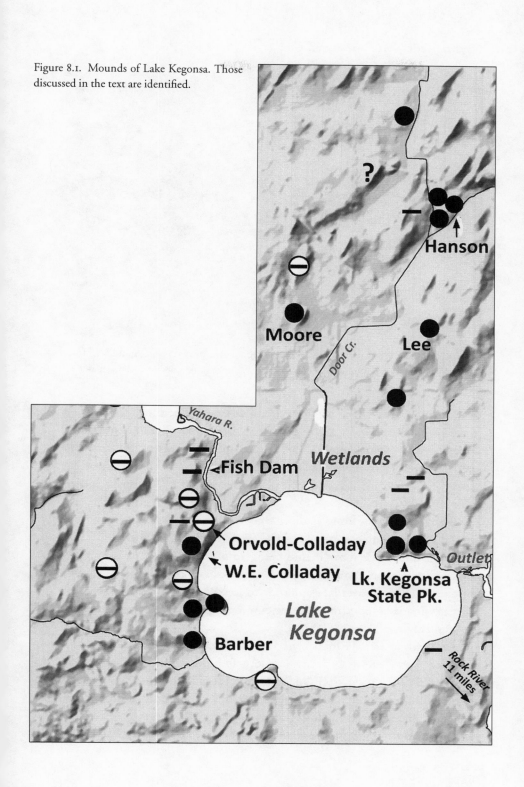

Figure 8.1. Mounds of Lake Kegonsa. Those discussed in the text are identified.

Figure 8.2. Adolf Hoeffler drawing of Lake Kegonsa area in 1852. Note mounds in foreground. These may be from the Orvold-Colladay group later described by McLachlan.

could still be seen in the early twentieth century.[1] The Ho-Chunk called the lake *Na-sa-koo-cha-tel-a* or "hard maple grove lake." Maple syrup and sugar were seasonal staples of the Native American diet at the time and were also used as trade items with American settlers. The spring sugaring time remains an important social occasion for many Wisconsin Indian people.

Being some miles from Madison, the mounds of Lake Kegonsa did not attract as much interest from early researchers; thus, many mounds disappeared under the plow before being recorded. T. H. Lewis mapped mounds here, and modern mound surveys have been conducted, but much of what is known is, again, due to Dr. W. G. McLachlan's work in the early 1920s "at odd times during summer vacations," often assisted by his son, Fergis.[2]

Early white settlers found the lake surrounded by oak savanna and crowded with mounds as drawn by German artist Adolf Hoeffler in 1852 (figure 8.2). The view from an unknown vantage point shows a large, high conical Indian mound, typical of earlier Woodland mound building, and what appears to be a cluster of smaller mounds nearby. Most of the 194 recorded mounds around the lake, however, appear to date from the

Late Woodland period, among them at least thirteen zoomorphic effigy forms, not including several that might be snakes. Large concentrations of mounds occurred near the west and northeast shores. Several smaller effigy mound groups lie several miles upstream along creeks that drain to the lake, thus providing insights into the expansion of mound ceremonial activity.

Like Waubesa, Lake Kegonsa is lower in elevation than the upper lakes and includes large wetland areas. Reflecting this lower-world environment, only four sky birds are recorded here along with one goose well away from the lake itself. Instead, the lake has a high proportion of linear mounds— 38 percent or nearly an identical proportion to that of Lake Waubesa. Other mound forms are water spirit and water mammals; bent, tapering, and curved snake-like forms; chain or compound mounds; and a great many conical mounds. At the Lee group, McLachlan mapped an unusual mound he thought could be a swan, but its shape cannot be verified since it has since disappeared under the plow. Charles Brown mapped a similar form, but with a suggestion of legs, quite some distance away in eastern Wisconsin (figure 8.3).

One large cluster of mounds, the Barber mound group, once spread itself across a high plateau southwest of the lakeshore. Indian garden beds were also located nearby at the lakeshore. According to Lewis, who mapped portions of the plateau in the early 1890s, the site contained at least fifty mounds in two groups. Lewis mapped two effigies that resemble water mammals but noted the nearby existence of other effigies, as well as conical, linear, and compound mounds (figure 8.4).[3] A number of springs flow from the edges of the plateau to an adjacent creek, accounting for the attraction to this place for purposes of ceremonial construction.

North of this, there were six mound groups located along the northwestern shore of Lake Kegonsa extending onto a peninsula called Colladay Point. A close relationship to geography is evident here. One set of linear mounds follows the east–west direction of the peninsula, while on a ridge north of this the linear mounds of the W. E. Colladay group orient north–south (figure 8.5). Water spirits, bears, and birds were among the few effigies found among linear and conical mounds in other larger groupings on this side of the lake.

Another concentration of mainly linear mounds was found in the vicinity of Williams or Sugarbush Point on the northeastern shore of Lake

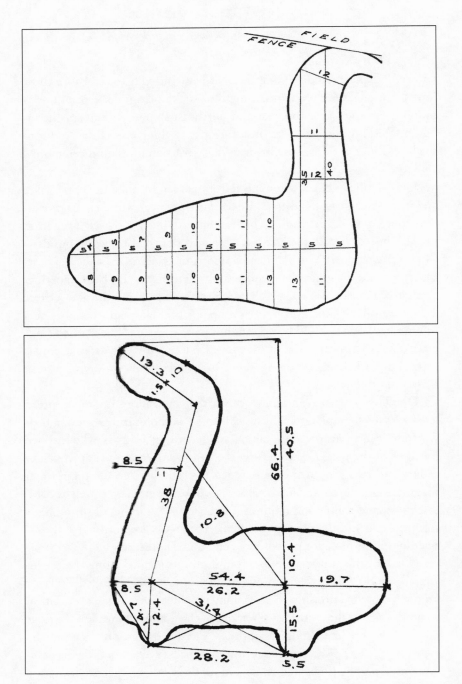

Figure 8.3. *Above*, "Swan" on Lake Kegonsa mapped by McLachlan. *Below*, similar mound from eastern Wisconsin mapped by Brown, suggesting that the swan may have been a different type of mound.

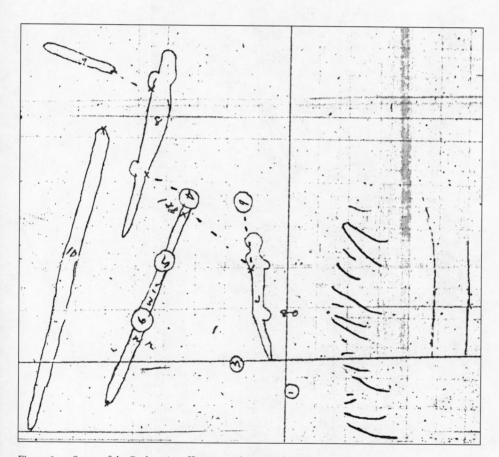

Figure 8.4. Some of the Barber site effigy mounds mapped by Lewis.

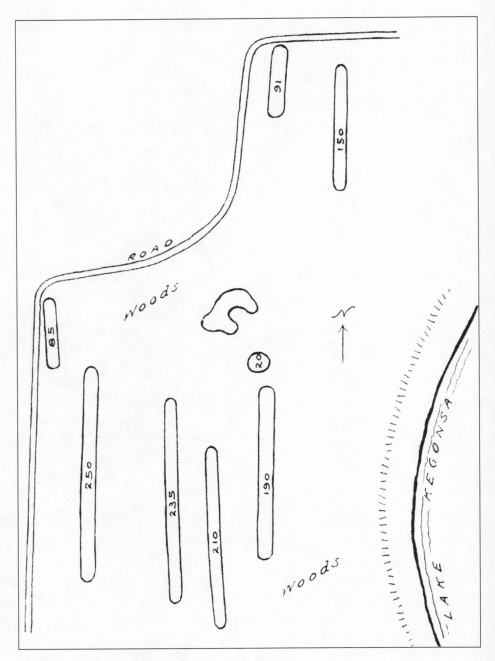

Figure 8.5. The W. E. Colladay group mapped by McLachlan.

Kegonsa and near the Yahara River outlet. Some linear mounds, part of once larger groupings, are preserved in Lake Kegonsa State Park. Ancient habitation sites and garden beds have been recorded in the vicinity.

Upstream well away from the lakeshore, smaller groups of mounds, all built during the Late Woodland, occupy drumlins. Three mounds of the Moore group remain on private land at the edge of a large wetland bordering Door Creek to the east (figure 8.6). McLachlan originally mapped the group, and it was located and mapped again as part of the Dane County Mound Identification project in 1991 using modern survey equipment.[4] The modern surveyors found the group in roughly the same condition as when McLachlan saw it. A linear mound follows the typical northeast/southwest–oriented drumlin while the panther-form water spirit and goose follow the slope down to a large wetland. This goose is perpendicular to the main axis of the landform, as is the case with many effigy mounds including other geese, and does not appear to have other directional significance. The orientations and symbolism of the remote Moore group, like much of the lower part of the Four Lakes ceremonial landscape, relate to the lower-world water realm.

Nearby, the ancient mound builders made two forms uncommon for the area at the Hanson group, also once situated along a ridge at the edge of the Door Creek marsh (figure 8.7). One is a flattened aerial perspective water spirit and the other a compound mound. Aerial perspective water spirit mounds occur throughout the effigy mound region but are most common in the eastern part. Only five of these long-tailed mounds are known to have existed in the Four Lakes mound district. The rest of the quite numerous water spirit mounds found here are of the panther shape shown in profile.

Compound or chain mounds are conical mounds joined with short linear earthworks, many time in a series. A total of thirteen compound mounds occurred at the Four Lakes mound district, mainly in the south or lower part. They were much more common to the west along the Mississippi River where they seem to be a part of initial Late Woodland mound ceremonial activity when only short linear and conical mounds were made.[5] It may be that compound mounds represent the symbolic unification of the upper and lower worlds at that time.

The occurrence of both of these forms here demonstrates the very wide distribution of mound forms and the placement of the Four Lakes mound

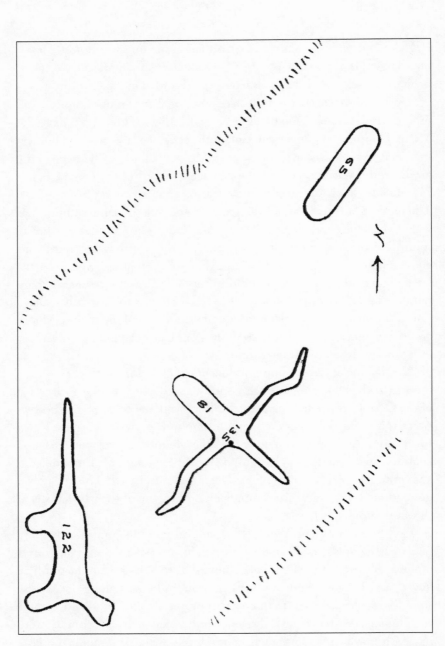

Figure 8.6. The Moore group on a ridge overlooking wetlands, based on a map by McLachlan.

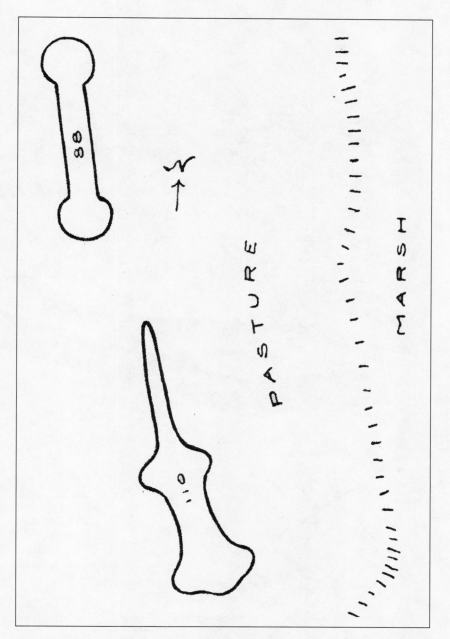

Figure 8.7. The Hanson mounds mapped by McLachlan.

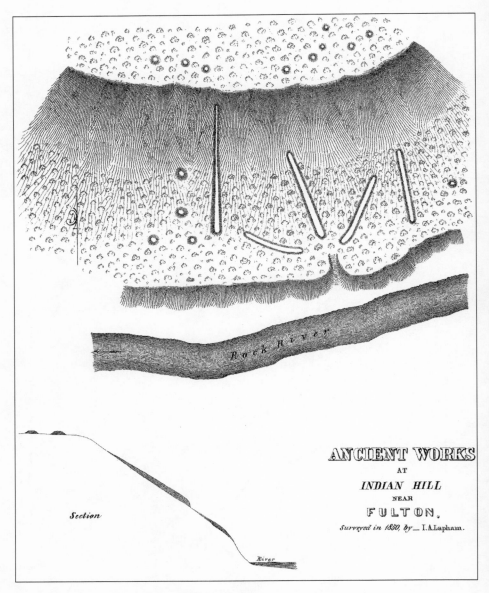

ANCIENT WORKS
AT
INDIAN HILL
NEAR
FULTON.
Surveyed in 1850, by I.A.Lapham.

Section

River

Rock River

Figure 8.8. Indian Hill mound group mapped by Lapham.

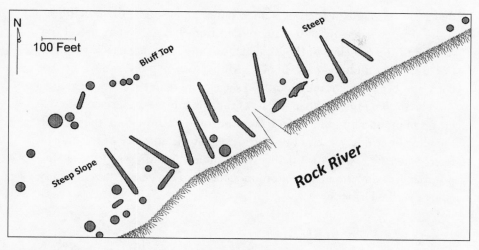

Figure 8.9. Indian Hill mound group as mapped by Rosebrough.

district in the center of overlapping areas of symbolic geography. They also provide additional information on the types of mounds that were being built as Late Woodland mound building expanded to more remote areas.

From Lake Kegonsa, the Yahara River meanders through the charming village of Stoughton and then through typical southern Wisconsin farmlands to its confluence with the Rock River eleven miles away. No mounds are found along this long stretch of the river, emphasizing the importance of the lakes in effigy and earlier mound ceremonial activity. In fact, the next mound group is not encountered until one reaches the Rock River. Here, the Indian Hill group is located on a high, steep hill along the Rock River one mile north of its confluence with the Yahara River. This group first drew the attention of Increase Lapham, who provided a map and description in his 1855 *Antiquities of Wisconsin*. Lapham showed conical mounds on the top and base of the hill, and three long tapering earthworks extending from a cutout along the river, possibly a former spring (figure 8.8). Another remarkable snake-like mound extends up the steep, eighty-foot-high slope. Investigators after Lapham clarified some of Lapham's locations, adding more conical mounds and one effigy mound to one side of the group (figure 8.9).[6]

One conical mound at Indian Hill dates back to the earliest mound building in the region, judging by its contents as reported by early mound diggers—red pigment (ocher) stained bones and a cache of "blue horn-stone" blades, referring to a stone traded from Indiana.[7] The use of red ocher and the presence of the Indiana hornstone are characteristic of the initial mound building in the Upper Midwest during the end of the Archaic and beginning of the Woodland stage more than 2,500 years ago.

The Indian Hill site, then, is one of those rare places that trace the evolution of mound building from its very beginnings through to the time of the effigy mounds. We end our tour here near the entrance of the Yahara River watershed with this microcosm of mound building history, an appropriate introduction to the monumental Four Lakes effigy mound landscape that lies farther up.

9 Landscapes of the Past, Questions and Issues for the Future

EIGHT HUNDRED YEARS AGO, pre-Columbian Indian people abandoned the region of Madison and the Four Lakes after thousands of years of continuous occupation. They left behind a visible legacy in the form of an incredible landscape sculpted from earth into ancestral spirit beings that continued to share their world and define human existence. Unparalleled preservation and documentation has allowed us to reconstruct much of this landscape. Integrated archaeological, ethnographic, and ethnohistoric research provides us with insights into the evolution and meaning of this wonderful monument, as well as similar landscapes found throughout the Upper Midwest.

In this book the origin of effigy mound landscapes has been traced to an even more distant time when Woodland people began the custom of making earthen mounds ca. 500 B.C. These early mounds functioned on several social and religious levels. At the most basic, the mounds were burial places that marked territories of bands of people and linked them to the land through their ancestors buried in these places. In at least some cases, the mounds reflected a part of a dual kinship system reflecting the upper and lower social worlds. On a more abstract yet critical level, ritual construction of the mounds represented cyclic re-creation of the world, merging life and death of humans in this continuous cycle.

After ca. A.D. 700, a complex society of Late Woodland people in southern Wisconsin and parts of adjoining states carried forward and elaborated these concepts in a unique and spectacular fashion. Using the natural landscape as their medium, Indian people sculpted vast three-dimensional ceremonial landscapes consisting of earthen images of birds, animals, and spirit beings that existed in a world invisible to most. These landscapes replicated the structure of their belief systems related to world creation and renewal, and also the kinship system that derived from these beliefs. As proposed here, the effigy mound landscape did not merely *symbolize* periodic re-creation of the world and its people in the form of their animal and spirit-being ancestors, but the landscape itself was perceived by the mound builders as creation in progress. Most mounds during this period continued to be used as burial places but many did not, underscoring that mound building transcended burial of the dead; the death of specific humans alone was not necessary to stimulate periodic earth- and life-renewal ritual ceremonies.

The effigy mound ceremonial added broader social, ideological, and even political dimensions to previous mound building. As proposed here and by others elsewhere, the effigy mound building ceremonials in southern Wisconsin and adjacent states integrated a number of groups of people, growing in population, into a larger ethnic identity. The complexity of effigy mound building and the enormity of many mounds, as detailed in these pages, argue for a far more complex society than has been previously surmised. Indeed, the climax of effigy mound building is correlated with the formation of new, complex societies throughout the Midwest as these cultures evolved from hunter-gatherers to farmers.

The subsequent demise of effigy mound landscape construction is also broadly correlated with the expansion of other peoples, most notably the Mississippians, for trade, alliance building, resource acquisition, territory, or other reasons. Other factors may have been at work as well, such as increased conflict, overexploitation of resources by larger populations, and climatic change, thus forcing economic and social changes.

Whatever the specific reasons, the changes follow a general pattern found elsewhere in the world where certain types of monument building linked formerly mobile people together as they made the transition to nonmigratory lifestyles based on agriculture. Eventually, as in other parts of the world, they nucleated into larger, more sedentary clusters of villages that replaced the need for special and seasonal ceremonial gathering places. Strongly defined clans that merged earlier further integrated these people since, as in modern times, intermarriage with other clans would have been required. Other social institutions, typical of Native American tribal societies (such as medicine and warrior groups), would also have reinforced a common identity because membership extended beyond both kinship and community boundaries. Archaeologists call this new social development the Oneota Tradition.

The well-documented effigy mound landscape of the Four Lakes mound district provides an informative case study of the effigy mound phenomena in one area. It illustrates the many general principles involved in the location and arrangement—and most importantly the close correspondence—between the natural environment and ideology. Analysis of this ideological or ceremonial landscape, along with a rich archaeological record, has also provided insights and ideas about the evolution of the effigy mound landscape that has it roots in earlier times.

However, much needs to be verified and clarified, and many questions remain. One interesting and important new question involves the nature of effigy mound society itself. Was it largely egalitarian as many assume—with social differences and status determined only by age, sex, personal achievements of individuals, and membership in the different but largely equal clans? Or does the very existence of some huge and awe-inspiring mounds and their exquisite arrangements reflect a more complex level of organization, a hierarchical society with some kinship groups and/or settlement areas exercising greater or lesser power and control?

A second older and larger issue concerns the precise dating of the effigy mound era. At present, a generally defined period of effigy mound construction between A.D. 700 and 1100 is based on comparatively few precise radiocarbon dates from the mounds themselves and none at all from the Four Lakes. Further, most of the dates that exist reflect older radiocarbon dating techniques that have since been greatly refined. The lack of precise dating hampers making firm correlations with other major changes and developments and would indeed go far in explaining the specific reasons for origins and demise. It could be, for example, that the climax of effigy mounding with truly monumental forms and groupings came as influence and movements of the great Cahokia-based Mississippian civilization spread north, generating instability and cultural insecurity. In this view, elaboration of mound building would be the result of the social need to define themselves as a people with ancient links to their land through widespread ceremonial constructions that depicted their distinctive beliefs, social arrangements, and origins from powerful animals and spirit beings that populated their universe.

But obtaining such dates is unlikely in the near future. Native Americans understandably object not only to the excavation of the graves of their ancestors, as many mounds clearly are, but also to destructive testing of previously excavated human remains. Most archaeologists are sympathetic to these concerns and also point to the mounds as precious and unique monuments of the past, not to be tampered with lightly. Mounds of all types are protected by Wisconsin state law, which is also supported and urged by the scientific community. In this light, it is clear that information on the emergence, proliferation, and demise of the effigy mound culture must continue to be extracted from nonburial sites, such as the large number of camps and villages, and from nondestructive analysis of surviving mound landscapes, as described in this book.

But continued analysis using a landscape approach is dependent on preservation of individual mounds and their geographical context. Wisconsin state law and the vigilance of the public has done a good job in the former matter, but enforcement has been an issue in those cases where there has been purposeful destruction. Additionally, roads, houses, and businesses continue to be constructed within and around the mounds, destroying the natural landscape that framed mound construction. Present law provides only a short five-foot buffer zone around an individual mound, which indeed allows for development within groupings. This facilitates destruction of the ancient landscapes, making it harder to understand both the meaning and the evolution of the mound groups through time. In this book, several examples of this ongoing problem have been provided for the Four Lakes mound district, most notably the Monona Mound, squeezed between lots on Lake Monona, and where quarry operations have removed the land around the remnants of the Ward group.

Public land stewards, conservation organizations, and Indian nations, such as the Ho-Chunk, continue to acquire and preserve parts of effigy mound landscapes. All of these efforts are to be applauded and hugely supported. However, aggressive new acquisition and conservation programs and laws must be developed since the land around and between the mounds—the sacred landscape that give them meaning—continues to disappear. In a global perspective, these "landscapes of creation" of the

Four Lakes and Upper Midwest—cosmological maps of their builder's worldview—are equivalent as world wonders to the megalithic landscapes of Europe and the Nasca Lines of Peru. We must recognize and celebrate this fact, preserving these magnificent places to honor the ancient mound builders and to further illuminate the human story.

Appendix

Selected Mound Sites Open to the Public

Lake Mendota Mound Sites That Can Be Visited

Governor Nelson State Park
County Highway M, Waunakee

The 422-acre Governor Nelson State Park is located on the northwestern shore of Lake Mendota. Five conical mounds and a panther or water spirit mound survive from an original group that also included a goose and a bird. A fortified Indian village was located north of the mounds near the beach. One panther-type water spirit mound is located in the south part of the park along Borchers Beach Road. Maps are available at the park.

Mendota Mental Health Institute
Troy Drive, Madison

Portions of two large mound groups are preserved on the grounds of Mendota Mental Health Institute, located on the northern shore of Lake Mendota. These include a bird with a 624-foot wingspan and a curve-tailed water spirit. Large conical and amorphous mounds, characteristic of those dating to before construction of the effigy mounds, occupy

a high point of land in the Farwell's Point group. One contained a rock enclosure or burial vault revealed by nineteenth-century digging. The mounds
are on the grounds of an active hospital, and security is present to protect
patient privacy; permission to visit the grounds is needed beforehand.

Burrows Park
Burrows Road, off Sherman Avenue, Madison

Burrows Park, a small city park on the eastern shore of
Lake Mendota, contains a reconstructed bird effigy mound with a wingspan of 128 feet. The bird was damaged early by looting, but was restored
by WPA workers under the direction of Charles E. Brown. A second effigy,
a fox or canine-like animal, was destroyed.

Observatory Hill
University of Wisconsin campus, Observatory Drive,
Madison

Two small effigy mounds, a bird and a unique two-tailed
water spirit, are located just west of the University of Wisconsin's Washburn Observatory on top of a hill that offers a majestic view of Lake Mendota. A panther-form water spirit and a linear mound were once located
below the hill but were obliterated by farming. The tails of the water spirit
mound have been marred by construction of sidewalks.

Willow Creek
University of Wisconsin campus, Observatory Drive,
Madison

Located along a campus bike path and a small creek, just
north of the University of Wisconsin Natatorium, the Willow Creek group
consists of three partially reconstructed mounds: a goose, a mound of in-
determinate form, and possibly the disturbed remnants of a long-tailed
water spirit. The goose was restored by Brown, but not accurately. It originally flew in the opposite direction.

Picnic Point
University of Wisconsin campus, off of University Bay
Drive, Madison

On the eastern shore of Picnic Point, toward the tip of

the peninsula, are one linear and one conical mound. On the western shore is a conical mound.

Pheasant Branch Conservancy
Pheasant Branch Road, Middleton
Conical and short linear mounds of the Pheasant Branch Hill mound group are on a high hill at the north end of the conservancy overlooking a large spring (Belle Fontaine) and extensive marshlands. A trail leads up the hill, but the preserved mounds on the hill are covered by thick vegetation and are difficult to see. Visitors are asked to stay on the trail. The top of the hill offers one of the most scenic views in the Four Lakes. A parking lot is on the west side of the conservancy along Pheasant Branch Road.

Blackhawk Country Club
Blackhawk Drive, Village of Shorewood Hills
The mounds preserved on the scenic Blackhawk Country Club golf course embody many principles on the arrangement of mounds in the Four Lakes area. Conical mounds are on top of a hill and a long, tapering linear mound runs down a long slope. A goose flies up the slope and bear mounds are located on a terrace below. A water spirit mound once paralleled the lakeshore. The country club welcomes visitors to the mounds but asks that visitors first check in at the clubhouse, so as to not interfere with members playing golf as well as for their own safety. However, there is a turnoff on Lake Mendota Drive from which the bear mounds along with a historic marker can be viewed.

Lake Wingra Mound Sites That Can Be Visited

Forest Hill Cemetery
Regent Street and Speedway Road, Madison
Established in 1858, historic Forest Hill Cemetery is the final resting place of many of Wisconsin's most prominent citizens, including eight governors. In among the more modern graves is an effigy mound group that consists of most of a goose, two water spirits or panthers, and a linear mound. The head of the bird effigy, which is on a slope that leads,

appropriately, to adjacent wetlands, was removed when a railroad was built adjacent to the area in the nineteenth century. Part of the tail of one panther and three additional linear mounds were destroyed during the early development of the cemetery. A walking-tour brochure for the cemetery is available at the cemetery office.

University of Wisconsin Arboretum
Arboretum Drive, Madison
Two Late Woodland effigy mound groups consisting of bird, panther or water spirit, linear, and conical mounds are located on either side of Arboretum Drive at the University of Wisconsin Arboretum. One group is situated immediately above several prominent springs considered sacred by Ho-Chunk who camped in this area into the twentieth century. These groups were restored by Charles E. Brown. A third mound group—linears and a conical—is not easily accessible. The Arboretum consists of over 1,260 acres of restored wetlands, oak savanna, and other floral communities, all of which give visitors a flavor of what the environment probably looked like at the time of the effigy mounds. Walking-tour maps are available at the visitor's center.

Vilas Park
Randall Avenue and Drake Street, Madison
The Late Woodland effigy mound group in Vilas Park contains a small hawk-like bird effigy, a linear mound, and six conical mounds. Two additional conical mounds and another bird effigy were destroyed. The plaque at the site is an example of the efforts undertaken by Charles E. Brown to call attention to the group and ensure preservation.

Vilas Park Circle
Vilas Avenue, Madison
The small city park was created to preserve a large effigy mound of a bear located on the west side of the circular park. This mound was once part of a larger group that included seven linear mounds radiating down the slope of the high hill, as well as several conical mounds.

Edgewood Campus
Edgewood College Drive, Madison

A bird, bear, and conical mounds are preserved on the Edgewood campus. Visitors are welcome to stroll the campus, but they are asked to first register at the Predolin Humanities Center.

Lake Monona Mound Sites That Can Be Visited

Lakeland Avenue Effigy Mound Parks
Lakeland Avenue, Madison

Two small city of Madison parks overlooking Lake Monona were created to preserve three mounds of the Elmside and Mills Woods groups. Hudson Park, located near the intersection of Lakeland and Hudson avenues, contains a panther-shape water spirit mound headed to the lake. The end of its slightly curved tail was removed by road construction. A short distance away and higher in elevation on the physical landscape is another park located at the intersection of Lakeland and Maple avenues that encloses two effigy mounds, a bear and another animal without a tail, variously identified to as a lynx, bear, or deer. The bronze sculpture *Let the Great Spirit Soar* by Henry Whitehorse honors the memory of the effigy mound people.

Outlet Mound
Midwood and Ridgewood Avenues, Monona

This is the last surviving large conical mound of the large Outlet group. It is about two thousand years old, built before the time of the effigy mounds. It is seven feet high and sixty feet in diameter and is located on a small parcel of land within a circular drive.

Woodland Park
Monona Drive, Monona

Two linear mounds, remnants of the long Tompkins-Brindler/Nichols group, follow the crest of the drumlin ridge just northeast of the water tower. The park, once covered by dense undergrowth, is being restored to an oak savanna. A pedestrian entrance to the park is on Monona Drive, but parking can be found near the Aldo Leopold Center off Femrite Drive. The entrance is about one-quarter mile east of Monona Drive on Femrite. A trail leads up to Woodland Park.

Edna Taylor Conservation Park
Femrite Drive, Monona

Remnants of the Pflaum-McWilliams mound group are located on a drumlin overlooking a marsh. These include long linear mounds that neatly follow the crest of the ridge, two of which were cut off by early cultivation and modern development. Three shorter linear mounds and a tailed effigy are found on the northwest slope. Two of the linear mounds were bisected by a sledding hill. Parking is at the entrance to the park on Femrite Drive. Trails take visitors to restored wetlands and oak savanna as well as the mounds.

Lake Waubesa Mound Sites That Can Be Visited

Goodland County Park
Waubesa Avenue, off of Goodland Park Road, Madison

Goodland County Park is located on the west shore of the lake off Goodland Park Road. Here there are three linear mounds (two with bent or curved ends) and one small or oval mound. They are located along both sides of the main park road. A road crossed one of the mounds, causing some disturbance.

Indian Mound Conservation Park
Exchange Street, McFarland

The Lewis group is located on the hill overlooking Lake Waubesa and the Village of McFarland. The group consists of conical, linear, and canine mounds along with a rare lifelike snake mound. Some mounds on top of the hill were disturbed during water tower construction, but now the mounds are carefully protected. Trails have been made to eliminate any impact on the mounds.

Lake Kegonsa Mound Sites That Can Be Visited

Kegonsa State Park
Door Creek Road, Stoughton

Kegonsa State Park is located on the east side of the lake. The park has maps showing locations of seven linear mounds along main trails. A Wisconsin state park sticker is required and can be purchased at the park, which is open year round.

Notes

Preface

1. Douglas T. Price and Gary M. Feinman, *Images of the Past* (New York: McGraw-Hill, 2005), 513–516.

2. Robert Hall, "Red Banks, Oneota, and the Winnebago: Views from a Distant Rock," *Wisconsin Archeologist* 74, no. 1–4 (1993): 51.

3. Robert A. Birmingham and Amy Rosebrough, "On the Meaning of Effigy Mounds," *Wisconsin Archeologist* 84, no. 1–2 (2003); Amy L. Rosebrough and Robert A. Birmingham, "Effigy Mound Landscapes of Wisconsin," paper presented at the 2003 Society of the American Archaeology Conference, Milwaukee, Wisconsin.

4. Nancy Oestreich Lurie, *Wisconsin Indians* (Madison: Wisconsin Historical Society Press, 2002), 21.

5. For an excellent discussion of various archaeological theoretical approaches, see James L. Pearson, *Shamanism and the Ancient Mind: A Cognitive Approach to Archaeology* (New York: Altimira Press, 2002).

6. Meghan C. L. Howley and John M. O'Shea, "Bear's Journey and the Study of Ritual in Archaeology," *American Antiquity* 71, no. 2 (2006).

7. Robert J. Salzer and G. Rajnovich, *The Gottschall Rockshelter: An Archaeological Mystery* (St. Paul, MN: Prairie Smoke Press, 2000).

8. Some examples are Pearson, *Shamanism and the Ancient Mind;* Grace Rajnovich, *Reading Rock Art: Interpreting the Indian Rock Paintings of the Canadian Shield* (Toronto: Natural Heritage/Natural History, 1994); James D. Keyser and David S. Whitney, "Sympathetic Magic in Western North American Rock Art," *American Antiquity* 71, no. 1 (2006).

9. Anthony F. Aveni, *Between the Lines: The Mystery of the Giant Ground Drawings of Ancient Nasca, Peru* (Austin: University of Texas Press, 2000).

10. William G. Gartner, "Late Woodland Landscapes of Wisconsin: Ridged Fields, Effigy Mounds and Territoriality," *Antiquity* 73, no. 281 (1999); Lynne Goldstein, "Landscapes and Mortuary Practices: A Case for Regional Perspectives," in *Regional Approaches to Mortuary Analysis*, ed. Lane Anderson Beck (New York: Plenum, 1995); Rosebrough and Birmingham, "Effigy Mound Landscapes of Wisconsin."

11. James E. Sneed and Robert W. Preucel, "The Ideology of Settlement: Landscapes in the Northern Rio Grande," in *Archaeologies of Landscape: Contemporary Perspectives*, ed. Wendy Asmore and A. Bernard Knapp (Malden, MA: Blackwell Publishers, 1999), 170. William Gartner takes a broader perspective and examines a landscape consisting of effigy mounds, habitation areas, and agricultural fields; see Gartner, "Late Woodland Landscapes of Wisconsin."

12. Ronald J. Mason, *Inconstant Companions: Archaeology and North American Indian Oral Traditions* (Tuscaloosa: University of Alabama Press, 2006).

Chapter 1. Spirits of Earth

1. John Locke, M.D., "Earthwork Antiquities in Wiskonsin Territory," U.S. 28th Cong., 1st sess., Senate Executive Document, 207, Washington, DC, 1844.

2. Based on records of the Office of the State Archaeologist, Wisconsin Historical Society.

3. James B. Stoltman and George W. Christiansen III, "The Late Woodland Stage in the Driftless Area of the Upper Mississippi Valley," in *Late Woodland Societies: Tradition and Transformation across the Midcontinent*, ed. Thomas E. Emerson, Dale L. McElrath, and Andrew C. Fortier (Lincoln: University of Nebraska Press, 2000); James L. Theler and Robert F. Boszhardt, "Collapse of Critical Resources and Culture Change: A Model for the Woodland to Oneota Transformation in the Upper Midwest," *American Antiquity* 71, no. 3 (2006).

4. Theler and Boszhardt, "Collapse of Critical Resources and Culture Change."

5. Robert F. Boszhardt, *Deep Cave Art in the Upper Mississippi Valley* (St. Paul, MN: Prairie Smoke Press, 2003).

6. Map by Samuel Stone and Leandes Judson dated 1836, Increase Lapham Papers, Box 32, Wisconsin Historical Society.

7. David V. Mollenhoff, *Madison: A History of the Formative Years*, 2nd ed. (Madison: University of Wisconsin Press, 2003), 46.

8. Robert Hall, "Red Banks, Oneota, and the Winnebago: Views from a Distant Rock," *Wisconsin Archeologist* 74, no. 1–4 (1993): 51.

9. Robert A. Birmingham and Leslie E. Eisenberg, *Indian Mounds of Wisconsin* (Madison: University of Wisconsin Press, 2000), 125–127.

10. Clark R. Mallam, *The Effigy Mound Manifestation: An Interpretive Model*, Report no. 9 (Iowa City: University of Iowa, Office of the State Archaeologist, 1979); Clark R. Mallam, "Birds, Bears, Panthers, 'Elephants' and Archaeologists,"

Wisconsin Archeologist 61, no. 3 (1980); Clark R. Mallam, "Ideology from the Earth: Effigy Mounds in the Midwest," *Archaeology* 35, no 4 (1982).

11. This idea is suggested for the "Alligator" mound of Ohio in Bradley T. Lepper and Tod A. Frolking, "Alligator Mound: Geographical and Iconographical Interpretations of a Late Prehistoric Effigy Mound in Central Ohio," *Cambridge Archaeological Journal* 13, no. 2 (2003).

12. Hall, "Red Banks, Oneota, and the Winnebago."

13. Sissel Schroeder, Kenneth Ritchie, Edward Swanson, and Lynnette Kleinsasser, "Structure Abandonment and Conflagrations at the Skare Site," paper presented at the 2003 Midwest Archaeological Conference, Milwaukee, Wisconsin.

14. David F. Overstreet, "Cultural Dynamics of the Late Prehistoric Period," in *Mounds, Modoc and MesoAmerica: Papers in Honor of Melvin F. Fowler,* ed. Steven R. Ahler (Springfield: Illinois State Museum 2000); James B. Stoltman, "A Reconsideration of the Cultural Processes Linking Cahokia to Its Northern Highlands during the Period A.D. 1000–1200," in Ahler, *Mounds, Modoc, and MesoAmerica.*

15. Robert Hall, "Rethinking Jean Nicolet's Route to the Ho-Chunk in 1634," in *Theory, Method, and Practice in Modern Archaeology,* ed. Robert J. Jeske and Douglas K. Charles (Westport, CT: Praeger Publishing, 2003).

16. Paul Radin, *The Winnebago Tribe* (Lincoln: University of Nebraska Press, 1970). Originally published as the *Thirty-Seventh Annual Report of the Bureau of American Ethnography,* 1923.

17. Ibid.

18. Historical research suggests that the first epidemics swept through the Midwest in the early seventeenth century, ahead of the Europeans. See Collin M. Betts, "Pots and Pox: The Identification of Protohistoric Epidemics in the Upper Mississippi Valley," *American Antiquity* 7, no. 2 (2006).

19. Kathleen Tigerman, ed., *Wisconsin Indian Literature: Anthology of Native Voices* (Madison: University of Wisconsin Press, 2006), 47.

20. Robert A. Birmingham and Lynne Goldstein, *Aztalan: Mysteries of an Ancient Indian Town* (Madison: Wisconsin Historical Society Press, 2005).

21. James L. Theler and Robert F. Boszhardt, *Twelve Millennia: Archaeology of the Upper Mississippi Valley* (Iowa City: University of Iowa Press, 2003).

22. Ibid.

23. Lynne Goldstein, "Landscapes and Mortuary Practices: A Case for Regional Perspectives," in *Regional Approaches to Mortuary Analysis,* ed. Lane Anderson Beck (New York: Plenum, 1995); W. C. McKern, "The Kletzien and Nitschke Mound Groups," *Bulletin of the Public Museum of the City of the Milwaukee* 3, no. 4 (1930).

24. Philip H. Salkin, *Archaeological Studies at Two Proposed Recreational Sites at Mendota Health Institute in Dane County, Wisconsin,* Reports of Investigation No. 1073 (Verona, WI: Archaeological Consulting and Services, 1988).

25. Birmingham and Eisenberg, *Indian Mounds of Wisconsin.*

26. McKern, "The Kletzien and Nitschke Mound Groups."

27. Ibid.

28. Stoltman, and Christiansen, "The Late Woodland Stage in the Driftless Area of the Upper Mississippi Valley," 508.

29. Christine Ella Ruth, "Death, Decay and Reconstruction: An Osteological Analysis of Effigy Mound Material from Wisconsin" (PhD. diss., University of Wisconsin–Milwaukee, 1998); Warren L. Wittry, "The Mendota Hills Bird Mound, Dane County," *Wisconsin Archeologist* 36, no. 2 (1955).

30. Goldstein, "Landscapes and Mortuary Practices," 114–115.

31. S. A Barrett and E. W Hawkes, "The Kratz Creek Mound Group," *Bulletin of the Public Museum of the City of Milwaukee* 3, no. 1 (1919); W. C. McKern, "The Neale and McClaughry Mound Groups," *Bulletin of the Public Museum of the City of Milwaukee* 3, no. 3 (1928); Chandler Rowe, *The Effigy Mound Culture of Wisconsin* (Milwaukee: Milwaukee Public Museum, 1956).

32. Radin, *Winnebago Tribe,* 139.

33. Chandler W. Rowe, "Preliminary Report on the Heller Mound Group," *Wisconsin Archeologist* 34, no. 2 (1953).

34. James L. Pearson, *Shamanism and the Ancient Mind: A Cognitive Approach to Archaeology* (New York: Altamira Press, 2002).

35. Good discussions of these concepts as represented by ancient Native American beliefs and iconography can be found in David S. Brose, James A. Brown, and David W. Penny, eds., *Ancient Art of the American Woodland Indians* (New York: Harry N. Abrams, in conjunction with the Detroit Institute of the Arts, 1985), 180–183; and Richard F. Townsend and Robert V. Sharp, eds., *Hero, Hawk, and Open Hand: American Indian Art of the Midwest and South* (Chicago: Art Institute of Chicago; New Haven: Yale University Press, 2004).

36. Radin, *Winnebago Tribe,* 237, 268, 391.

37. Ibid., 391.

38. Hall, "Red Banks, Oneota, and the Winnebago."

39. Robert F. Boszhardt, "An Etched Pipe from Southeastern Minnesota," *Archaeology News* 24, no. 2 (June 2006).

40. Radin, *Winnebago Tribe,* 302.

41. Dorothy Moulding Brown, *Wisconsin Indian Place-Name Legends* (Madison: Wisconsin Folklore Booklets, 1947), 14; Henry Ellsworth Cole, *Baraboo, Dells, and Devil's Lake Region* (Baraboo, WI: Baraboo Publishing Co., 1920).

42. Hall, "Red Banks, Oneota, and the Winnebago."

43. Radin, *Winnebago Tribe,* 159, 178, 193; George Christiansen III, "The Burial Mound Research Project" (Madison: Office of the State Archaeologist, Wisconsin Historical Society, 1997); Birmingham and Eisenberg, *Indian Mounds of Wisconsin,* 115; Robert A. Birmingham and Amy Rosebrough, "On the Meaning of Effigy Mounds," *Wisconsin Archeologist* 84, no. 1–2 (2003).

44. Jane E. Buikstra and Douglas K. Charles, "Centering the Ancestors: Cemeteries, Mounds and Landscapes of the Ancient North American Continent," in

Archaeologies of Landscape: Contemporary Perspectives, ed. Wendy Asmore and A. Bernard Knapp (Malden, MA: Blackwell Publishers, 1999).

45. Melvin L. Fowler, Jerome Rose, Barbara Vander Leest, and Steven R. Ahler, *The Mound 72 Area: Dedicated Space in Early Cahokia,* Illinois State Museum Reports of Investigations (Springfield: Illinois State Museum Society, 1999).

46. Louise S. Spindler, "The Menominee," in *Handbook of North American Indians,* vol. 15, *Northeast,* ed. Bruce G. Trigger (Washington, DC: Smithsonian Institution Press, 1978).

47. Radin, *Winnebago Tribe,* 194.

48. Mallam, "Birds, Bears, Panthers, 'Elephants' and Archaeologists."

49. Buikstra and Charles, "Centering the Ancestors."

50. Christopher Chippendale, *Stonehenge Complete* (London: Thames and Hudson, 2004).

51. Radin, *Winnebago Tribe,* 140.

52. G. A. Bailey, ed., *The Osage and the Invisible World from the Works of Francis La Flesche* (Norman: University of Oklahoma Press, 1995), 40–41.

53. Biloine Whiting Young and Melvin L. Fowler, *Cahokia, the Great Native American Metropolis* (Urbana: University of Illinois Press, 2000); John E. Kelly, "Redefining Cahokia: Principles and Elements of Community Organization," *Wisconsin Archeologist* 77, no. 3–4 (1996).

54. William G. Gartner, "Archaeoastronomy as Sacred Geography," *Wisconsin Archeologist* 77, no. 3–4 (1996); Peter Nabokov and Robert Easton, *Native American Architecture* (Oxford: Oxford University Press, 1989).

55. These forms are keys to the interpretation of effigy mounds. Other possible interpretations are that some represent medicine people who often wear buffalo horn headdresses or even important Native American culture heros (see Birmingham and Eisenberg, *Indian Mounds of Wisconsin,* 121).

56. Birmingham and Eisenberg, *Indian Mounds of Wisconsin*; Birmingham and Rosebrough, "On the Meaning of Effigy Mounds"; Amy L. Rosebrough and Robert A. Birmingham, "Effigy Mound Landscapes of Wisconsin" (paper presented at the 2003 Society of the American Archaeology Conference, Milwaukee, Wisconsin).

57. Birmingham and Eisenberg, *Indian Mounds of Wisconsin,* 115; Birmingham and Rosebrough, "On the Meaning of Effigy Mounds."

58. Birmingham and Eisenberg, *Indian Mounds of Wisconsin,* 90, 122–124.

59. Charles E. Brown, "The Springs of Lake Wingra," *Wisconsin Magazine of History,* o.s., 10, no. 3 (1927); Robert H. Hall, *Archaeology of the Soul: North American Belief and Ritual* (Urbana: University of Illinois Press, 1997), 19.

60. Rosebrough and Birmingham, "Effigy Mound Landscapes of Wisconsin."

61. Ray Hively and Robert Horn, "Geometry and Astronomy in Prehistoric Ohio," *Archaeoastronomy* 4 (1984); William F. Romain, *Mysteries of the Hopewell: Astronomers, Geometers, and Magicians of the Eastern Woodlands* (Akron, OH: University of Akron Press, 2000); Mark J. Lynott, review of *Mysteries of the Hopewell:*

Astronomers, Geometers, and Magicians of the Eastern Woodlands, by W. F. Romain, *Hopewell Archeology* 4, no. 2 (2001). For different discussions of mound astronomical orientations see Birmingham and Eisenberg, *Indian Mounds of Wisconsin,* and James P. Scherz, *Wisconsin's Effigy Mounds* (Madison, WI: Ancient Earthworks Society, 1991).

Chapter 2. The Ancient Mound Builders

1. Lee Clayton and John W. Attig, "Pleistocene Geology of Dane County, Wisconsin," *Geological and Natural History Bulletin* 95 (1997).

2. Clovis points have been dated to thirteen thousand years ago elsewhere in North America. There is growing evidence that the first people in North American came from Asia long before this date, making other types of stone points and tools.

3. Marjorie Green Winkler, "Late Quaternary Climate, Fire, and Vegetation Dynamics," in *Sediment Records of Biomass Burning and Global Change,* ed. James S. Clark, Helene Cachier, Johann G. Goldammer, and Brina Stocks (Berlin Heidelberg: Springer-Verlag, 1997); M. G. Winkler, A. M. Swain, and J. E. Kutzbach, "Middle Holocene Dry Period in the Northern Midwestern United States: Lake Levels and Pollen Stratigraphy," *Quaternary Research* 25 (1986).

4. David F. Barton, "Skare Site Projectile Points," *Wisconsin Archeologist* 77, no. 1–2 (1996): 82; Sissel Schroeder, "Evidence for Paleoindians in Wisconsin and the Skare Site," *Plains Anthropologist* 52 (2007).

5. Sissel Schroeder, Kenneth Ritchie, Edward Swanson, and Lynnette Kleinsasser, "Structure Abandonment and Conflagrations at the Skare Site" (paper presented at the 2003 Midwest Archaeological Conference, Milwaukee, Wisconsin).

6. James Stoltman and Thomas Pleger, "The Archaic in Wisconsin," in *Archaic Societies: Diversity and Complexity across the Midcontinent,* ed. Thomas E. Emerson, Dale L. McElrath, and Andrew C. Fortier (Albany: State University of New York Press, 2009). Radiocarbon samples are taken from organic material, and the decay of a radioactive carbon isotope is measured at a known rate after the death of the organism. Because of fluctuations in carbon in the earth atmosphere through time, radiocarbon dates are now calibrated using dated tree rings, which has led to refinements of earlier prehistoric chronologies.

7. Norman M. Meinholz and Steven R. Kuehn, *The Deadman Slough Site: Late Paleoindian/Early Archaic and Woodland Occupations along the Flambeau River, Price County, Wisconsin* (Madison: State Historical Society of Wisconsin, 1996).

8. Ronald J. Mason and Carol Irwin, "An Eden-Scottsbluff Burial in Northeastern Wisconsin," *American Antiquity* 26 (1960).

9. Winkler, Swain, and Kutzbach, "Middle Holocene Dry Period in the Northern Midwestern United States"; Reid A. Bryson and Robert U. Bryson, *The History of Woodland Climatic Environments: As Simulated with Archaeoclimatic Models* (Madison: University of Wisconsin Climatic Research Center, 2000).

10. Steve Woverton, "The Effects of the Hypsithermal on Prehistoric Foraging Efficiency in Missouri," *American Antiquity* 70, no. 1 (2005).

11. Winker, Swain, and Kutzbach, "Middle Holocene Dry Period in the Northern United States"; Robert S. Elarson, "Vegetation of Dane County in 1935," *Transactions of the Wisconsin Academy of Sciences, Arts and Letters* 39 (1949).

12. For a summary of this evidence, see James L. Theler and Robert F. Boszhardt, *Twelve Millennia: Archaeology of the Upper Mississippi Valley* (Iowa City: University of Iowa Press, 2003).

13. K. Hamilton, D. Tennesson, S. Slossman, and M. Bauman, *Archaeological Investigations of the Alternate Corridor Alignments for the Proposed Reconstruction of USH 12 between Middleton and Sauk County, Dane County*, Museum Archaeology Program Research Report No. 46 (Madison: Wisconsin Historical Society, 1995); Norman M. Meinholz and Jennifer Kolb, *The Statz Site: A Late Woodland Community and Archaic Workshop in Dane County Wisconsin* (Madison: State Historical Society of Wisconsin, 1996); Marlin F. Hawley, "Excavations at the Murphy (47 DA-736) and River Quarry (47 DA-768) Sites," *WisArch News* 4 (2002).

14. Winkler, Swain, and Kutzbach, "Middle Holocene Dry Period in the Northern United States"; Tristram R. Kidder, "Climate Change and the Archaic to Woodland Transition (3000–2500 Cal. BP) in the Mississippi River Basin," *American Antiquity* 69, no. 2 (2006); James C. Knox, "North American Paleofloods and Future Floods: Responses to Climate Change," in *Paleohydrology: Understanding Global Change*, ed. K. J. Gregory and G. Benito (New York: John Wiley and Sons, 1993).

15. Stoltman and Pleger, "The Archaic in Wisconsin."

16. Thomas C. Pleger, "Old Copper and Red Ochre Social Complexity," *Midcontinental Journal of Archaeology* 25, no. 2 (2000).

17. David F. Overstreet, "The Convent Knoll Site (47Wk327): A Red Ochre Cemetery in Waukesha, Wisconsin," *Wisconsin Archeologist* 6, no 1 (1980); Stoltman and Pleger, "The Archaic in Wisconsin."

18. Katherine P. Stevenson, Robert F. Boszhardt; Charles R. Moffat, Philip H. Salkin, Thomas C. Plegar, James L. Theler, and Constance M. Arizigian, "The Woodland Stage," in "Wisconsin Archaeology," ed. Robert A. Birmingham, Carol I. Mason, and James B. Stoltman, special issue of *Wisconsin Archeologist* 78, no.1–2 (1997).

19. Charles E. Brown and Theodore T. Brown, "Indian Villages and Campsites of the Lower Rock River," *Wisconsin Archeologist* 9, no. 1 (1929): 43.

20. Philip H. Salkin, "The Lake Farms Phase: The Early Woodland Stage in Central Wisconsin as Seen from the Lake Farms Archaeological District," in *Early Woodland Archaeology*, ed. Ken Farnsworth and Thomas Emerson (Kampsville, IL: Center for American Archaeology Research, 1986).

21. David W. Benn, "The Woodland People and the Roots of Oneota," in *Oneota Archaeology, Past, Present, and Future*, ed. William Green, Report No. 20 (Iowa City: University of Iowa, Office of the State Archaeologist, 1995), 103.

22. Howard Van Langden and Thomas F. Kehoe, "Hilgen Springs Park Mounds," *Wisconsin Archeologist* 52, no. 1 (1971); Robert L. Hall, *Archaeology of the Soul: North American Belief and Ritual* (Urbana: University of Illinois Press, 1997), 17–24.

23. Philip H. Salkin, *Archaeological Mitigation Excavations at the Airport Village Site (47Da2) in Dane County, Wisconsin*, Reports of Investigations No. 871 (Verona, WI: Archaeological Consulting and Services, 1994).

24. Victoria Dirst, *Research in Pursuit of the Past at Governor Nelson Park, Dane County, Wisconsin* (Madison: Bureau of Parks and Recreation, Wisconsin Department of Natural Resources, 1988).

25. Hall, *Archaeology of the Soul.*

26. W. C. McKern, "A Wisconsin Variant of the Hopewell Culture," *Bulletin of the Public Museum of the City of Milwaukee* 10, no. 2 (1931).

27. Christopher Carr and D. Troy Case, eds., *Gathering Hopewell: Society, Ritual, and Ritual Interaction* (New York: Springer Science and Media, 2006).

28. James B. Stoltman, "Tillmont (47CR460): A Stratified Prehistoric Site in the Upper Mississippi River Valley," *Wisconsin Archeologist* 86, no. 2 (2005).

29. Jane E. Buikstra and Douglas K. Charles, "Centering the Ancestors: Cemeteries, Mounds and Landscapes of the Ancient North American Continent," in *Archaeologies of Landscape: Contemporary Perspectives*, ed. Wendy Asmore and A. Bernard Knapp (Malden, MA: Blackwell Publishers, 1999), 216.

30. Charles E. Brown Papers, Wisconsin Historical Society; Charles E. Brown, "Lake Monona," *Wisconsin Archeologist* 1, no. 4 (1922); Charlotte T. Bakken, "Preliminary Investigations at the Outlet Site," *Wisconsin Archeologist* 31, no. 2 (1950); A. H. Whiteford, "A Report on Outlet Site on Lake Monona," *Wisconsin Archeologist* 30, no. 1 (1949); David A. Baerreis and Margaret M. Bender, "The Outlet Site (47 DA 3): Some Dating Problems and a Reevaluaton of the Presence of Corn in the Diet of Middle and Late Woodland Peoples in Wisconsin," *Midcontinental Journal of Archaeology* 9, no. 2 (1984).

31. Baerreis and Bender, "The Outlet Site (47 DA 3)"; David A. Baerreis, Margaret Bender, R. A. Bryson, and Raymond L. Steventon, "University of Wisconsin Radiocarbon Dates XIV," *Radiocarbon* 24, no. 1 (1982): 87.

32. Whiteford, "A Report on Outlet Site on Lake Monona."

33. Hall, *Archaeology of the Soul*, 19.

34. J. M. De Hart, "The Antiquities and Platycnemism of the Mound Builders of Wisconsin," *Transactions of the Wisconsin Academy of Sciences, Arts, and Letters* 4 (1876–1877); Cyrus Thomas, *Report on the Mound Explorations of the Bureau of Ethnology*, Twelfth Annual Report of the Bureau of American Ethnology, 1890–1891 (Washington, DC: Smithsonian Institution Press, 1985).

35. Charles E. Brown Papers, Box 21, Wisconsin Historical Society.

36. Bryson and Bryson, *The History of Woodland Climatic Environments*, 8.

37. Theler and Boszhardt, *Twelve Millennia*, 127; Salkin, *Archaeological Mitigation Excavations at the Airport Village Site.*

38. Evidence for corn at effigy mound period sites is presented in George W. Christiansen, *Archaeological Investigations along STH 60 between CTH W and STH 80 in Richwood and Eagle Townships in Richland County, Wisconsin* (Milwaukee: Great Lakes Archaeological Research Center, 2002); William G. Gartner, "The Late Woodland Landscapes of Wisconsin: Ridged Fields, Effigy Mounds, and Territoriality," *Antiquity* 73, no. 281 (1999); James B. Stoltman and George W. Christiansen III, "The Late Woodland Stage in the Driftless Area of the Upper Mississippi Valley," in *Late Woodland Societies: Tradition and Transformation across the Midcontinent*, ed. Thomas E. Emerson, Dale L. McElrath, and Andrew C. Fortier (Lincoln: University of Nebraska Press, 2000).

39. E. F. Dietz, David A. Baerreis, Robert Nero, and Hugh C. Cutler, "A Report on the Dietz Site," *Wisconsin Archeologist* 37, no. 1 (1956); Philip Salkin, *Archaeological Mitigation Excavations at the Sticker Pond I Site (47DA424) in Middleton, Dane County, Wisconsin*, Reports of Investigations No. 353 (Verona, WI: Archaeological Consulting and Services, 1987).

40. Bryson and Bryson, "The History of Woodland Climatic Environments."

41. Timothy R. Pauketat, *Ancient Cahokia and the Mississippians* (Cambridge: University of Cambridge Press, 2004); Larry V. Benson, Timothy R. Pauketat, and Edward Cook, "Cakokia's Boom and Bust in the Context of Climate Change," *American Antiquity* 74, no. 3 (2009).

42. Dirst, *Research in Pursuit of the Past at Governor Nelson Park.*

43. Hamilton et al., *Archaeological Investigations of the Alternate Corridor Alignments for the Proposed Reconstruction of USH 12*; Meinholz and Kolb, *The Statz Site.*

44. Philip H. Salkin, "The Horicon and Kekoskee Phases: Cultural Complexity in the Woodland Stage in Southwestern Wisconsin," in *Late Woodland Societies: Tradition and Transformation across the Midcontinent*, ed. Thomas E. Emerson, Dale L. McElrath, and Andrew C. Fortier (Lincoln: University of Nebraska Press, 2000); Stoltman and Christiansen, "The Late Woodland Stage in the Driftless Area of the Upper Mississippi Valley"; John Martin Kelly, "Delineating the Spatial and Temporal Boundaries of Late Woodland Collared Wares from Wisconsin and Illinois" (master's thesis, Department of Anthropology, University of Wisconsin–Milwaukee, 2002).

45. W. C. McKern, "The Kletzien and Nitschke Mound Groups," *Bulletin of the Public Museum of the City of the Milwaukee* 3, no. 4 (1930).

46. Philip H. Salkin, *Archaeological Studies at Two Proposed Recreational Sites at the Mendota Mental Health Institute in Dane County, Wisconsin*, Reports of Investigations No. 1073 (Verona, WI: Archaeological Consulting Services, 1988).

47. Robert A. Birmingham and Lynne Goldstein, *Aztalan: An Ancient Indian Town* (Madison: Wisconsin Historical Society Press, 2006).

48. Pauketat, *Ancient Cahokia and the Mississippians*, 79.

49. Robert J. Salzer and G. Rajnovich, *The Gottschall Rockshelter: An Archaeological Mystery* (St. Paul, MN: Prairie Smoke Press, 2000).

50. James B. Stoltman, "A Reconsideration of the Cultural Processes Linking Cahokia to Its Northern Highlands during the Period A.D. 1000–1200," in *Mounds, Modoc, and MesoAmerica: Papers in Honor of Melvin L. Fowler*, ed. Steve Ahler (Springfield: Illinois State Museum, 2000); Stoltman and Christiansen, "The Late Woodland Stage in the Driftless Area of the Upper Mississippi Valley."

51. Robert Hall, *The Archaeology of Carcajou Point*, 2 vols. (Madison: University of Wisconsin Press, 1962); David F. Overstreet, "Oneota Prehistory and History," in "Wisconsin Archaeology," ed. Robert A. Birmingham, Carol I. Mason, and James B. Stoltman, special issue of *Wisconsin Archeologist* 78, no. 1–2 (1997).

52. Hall, *Archaeology of Carcajou Point*; Robert J. Jeske, "Crescent Bay Hunt Club: Radiocarbon Dates and Research Summary," in *Program in Midwestern Archaeology (Southeastern Wisconsin Archaeology Program): 2000–2001*, ed. R. J. Jeske, Archaeological Research Laboratory Report of Investigations No. 148 (University of Wisconsin–Milwaukee, 2001); Overstreet, "Oneota Prehistory and History."

53. Dirst, *Research in Pursuit of the Past at Governor Nelson Park*.

54. Charles E. Brown, "Undescribed Groups of Lake Mendota Mounds," *Wisconsin Archeologist*, o.s., 11, no. 1 (1912).

55. S. A. Barrett, "Ancient Aztalan," *Bulletin of the Museum of the City of Milwaukee* (1933): 256–257.

56. Schroeder et al., "Structure Abandonment and Conflagrations at the Skare Site."

57. John H. Kinzie, *Schedule of the Number and Names of the Different Winnebago Villages, Number of Lodges and Persons in Each, with the Names of the Head Chiefs in Each Village, Oct. 1, 1829* (Indian Office Files, Michigan, 1829–1832; copy at the Wisconsin Historical Society).

58. Charles J. Kappler, comp. and ed., *Indian Treaties 1778–1883* (New York: Interland Publishing, 1972).

59. Nancy Oestreich Lurie, *Wisconsin Indians* (Madison: Wisconsin Historical Society Press, 2002).

60. Robert A. Birmingham and Leslie Eisenberg, *Indian Mounds of Wisconsin* (Madison: University of Wisconsin Press, 2000), 175–177.

Chapter 3. The Effigy Mound Landscape of Madison and the Four Lakes

1. Richard C. Taylor, "Notes Respecting Certain Indian Mounds and Earthworks in the Form of Animal Effigies, Chiefly in Wisconsin Territory, U.S.," *American Journal of Science and Art* 34 (1838).

2. John Locke, M.D., "Earthwork Antiquities in Wiskonsin Territory," U.S. 28th Cong., 1st sess., Senate Executive Document, 207, Washington, D.C., 1844.

3. Increase A. Lapham, *Antiquities of Wisconsin, as Surveyed and Described* (Washington, DC: Smithsonian Institution, 1855; reprint, Madison: University of Wisconsin Press, 2001), 40.

4. Theodore H. Lewis, *The Northwestern Archaeological Survey: Fieldbooks and Related Volumes, 1880–1895*, Minnesota Historical Society Archives; Fred A. Finney, "The Archaeological Legacy of Theodore H. Lewis: Letters, Papers, and Articles," *Wisconsin Archeologist* 87, no. 1–2 (2007).

5. A. B. Stout and H. L. Skavlem, "The Archaeology of the Lake Koshkonong Region," *Wisconsin Archeologist*, o.s., 7, no. 2 (1908).

6. Much of the following material on Brown is extracted from Robert A. Birmingham, "Charles E. Brown and the Mounds of Madison," *Historic Madison: A Journal of the Four Lakes Region* 13 (1996).

7. W. G. McLachlan, "The Mounds of the Lake Waubesa Region," *Wisconsin Archeologist*, o.s., 12, no. 4 (1914): 158–161; Charles E. Brown, "Lake Wingra," *Wisconsin Archeologist*, o.s., 14, no. 3 (1915); W. G. McLachlan, "The Lake Kegonsa Region," *Wisconsin Archeologist* 4, no 4 (1925).

8. Letter from Julien M. Wilkinson, UW Office of the President, to Brown, June 1 1939; letter from A. F. Gallistel, UW Buildings and Grounds, to Brown, July 5, 1939; both in Charles E. Brown Papers, Box 21, Wisconsin Historical Society.

9. Robert W. Peterson, "A Survey of the Destruction of Effigy Mounds in Wisconsin and Iowa—A Perspective," *Wisconsin Archeologist* 65, no. 1 (1985).

10. Robert J. Salzer and Larry A. Johns, *Report of the Dane County Identification Project, Dane County Park Commission, 1992* (on file, Office of the State Archaeologist, Wisconsin Historical Society).

11. For example, James P. Scherz and Buck Trawicky, *Survey Report, Hudson Park Mound Group, Dane County, Madison, Wisconsin, 1990* (Madison, WI: Ancient Earthworks Society, 1990); James P. Scherz, *Wisconsin's Effigy Mounds* (Madison, WI: Ancient Earthworks Society, 1991).

12. George W. Christiansen III, *2004 Archaeological Investigations on the University of Wisconsin–Madison, City of Madison, Dane County* (Milwaukee: Great Lakes Archaeological Research Center, 2005).

13. However, state law allows the Wisconsin Historical Society to restrict access to information about site locations to prevent unauthorized digging and looting.

14. Robert A. Birmingham and Leslie Eisenberg, *Indian Mounds of Wisconsin* (Madison: University of Wisconsin Press, 2000).

15. Lynne Goldstein, "Landscapes and Mortuary Practices: A Case for Regional Perspectives," in *Regional Approaches to Mortuary Analysis*, ed. Lane Anderson Beck (New York: Plenum, 1995).

Chapter 4. Yahara Inlet and Mendota

1. Charles E. Brown, *Lake Mendota Indian Legends* (Madison, WI: State Historical Museum, 1927), 3–4; Dorothy Moulding Brown, *Wisconsin Indian Place-Name Legends* (Madison: Wisconsin Folklore Booklets, 1947), 13–14; a slightly shorter version exists in James Davie Butler, "Taychoperah, the Four Lakes Country," *Wisconsin Historical Collections* 10 (1885): 64–65.

2. Major sources of information on Lake Mendota mounds come from Charles E. Brown, "Undescribed Groups of Lake Mendota Mounds," *Wisconsin Archeologist*, o.s., 11, no. 1 (1912); Charles E. Brown Papers, Wisconsin Historical Society; George W. Christiansen III, *2004 Archaeological Investigations on the University of Wisconsin–Madison, City of Madison, Dane County* (Milwaukee: Great Lakes Archaeological Research Center Reports of Investigation, 2005); Theodore H. Lewis, *The Northwestern Archaeological Survey*, Notebook 24, 1885, 1888, Minnesota Historical Society Archives; Robert J. Salzer and Larry A. Johns, *Report of the Dane County Identification Project, Dane County Park Commission, 1992* (on file, Office of the State Archaeologist, Wisconsin Historical Society).

3. Brown, *Lake Mendota Indian Legends*.

4. Victoria Dirst, *Research in Pursuit of the Past at Governor Nelson State Park, Dane County, Wisconsin* (Madison: Bureau of Parks and Recreation, Wisconsin Department of Natural Resources, 1988).

5. Philip H. Salkin, *Archaeological Studies at Two Proposed Recreational Sites at the Mendota Mental Health Institute in Dane County, Wisconsin* (Verona, WI: Archaeological Consulting and Services, 1988).

6. T. H. Lewis, "Notice of Some Recently Discovered Effigy Mounds," *Science*, o.s., 5, no. 106 (February 13, 1885).

7. Christiansen, *2004 Archaeological Investigations on the University of Wisconsin–Madison*.

8. For a list of the numerous references and maps for this significant group, see Amy Rosebrough, *National Register Nomination form for the Observatory Hill Mound Group* (Madison: Historic Preservation Division, Wisconsin Historical Society, 2003).

9. Gary J. Maier, *The Eagle's Voice: Tales Told by Indian Effigy Mounds* (Madison, WI: Prairie Oak Press, 2001).

10. Elizabeth McCoy, Edwin Broun Fred, and Eleanore Oimoen, *"Seeing" the University of Wisconsin–Madison Today* (Madison: University of Wisconsin Foundation, 1978).

11. Notes on Merrill Springs, Charles E. Brown Papers, Box 21, Wisconsin Historical Society.

12. Maier, *The Eagle's Voice*.

13. These azimuths for the sun's rising and setting assume a flat horizon. Obstruction and topography would make a difference in actual sighting since the sun does not rise or set straight up or down but rather arcs.

14. Lewis, *Northwestern Archaeological Survey*, Notebook 27:11.

15. Salzer and Johns, *Report of the Dane County Identification Project*.

16. Brown, "Undescribed Groups of Lake Mendota Mounds."

17. Letter from Ferdinand J. Heim to Charles E. Brown, July 8, 1937, Charles E. Brown Papers, Wisconsin Historical Society.

18. Limited archaeological excavations were conducted in the mound by the

Wisconsin Historical Society to acquire more information about mounds in the area but most of the form remains undisturbed.

Chapter 5. Wingra

1. Charles E. Brown, "Lake Wingra," *Wisconsin Archeologist*, o.s., 14, no. 3 (1915).
2. Charles E. Brown, "The Springs of Lake Wingra," *Wisconsin Magazine of History* 10, no. 3 (1927).
3. Ibid.
4. Brown, "Lake Wingra," 115.
5. Theodore H. Lewis, *The Northwestern Archaeological Survey*, Notebook 27: 24–25, Minnesota Historical Society Archives; T. H. Lewis, "A New Departure in Effigy Mounds," *Science*, o.s., 13, no. 318 (March 8, 1889).
6. Increase Lapham, *Milwaukee Daily Sentinel*, Jan. 2. 1860.
7. Ibid.
8. Brown, "Lake Wingra," 89.
9. Ibid., 99–100.
10. Robert A. Birmingham and Leslie Eisenberg, *Indian Mounds of Wisconsin* (Madison: University of Wisconsin Press, 2000), 177–179.
11. Robert A. Birmingham, "Charles E. Brown and the Mounds of Madison," *Historic Madison: A Journal of the Four Lakes Region* 13 (1996).
12. Ibid.

Chapter 6. Lake Monona

1. Charles E. Brown, "Lake Monona," *Wisconsin Archeologist* 1, no. 4 (1922); Charles E. Brown Papers, "Lake Monona," Wisconsin Historical Society.
2. Theodore H. Lewis, *The Northwestern Archaeological Survey*, Notebook 27: 15–21, Minnesota State Historical Society Archives; Charles E. Brown Papers, "Lake Monona." A map based on Lewis's survey of the Mills Woods was produced by James P. Scherz and Buck Trawicky in *Survey Report, Hudson Park Mound Group, Dane County, Madison, Wisconsin* (Madison, WI: Ancient Earthworks Society, 1990).
3. Increase A. Lapham, *Antiquities of Wisconsin, as Surveyed and Described* (Washington, DC: Smithsonian Institution, 1855; reprint, Madison: University of Wisconsin Press, 2001), 40, plate 32.
4. David A. Baerreis, "Further Information on the Frost Woods Mound Group (DA1)," *Wisconsin Archeologist* 35, no. 2 (1954).
5. W. G. McLachlan, "The Mounds of the Lake Waubesa Region," *Wisconsin Archeologist*, o.s., 12, no. 4 (1914): 158–161.
6. Robert A. Birmingham, "Charles E. Brown and the Mounds of Madison," *Historic Madison: A Journal of the Four Lakes Region* 13 (1996).

Chapter 7. Waubesa

1. Charles E. Brown Papers, "Lake Waubesa," Wisconsin Historical Society.
2. Theodore H. Lewis, *The Northwestern Archaeological Survey*, Notebook 27: 54, Minnesota Historical Society Archives; W. G. McLachlan, "The Mounds of the Lake Waubesa Region," *Wisconsin Archeologist* 12, no. 4 (1914): 139–142.
3. Lewis, *Northwestern Archaeological Survey*, Notebook 27:56; McLachlan, "Mounds of the Lake Waubesa Area," 133–134.
4. McLachlan, "Mounds of the Lake Waubesa Area," 123.
5. Ibid., 112.

Chapter 8. Kegonsa and the Mouth of the Yahara

1. W. G. McLachlan, "The Lake Kegonsa Region," *Wisconsin Archeologist* 4, no. 4 (1925).
2. Ibid.
3. Theodore H. Lewis, *The Northwestern Archaeological Survey*, Notebook 32: 6–8, Supplementary Notebook 1:113, Minnesota Historical Society Archives.
4. Robert. J Salzer and Larry A. Johns, *Report of the Dane County Identification Project, Dane County Park Commission, 1992* (on file, Office of the State Archaeologist, Wisconsin Historical Society).
5. Amy L. Rosebrough and Robert A. Birmingham, "Effigy Mound Landscapes of Wisconsin" (paper presented at the 2003 Society of the American Archaeology Conference, Milwaukee, Wisconsin).
6. Charles E. Brown and Theodore T. Brown, "Indian Villages and Campsites of the Lower Rock River," *Wisconsin Archeologist* 9, no. 1 (1929): 43; H. L. Skavlem, "Indian Hill Mounds," *Wisconsin Archeologist* 13, no. 2 (1914).
7. Brown and Brown, "Indian Villages and Campsites of the Lower Rock River."

Bibliography

Aveni, Anthony F. *Between the Lines: The Mystery of the Giant Ground Drawings of Ancient Nasca, Peru*. Austin: University of Texas Press, 2000.

Baerreis, David A. "The Blackhawk Village (Da-5), Dane County, Wisconsin." *Journal of the Iowa Archeological Society* 2, no. 4 (1953): 5–20.

———. "Further Information on the Frost Woods Mound Group (DA1)." *Wisconsin Archeologist* 35, no. 2 (1954): 43–48.

Baerreis, David A., and Margaret M. Bender. "The Outlet Site (47 DA 3): Some Dating Problems and a Reevaluaton of the Presence of Corn in the Diet of Middle and Late Woodland Peoples in Wisconsin." *Midcontinental Journal of Archaeology* 9, no. 2 (1984): 143–154.

Baerreis, David A., Margaret Bender, R. A. Bryson, and Raymond L. Steventon. "University of Wisconsin Radiocarbon Dates XIV." *Radiocarbon* 24, no. 1 (1982): 83–100.

Bailey, G. A., ed. *The Osage and the Invisible World from the Works of Francis La Flesche*. Norman: University of Oklahoma Press, 1995.

Bakken, Charlotte T. "Preliminary Investigations at the Outlet Site." *Wisconsin Archeologist* 31, no. 2 (1950): 43–70.

Barrett, John C. "Mythical Landscapes of the British Iron Age." In *Archaeologies of Landscape: Contemporary Perspectives*, edited by Wendy Asmore and A. Bernard Knapp, 253–265. Malden, MA: Blackwell Publishers, 1999.

Barrett, S. A. "Ancient Aztalan." *Bulletin of the Public Museum of the City of Milwaukee* 13 (1933).

Barrett, S. A., and E. W Hawkes. "The Kratz Creek Mound Group." *Bulletin of the Public Museum of the City of Milwaukee* 3, no. 1 (1919): 1–138.

Barton, David A. "Skare Site Projectile Points." *Wisconsin Archeologist* 77, no. 1–2 (1996): 82.

Benn, David W. "The Woodland People and the Roots of Oneota." In *Oneota*

Archaeology, Past, Present, and Future, edited by William Green. Report No. 20. Iowa City: University of Iowa, Office of the State Archaeologist, 1995.

Benson, Larry V., Timothy R. Pauketat, and Edward R. Cook. "Cahokia's Boom and Bust in the Context of Climate Change." *American Antiquity* 74, no. 3 (2009): 467–484.

Berres, Thomas E. *Power and Gender in Oneota Culture: A Study of a Late Prehistoric People*. DeKalb: Northern Illinois University Press, 2001.

Betts, Collin M. "Pots and Pox: The Identification of Protohistoric Epidemics in the Upper Mississippi Valley." *American Antiquity* 7, no. 2 (2006): 233–259.

Birmingham, Robert A. "Charles E. Brown and the Mounds of Madison." *Historic Madison: A Journal of the Four Lakes Region* 13 (1996): 17–29.

Birmingham, Robert A., and Leslie Eisenberg. *Indian Mounds of Wisconsin*. Madison: University of Wisconsin Press, 2000.

Birmingham, Robert A., and Lynne Goldstein. *Aztalan: Mysteries of an Ancient Indian Town*. Madison: Wisconsin Historical Society Press, 2005.

Birmingham, Robert A., and Katherine H. Rankin. *Native American Mounds of Madison*, 2nd ed. Madison: City of Madison and the Wisconsin Historical Society, 1996.

Birmingham, Robert A., and Amy Rosebrough. "On the Meaning of Effigy Mounds." *Wisconsin Archeologist* 84, no. 1–2 (2003): 21–36.

Boszhardt, Robert F. *Deep Cave Art in the Upper Mississippi Valley*. St. Paul, MN: Prairie Smoke Press, 2003.

———. "An Etched Pipe from Southeastern Minnesota." *Archaeology News* (Mississippi Valley Archaeology Center at University of Wisconsin–La Crosse) 24, no. 2 (June 2006): 1–2.

Boszhardt, Robert F., and Jeremy L. Nienow. *Late Woodland Radiocarbon Dates from Wisconsin*. La Crosse: Mississippi Valley Archaeology Center at University of Wisconsin–La Crosse, 1995.

Brose, David S., James A. Brown, and David W. Penny, eds. *Ancient Art of the American Woodland Indians*. New York: Harry N. Abrams, in conjunction with the Detroit Institute of the Arts, 1985.

Brown, Charles E. "The Heim Effigy Mound." *Wisconsin Archeologist* 18, no. 2 (1938): 39–41.

———. *Lake Mendota Indian Legends*. Madison, WI: State Historical Museum, 1927.

———. "Lake Monona." *Wisconsin Archeologist* 1, no. 4 (1922): 119–167.

———. "Lake Wingra." *Wisconsin Archeologist*, o.s., 14, no. 3 (1915): 75–115.

———. "The Preservation of the Man Mound." *Wisconsin Archeologist*, o.s., 7, no. 4 (1908): 140–154.

———. "The Springs of Lake Wingra." *Wisconsin Magazine of History* 10, no. 3 (1927): 298–303.

———. "Undescribed Groups of Lake Mendota Mounds." *Wisconsin Archeologist*, o.s., 11, no. 1 (1912): 7–32.

———. "Waukesha County: Northern Townships." *Wisconsin Archeologist* 2, no. 4 (1923): 43.

Brown, Charles E., and Theodore T. Brown. "Indian Villages and Campsites of the Lower Rock River." *Wisconsin Archeologist* 9, no. 1 (1929): 7–93.

Brown, Dorothy Moulding. *Wisconsin Indian Place-Name Legends*. Madison: Wisconsin Folklore Booklets, 1947.

Bryson, Reid A., and Robert U. Bryson. *The History of Woodland Climatic Environments: As Simulated with Archaeoclimatic Models*. Madison: University of Wisconsin Climatic Research Center, 2000.

Buikstra, Jane E., and Douglas K. Charles. "Centering the Ancestors: Cemeteries, Mounds, and Landscapes of the Ancient North American Continent." In *Archaeologies of Landscape: Contemporary Perspectives*, edited by Wendy Asmore and A. Bernard Knapp, 219–228. Malden, MA: Blackwell Publishers, 1999.

Butler, James Davie. "Taychoperah, the Four Lakes Country." *Wisconsin Historical Collections* 10 (1885): 64–89.

Canfield, William. *Outline Sketches of Sauk County: Including Its History, from the First Marks of Man's Hand to 1861, and Its Topography, Both Written and Illustrated*. Baraboo, WI: A. N. Kellogg, 1861.

Carr, Christopher, and D. Troy Case, eds. *Gathering Hopewell: Society, Ritual, and Ritual Interaction*. New York: Springer Science and Media, 2006.

Chippendale, Christopher. *Stonehenge Complete*. London: Thames and Hudson, 2004.

Christiansen, George W., III. *Archaeological Investigations along STH 60 between CTH W and STH 80 in Richwood and Eagle Townships in Richland County, Wisconsin*. Milwaukee: Great Lakes Archaeological Research Center, 2002.

———. "The Burial Mound Research Project." Madison: Office of the State Archaeologist, Wisconsin Historical Society, 1997.

———. *2004 Archaeological Investigations on the University of Wisconsin–Madison, City of Madison, Dane County*. Milwaukee: Great Lakes Archaeological Research Center Reports of Investigation, 2005.

Clayton, Lee, and John W. Attig. "Pleistocene Geology of Dane County, Wisconsin." *Geological and Natural History Bulletin* 95 (1997).

Cole, Henry Ellsworth. *Baraboo, Dells, and Devil's Lake Region*. Baraboo, WI: Baraboo Publishing Co., 1920.

De Hart, J. M. "The Antiquities and Platycnemism of the Mound Builders of Wisconsin." *Transactions of the Wisconsin Academy of Sciences, Arts, and Letters* 4 (1876–1877): 188–200.

Dietz, E. F., David A. Baerreis, Robert Nero, and Hugh C. Cutler. "A Report on the Dietz Site." *Wisconsin Archeologist* 37, no. 1 (1956): 1–19.

Dirst, Victoria. *An Excavation Near the Morris Park Mounds at Governor Nelson State Park, Dane County. Wisconsin*. Madison: Bureau of Parks and Recreation, Wisconsin Department of Natural Resources, 1985.

———. *Research in Pursuit of the Past at Governor Nelson State Park, Dane*

County, Wisconsin. Madison: Bureau of Parks and Recreation, Wisconsin Department of Natural Resources, 1988.

Elarson, Robert S. "Vegetation of Dane County in 1935." *Transactions of the Wisconsin Academy of Sciences, Arts and Letters* 39 (1949): 31–45.

Emerson, Thomas E. "Water, Serpents, and the Underworld: An Exploration into Cahokia Symbolism." In *The Southeastern Ceremonial Complex; Artifacts and Analysis: The Cottonlandia Conference,* edited by Patricia Galloway, 45–92. Lincoln: University of Nebraska Press, 1989.

Finney, Fred. "The Archaeological Legacy of Theodore H. Lewis: Letters, Papers, and Articles." Special issue, *Wisconsin Archeologist* 87, no. 1–2 (2007).

Finney, Fred A., and James B. Stoltman. "The Fred Edwards Site: A Case of Stirling Phase Cultural Contact in Southwestern Wisconsin." In *New Perspectives on Cahokia: Views from the Periphery*, edited by James Stoltman, 229–252. Monographs in World Prehistory. Madison, WI: Prehistory Press, 1991.

Fowler, Melvin L., ed. "Ancient Skies and Sky Watchers of Cahokia: Woodhenges, Eclipses, and Cahokian Cosmology." Special issue, *Wisconsin Archeologist* 77, no. 3–4 (1996).

Fowler, Melvin L., Jerome Rose, Barbara Vander Leest, and Steven R. Ahler. *The Mound 72 Area: Dedicated Space in Early Cahokia.* Illinois State Museum Reports of Investigations. Springfield: Illinois State Museum Society, 1999.

Gartner, William G. "Archaeoastronomy as Sacred Geography." *Wisconsin Archeologist* 77, no. 3–4 (1996): 128–150.

———. "The Late Woodland Landscapes of Wisconsin: Ridged Fields, Effigy Mounds and Territoriality." *Antiquity* 73, no. 281 (1999): 671–683.

Goldstein, Lynne. "Landscapes and Mortuary Practices: A Case for Regional Perspectives." In *Regional Approaches to Mortuary Analysis*, edited by Lane Anderson Beck, 101–120. New York: Plenum, 1995.

Green, William, and Roland L. Rodell. "The Mississippian Presence and Cahokia Interaction at Trempealeau, Wisconsin." *American Antiquity* 59 (1994): 334–358.

Hall, Robert. *The Archaeology of Carcajou Point*, 2 vols. Madison: University of Wisconsin Press, 1962.

———. *Archaeology of the Soul: North American Belief and Ritual.* Urbana: University of Illinois Press, 1997.

———. "Red Banks, Oneota, and the Winnebago: Views from a Distant Rock." *Wisconsin Archeologist* 74, no. 1–4 (1993): 10–79.

———. "Rethinking Jean Nicolet's Route to the Ho-Chunk in 1634." In *Theory, Method, and Practice in Modern Archaeology*, ed. Robert J. Jeske and Douglas K. Charles, 238–251. Westport, CT: Praeger Publishing, 2003.

Hamilton, K., D. Tennesson, S. Slossman, and M. Bauman. *Archaeological Investigations of the Alternate Corridor Alignments for the Proposed Reconstruction of USH 12 between Middleton and Sauk County, Dane County*. Museum Archaeology Program Research Report No. 46. Madison: Wisconsin Historical Society, 1995.

Hawley, Marlin F. "Excavations at the Murphy (47 DA-736) and River Quarry (47 DA-768) Sites." *WisArch News* 4, no. 1 (2002): 1–3.

Highsmith, Hugh. *The Mounds of Koshkonong and Rock River: A History of Ancient Indian Earth Works in Wisconsin.* Fort Atkinson, WI: Highsmith Press, 1997.

Hively, Ray, and Robert Horn. "Geometry and Astronomy in Prehistoric Ohio." *Archaeoastronomy* 4 (1984): s1–s20.

Howey, Meghan C. L., and John M. O'Shea. "Bear's Journey and the Study of Ritual in Archaeology." *American Antiquity* 71, no. 2 (2006): 261–282.

Hurley, William M. *An Analysis of Effigy Mound Complexes in Wisconsin.* Anthropological Papers. Ann Arbor: University of Michigan, Museum of Anthropology, 1975.

Jeske, Robert J. "Crescent Bay Hunt Club: Radiocarbon Dates and Research Summary." In *Program in Midwestern Archaeology (Southeastern Wisconsin Archaeology Program): 2000–2001,* edited by R. J. Jeske, 4–12. Archaeological Research Laboratory Report of Investigations No. 148. University of Wisconsin–Milwaukee, 2001.

Kappler, Charles J., comp. and ed. *Indian Treaties 1778–1883.* New York: Interland Publishing, 1972.

Kelly, John E. "Redefining Cahokia: Principles and Elements of Community Organization." *Wisconsin Archeologist* 77, no. 3–4 (1996): 97–119.

Kelly, John Martin. "Delineating the Spatial and Temporal Boundaries of Late Woodland Collared Wares from Wisconsin and Illinois." Master's thesis, Department of Anthropology, University of Wisconsin–Milwaukee, 2002.

Keyser, James D., and David S. Whitney. "Sympathetic Magic in Western North American Rock Art." *American Antiquity* 71, no. 1 (2006): 3–26.

Kidder, Tristram R. "Climate Change and the Archaic to Woodland Transition (3000–2500 Cal. BP) in the Mississippi River Basin." *American Antiquity* 69, no. 2 (2006): 195–232.

Kinzie, John H. *Schedule of Number and Names of the Different Winnebago Villages, Number of Lodges and Persons in Each, with the Names of the Head Chiefs of Each Village, Oct. 1, 1829.* Indian Office Papers, Wisconsin Historical Society.

Knox, James C. "North American Paleofloods and Future Floods: Responses to Climate Change." In *Paleohydrology: Understanding Global Change,* edited by K. J. Gregory and G. Benito. New York: John Wiley and Sons, 1993.

Lapham, Increase. *Antiquities of Wisconsin, as Surveyed and Described.* Smithsonian Contributions to Knowledge. Washington, DC: Smithsonian Institution, 1855. Reprint, Madison: University of Wisconsin Press, 2001.

Lepper, Bradley T., and Tod A. Frolking. "Alligator Mound: Geographical and Iconographical Interpretations of a Late Prehistoric Effigy Mound in Central Ohio." *Cambridge Archaeological Journal* 13, no. 2 (2003): 147–167.

Lewis, Theodore H. "A New Departure in Effigy Mounds." *Science,* o.s., 13, no. 318 (March 8, 1889): 187–189.

———. "Cave Drawings in Minnesota, Iowa, and Wisconsin." *Appleton's Annual Cyclopedia and Register of Important Events, 1889* 14 (1890): 114–122.

———. "Notice of Some Recently Discovered Effigy Mounds." *Science,* o.s., 5, no. 106 (February 13, 1885): 131–132.

Locke, John, M.D. "Earthwork Antiquities in Wiskonsin Territory." U.S. 28th Congress 1st Session, Senate Executive Document, 1844: 207. Reprinted in *Wisconsin Archeologist* 11, no. 1 (1931): 20–29.

Lowe, David. "Rock Art Survey of the Blue Mounds Creek and Mill Drainages in Iowa and Dane Counties, Wisconsin." *Wisconsin Archeologist* 68, no. 4 (1987): 341–375.

Lurie, Nancy Oestreich. *Wisconsin Indians.* Madison: Wisconsin Historical Society Press, 2002.

Lynott, Mark J. Review of *Mysteries of the Hopewell: Astronomers, Geometers, and Magicians of the Eastern Woodlands,* by W. F. Romain. *Hopewell Archeology* 4, no. 2 (2001): 8–9.

Maier, Gary J. *The Eagle's Voice: Tales Told by Indian Effigy Mounds.* Madison, WI: Prairie Oak Press, 2001.

Mallam, Clark R. "Birds, Bears, Panthers, 'Elephants,' and Archaeologists." *Wisconsin Archeologist* 61, no. 3 (1980): 375–384.

———. *The Effigy Mound Manifestation: An Interpretive Model.* Report No. 9. Iowa City: University of Iowa, Office of the State Archaeologist, 1979.

———. "Ideology from the Earth: Effigy Mounds in the Midwest." *Archaeology* 35, no. 4 (1982): 60–64.

Martin, Lawrence. *The Physical Geography of Wisconsin.* Bulletin 36. Madison: Wisconsin Geological and History Survey, 1916. Reprint, Madison: University of Wisconsin Press, 1965.

Mason, Ronald J. *Inconstant Companions: Archaeology and North American Indian Oral Traditions.* Tuscaloosa: University of Alabama Press, 2006.

Mason, Ronald J., and Carol Irwin. "An Eden-Scottsbluff Burial in Northeastern Wisconsin." *American Antiquity* 26 (1960): 43–57.

McCoy; Elizabeth, Edwin Broun Fred, and Eleanore Oimoen. *"Seeing" the University of Wisconsin–Madison Today.* Madison: University of Wisconsin Foundation, 1978.

McKern, W. C. "The Kletzien and Nitschke Mound Groups." *Bulletin of the Public Museum of the City of the Milwaukee* 3, no. 4 (1930): 417–572.

———. "The Neale and McClaughry Mound Groups." *Bulletin of the Public Museum of the City of Milwaukee* 3, no. 3 (1928): 215–416.

———. "A Wisconsin Variant of the Hopewell Culture." *Bulletin of the Public Museum of the City of Milwaukee* 10, no. 2 (1931): 185–328.

McKusick, Marshall. "Exploring Turkey River Mounds." *Palimpsest* 45 (1964): 473–485.

McLachlan, W. G. "The Lake Kegonsa Region." *Wisconsin Archeologist* 4, no. 4 (1925): 181–206.

———. "The Mounds of the Lake Waubesa Region." *Wisconsin Archeologist*, o.s., 12, no. 4 (1914): 107–166.

Mead, Barbara. "The Rehbain I Site (47-RI-81)." *Wisconsin Archeologist* 60, no. 2 (1979): 91–182.

Meinholz, Norman M., and Jennifer Kolb. *The Statz Site: A Late Woodland Community and Archaic Workshop in Dane County Wisconsin*. Archaeology Research Series. Madison: State Historical Society of Wisconsin, 1996.

Meinholz, Norman M., and Steven R. Kuehn. *The Deadman Slough Site: Late Paleoindian/Early Archaic and Woodland Occupations along the Flambeau River, Price County, Wisconsin*. Archaeology Research Series. Madison: State Historical Society of Wisconsin, 1996.

Mickelson, David. *Landscapes of Dane County, Wisconsin*. Wisconsin Geological and Natural History Educational Series. Madison: Wisconsin Geological and Natural History Survey, 2007.

Milner, George R. *The Moundbuilders: Ancient Peoples of Eastern North America*. London: Thames and Hudson, 2004.

Mollenhoff, David V. *Madison: A History of the Formative Years*, 2nd ed. Madison: University of Wisconsin Press, 2003.

Nabokov, Peter, and Robert Easton. *Native American Architecture*. Oxford: Oxford University Press, 1989.

Overstreet, David F. "The Convent Knoll Site (47Wk327): A Red Ochre Cemetery in Waukesha, Wisconsin." *Wisconsin Archeologist* 6, no. 1 (1980): 34–90.

———. "Cultural Dynamics of the Late Prehistoric Period." In *Mounds, Modoc and MesoAmerica: Papers in Honor of Melvin F. Fowler*, edited by Steven R. Ahler, 405–438. Illinois State Museum Scientific Papers. Springfield: Illinois State Museum, 2000.

———. "Dreaded Dolostone and Old Smudge Stories: A Response to Critiques of Emergent Oneota 14C Dates from Eastern Wisconsin." In "Papers in Honor of Carol I. Mason," edited by Thomas C. Pleger, Robert A. Birmingham, and Carol I. Mason, 33–86. Special issue, *Wisconsin Archeologist* 82, no. 1–2 (2001).

———. "Oneota Prehistory and History." In "Wisconsin Archaeology," edited by Robert A. Birmingham, Carol I. Mason, and James B. Stoltman, 250–297. Special issue, *Wisconsin Archeologist* 78, nos. 1–2 (1997).

Pauketat, Timothy R. *Ancient Cahokia and the Mississippians*. Cambridge: University of Cambridge Press, 2004.

Pearson, James L. *Shamanism and the Ancient Mind: A Cognitive Approach to Archaeology*. New York: Altamira Press, 2002.

Peet, Stephen D. *Emblematic Mounds and Animal Effigies*. Prehistoric America. Chicago: American Antiquarian, 1890.

Peterson, Robert W. "A Survey of the Destruction of Effigy Mounds in Wisconsin and Iowa—A Perspective." *Wisconsin Archeologist* 65, no. 1 (1985): 1–31.

Pleger, Thomas C. "Old Copper and Red Ochre Social Complexity." *Midcontinental Journal of Archaeology* 25, no. 2 (2000): 169–190.

Price, Douglas T., and Gary M. Feinman. *Images of the Past*. New York: McGraw-Hill, 2005.

Radin, Paul. *The Road to Life and Death*. Bollingen Series. New York: Pantheon Books, 1945.

———. *The Winnebago Tribe*. Lincoln: University of Nebraska Press, 1970. Originally published as the *Thirty-Seventh Annual Report of the Bureau of American Ethnography*, 1923.

Rajnovich, Grace. *Reading Rock Art: Interpreting the Indian Rock Paintings of the Canadian Shield*. Toronto: Natural Heritage/Natural History, 1994.

Rodell, Roland. "The Diamond Bluff Site Complex and Cahokia Influence in the Red Wing Locality." In *New Perspectives on Cahokia: View form the Periphery*, edited by James B. Stoltman, 253–280. Madison, WI: Prehistory Press, 1991.

Romain, William F. *Mysteries of the Hopewell: Astronomers, Geometers, and Magicians of the Eastern Woodlands*. Akron, OH: University of Akron Press, 2000.

Rosebrough, Amy L. *National Register Nomination for the Observatory Hill Mound Group*. Madison: Historic Preservation Division, Wisconsin Historical Society, 2003.

Rosebrough, Amy L., and Robert A. Birmingham. "Effigy Mound Landscapes of Wisconsin." Paper presented at the 2003 Society of the American Archaeology Conference, Milwaukee, Wisconsin.

Rowe, Chandler W. *The Effigy Mound Culture of Wisconsin*. Milwaukee Public Museum Publications in Anthropology. Milwaukee: Milwaukee Public Museum, 1956.

———. "Preliminary Report on the Heller Mound Group." *Wisconsin Archeologist* 34, no. 2 (1953): 144–148.

Ruth, Christine Ella. "Death, Decay and Reconstruction: An Osteological Analysis of Effigy Mound Material from Wisconsin." PhD diss., University of Wisconsin–Milwaukee, 1998.

Salkin, Philip H. *Archaeological Mitigation Excavations at the Airport Village Site (47Da2) in Dane County, Wisconsin*. Reports of Investigations No. 871. Verona, WI: Archaeological Consulting and Services, 1994.

———. *Archaeological Mitigation Excavations at the Sticker Pond I Site (47DA424) in Middleton, Dane County, Wisconsin*. Reports of Investigations No. 353. Verona, WI: Archaeological Consulting and Services, 1987.

———. *Archaeological Studies at Two Proposed Recreational Sites at the Mendota Mental Health Institute in Dane County, Wisconsin*. Reports of Investigations No. 1073. Verona, WI: Archaeological Consulting and Services, 1988.

———. "The Horicon and Kekosgee Phases: Cultural Complexity in the Woodland Stage in Southwestern Wisconsin." In *Late Woodland Societies: Tradition and Transformation across the Midcontinent*, edited by Thomas E. Emerson, Dale L. McElrath, and Andrew C. Fortier, 525–542. Lincoln: University of Nebraska Press, 2000.

———. "The Lake Farms Phase: The Early Woodland Stage in Central Wisconsin as Seen from the Lake Farms Archaeological District." In *Early Woodland Archaeology*, edited by Ken Farnsworth and Thomas Emerson, 92–120. Kampsville Seminars in Archaeology. Kampsville, IL: Center for American Archaeology Research, 1986.

Salzer, Robert J., and Larry A. Johns. *Report of the Dane County Identification Project. Dane County Park Commission, 1992*. Report on file, Office of the State Archaeologist, Wisconsin Historical Society.

Salzer, Robert J., and G. Rajnovich. *The Gottschall Rockshelter: An Archaeological Mystery*. St. Paul, MN: Prairie Smoke Press, 2000.

Scherz, James P. *Wisconsin's Effigy Mounds*. Madison, WI: Ancient Earthworks Society, 1991.

Scherz, James P., and Buck Trawicky. *Survey Report, Hudson Park Mound Group, Dane County, Madison, Wisconsin*. Madison, WI: Ancient Earthworks Society, 1990.

Schroeder, Sissel. "Evidence for Paleoindians in Wisconsin and the Skare Site." *Plains Anthropologist* 52 (2007): 63–91.

Schroeder, Sissel, Kenneth Ritchie, Edward Swanson, and Lynnette Kleinsasser. "Structure Abandonment and Conflagrations at the Skare Site." Paper presented at the 2003 Midwest Archaeological Conference, Milwaukee, Wisconsin.

Schoolcraft, Henry Rowe. *The Indian Tribes of the United States*. Philadelphia: Lippincott, 1884.

Skavlem, H. L. "Indian Hill Mounds." *Wisconsin Archeologist* 13, no. 2 (1914): 93–96.

Skinner, Alanson. "Social Life and Ceremonial Bundles of the Menominee Indians." *Anthropological Papers of the American Museum of Natural History* 13, no. 1 (1913): 1–165.

Sneed, James E., and Robert W. Preucel. "The Ideology of Settlement: Landscapes in the Northern Rio Grande." In *Archaeologies of Landscape: Contemporary Perspectives*, edited by Wendy Asmore and A. Bernard Knapp, 169–200. Malden, MA: Blackwell Publishers, 1999.

Spindler, Louise S. "The Menominee." In *Handbook of North American Indians*, vol. 15, *Northeast*, edited by Bruce G. Trigger, 708–724. Washington, DC: Smithsonian Institution Press, 1978.

Stevenson, Katherine P., Robert F. Boszhardt, Charles R. Moffat, Philip H. Salkin, Thomas C. Pleger, James L. Theler, and Constance M. Arizigian. "The Woodland Stage." In "Wisconsin Archaeology," edited by Robert A. Birmingham, Carol I. Mason, and James B. Stoltman, 140–201. Special issue, *Wisconsin Archeologist* 78, no. 1–2 (1997).

Stoltman, James B. "A Reconsideration of the Cultural Processes Linking Cahokia to Its Northern Highlands during the Period A.D. 1000–1200." In *Mounds, Modoc, and MesoAmerica: Papers in Honor of Melvin L. Fowler*, edited by Steve

Ahler, 439–454. Illinois State Museum Scientific Papers. Springfield: Illinois State Museum, 2000.

―――. "Tillmont (47CR460): A Stratified Prehistoric Site in the Upper Mississippi River Valley." Special Issue, *Wisconsin Archeologist* 86, no. 2 (2005).

Stoltman, James B., and George W. Christiansen III. "The Late Woodland Stage in the Driftless Area of the Upper Mississippi Valley." In *Late Woodland Societies: Tradition and Transformation across the Midcontinent*, edited by Thomas E. Emerson, Dale L. McElrath, and Andrew C. Fortier, 497–524. Lincoln: University of Nebraska Press, 2000.

Stoltman, James B., and Thomas Pleger. "The Archaic in Wisconsin." In *Archaic Societies: Diversity and Complexity across the Midcontinent*, edited by Dale L. McElrath and Andrew C. Fortier, 697–723. Albany: State University of New York Press, 2009.

Stout, A. B., and H. L. Skavlem. "The Archaeology of the Lake Koshkonong Region." *Wisconsin Archeologist*, o.s., 7, no. 2 (1908): 47–102.

Tanner, Helen Hornbeck, ed. *Atlas of Great Lakes Indian History*. Norman: University of Oklahoma Press, 1987.

Taylor, Richard C. "Notes Respecting Certain Indian Mounds and Earthworks in the Form of Animal Effigies, Chiefly in Wisconsin Territory, U.S." *American Journal of Science and Art* 34 (1838): 88–104.

Theler James L., and Robert F. Boszhardt. "Collapse of Critical Resources and Culture Change: A Model for the Woodland to Oneota Transformation in the Upper Midwest." *American Antiquity* 71, no. 3 (2006): 433–472.

―――. *Twelve Millennia: Archaeology of the Upper Mississippi Valley*. Iowa City: University of Iowa Press, 2003.

Thomas, Cyrus. *Report on the Mound Explorations of the Bureau of Ethnology*. Twelfth Annual Report of the Bureau of American Ethnology, 1890–1891. Washington, DC: Smithsonian Institution Press, 1985.

Tigerman, Kathleen, ed. *Wisconsin Indian Literature: Anthology of Native Voices*. Madison: University of Wisconsin Press, 2006.

Townsend, Richard F., and Robert V. Sharp, eds. *Hero, Hawk, and Open Hand: American Indian Art of the Midwest and South*. Chicago: Art Institute of Chicago; New Haven: Yale University Press, 2004.

Van Langden, Howard, and Thomas F. Kehoe. "Hilgen Springs Park Mounds." *Wisconsin Archeologist* 52, no. 1 (1971): 1–19.

Whiteford, A. H. "A Report on the Outlet Site on Lake Monona." *Wisconsin Archeologist* 30, no. 1 (1949): 22–35.

Winkler, Marjorie Green. "Late Quaternary Climate, Fire, and Vegetation Dynamics." In *Sediment Records of Biomass Burning and Global Change*, edited by James S. Clark, Helene Cachier, Johann G. Goldammer, and Brina Stocks, 329–346. NATO ASI Series. Berlin: Springer-Verlag, 1997.

Winkler, M. G., A. M. Swain, and J. E. Kutzbach. "Middle Holocene Dry Period in the Northern Midwestern United States: Lake Levels and Pollen Stratigraphy." *Quaternary Research* 25 (1986): 235–250.

Wittry, Warren L. "The Mendota Hills Bird Mound, Dane County." *Wisconsin Archeologist* 36, no. 2 (1955): 53–55.

Woverton, Steve. "The Effects of the Hypsithermal on Prehistoric Foraging Efficiency in Missouri." *American Antiquity* 70, no. 1 (2005): 91–106.

Young, Biloine Whiting, and Melvin L. Fowler. *Cahokia, the Great Native American Metropolis*. Urbana: University of Illinois Press, 2000.

Illustration Credits

Figure P.1, photo by Robert Birmingham

Figure P.2, drawing by Julia Meyerson, from Anthony Aveni, *Between the Lines: The Mystery of the Giant Ground Drawings of Ancient Nasca, Peru*, © 2000; reproduced with permission of the author and the University of Texas Press

Figure P.3, photo by Robert Birmingham

Figure 1.1, from Lapham, *The Antiquities of Wisconsin*; reproduced with permission of the University of Wisconsin Press

Figure 1.2, based on a map by Amy Rosebrough, Wisconsin Historical Society

Figure 1.3, reproduced courtesy of the Mississippi Valley Archaeology Center at the University of Wisconsin–La Crosse

Figure 1.4, map by Amelia Janes with additions by Robert Birmingham

Figure 1.5, Increase Lapham Papers, Wisconsin Historical Society Archives; reproduced with permission of the Wisconsin Historical Society

Figure 1.6, reproduced with permission of the Milwaukee Public Museum, neg. 48310

Figure 1.7, map by Amelia Janes with additions by Robert Birmingham

Figure 1.8, map by Amy Rosebrough, Wisconsin Historical Society, with additions by Robert Birmingham, from McKern, "The Neale and McCloughry Mound Groups"

Figure 1.9a, from Lowe, "Rock Art Survey of the Blue Mounds Creek and Mill Drainages in Iowa and Dane Counties, Wisconsin"; reproduced with permission of the Wisconsin Archeological Society

Figure 1.9b, reproduced with permission of the Office of the State Archeologist, Wisconsin Historical Society

Figure 1.9c, reproduced with permission of the University of Wisconsin–Waukesha

Figure 1.10, from Lapham, *The Antiquities of Wisconsin*; reproduced with permission of the University of Wisconsin Press

Figure 1.11a, illustration by Julia Fauci, from Berres, *Power and Gender in One-ota Culture*; reproduced with permission of the Northern Illinois University Press

Figure 1.11b, from Skinner, "Social Life and Ceremonial Bundles of the Menominee Indians"

Figure 1.11c, drawing by Robert Birmingham

Figure 1.11d, Wisconsin Historical Society, WHi-34556

Figure 1.12a, from Lewis, "Cave Drawings in Minnesota, Iowa, and Wisconsin"

Figure 1.12b, reproduced courtesy of the Mississippi Valley Archaeology Center at the University of Wisconsin–La Crosse

Figure 1.12c, illustration by Julia Fauci, from Berres, *Power and Gender in Oneota Culture*; reproduced with permission of the Northern Illinois University Press

Figure 1.13a, drawing by Richard Nolan

Figure 1.13b, reproduced courtesy of the Mississippi Valley Archaeology Center at the University of Wisconsin–La Crosse

Figure 1.14, from Canfield, *Outline Sketches of Sauk County*

Figure 1.15, courtesy of the Ohio Historical Society

Figure 1.16, from Lapham, *The Antiquities of Wisconsin*; reproduced with permission of the University of Wisconsin Press

Figure 1.17, map by Robert Birmingham based on information from Dodge County Parks and McKern, "The Kletzien and Nitchske Mound Groups"

Figure 2.1, aerial photograph by Donna Harris, drumlin map by Susan L. Hunt, in Mickelson, *Landscapes of Dane County, Wisconsin*; reproduced with permission of the Natural History and Geological Society

Figure 2.2, map by Amelia Janes, adapted from a map in Mollenhoff, *Madison*; reproduced with permission of David Mollenhoff

Figure 2.3, reproduced with permission of Robert Granflaten, Wisconsin Historical Society

Figure 2.4, reproduced courtesy of the Office of the State Archeologist, Wisconsin Historical Society

Figure 2.5, base relief map by Mapping Specialists, Ltd.

Figure 2.6 left and right, from Stevenson et al., "The Woodland Stage"; reproduced with permission of the Wisconsin Archeological Society

Figure 2.7, photo by Kevin Birmingham

Figure 2.8, from Dirst, *An Excavation Near the Morris Park Mounds*, reproduced with permission of the Wisconsin Department of Natural Resources

Figure 2.9 right, reproduced with permission of the Milwaukee Public Museum, neg. 401889

Figure 2.9 left, reproduced with permission of the Milwaukee Public Museum, neg. 70292

Figure 2.10, map by Robert Birmingham based on drawing by Charles E. Brown

Figure 2.11, reproduced with permission of James Stoltman, Department of Anthropology, University of Wisconsin–Madison

Figure 2.12 above, from De Hart, "The Emblematic Mounds of Wisconsin"

Figure 2.12 below, photo by Robert Birmingham

Figure 2.13 above and below, Charles E. Brown Papers, box 21, Wisconsin Historical Society Archives

Figure 2.14, from Bryson and Bryson, *The History of Woodland Climatic Environments*

Figure 2.15, from Dirst, *Research in Pursuit of the Past at Governor Nelson Park, Dane County, Wisconsin*, with additions by Robert Birmingham; reproduced with permission of the Wisconsin Department of Natural Resources

Figure 2.16 above, from Meinholz and Kolb, *The Statz Site*; reproduced with permission of the Museum Archaeology Program of the Wisconsin Historical Society

Figure 2.16 below, photo by Robert Birmingham

Figure 2.17, reproduced with permission of Robert Granflaten, Wisconsin Historical Society

Figure 2.18, reproduced courtesy of Fred Finney

Figure 2.19, reproduced with permission of the Milwaukee Public Museum, neg. 70129

Figure 2.20, base map by Earth Information Technology

Figure 2.21, photo by Daniel Seurer

Figure 2.22, Charles E. Brown Papers, Box 21, Wisconsin Historical Society Archives, with additions by Robert Birmingham

Figure 2.23, reproduced with permission of Sissel Schroeder, Department of Anthropology, University of Wisconsin–Madison

Figure 2.24, from Schoolcraft, *The Indians Tribes of the United States*

Figure 3.1, Wisconsin Historical Society, WHi(X3)50551

Figure 3.2, from Lapham, *The Antiquities of Wisconsin*; reproduced with permission of the University of Wisconsin Press

Figure 3.3, Wisconsin Historical Society, WHi-2758

Figure 3.4, reproduced courtesy of the Goodhue County Historical Society, Red Wing, Minnesota

Figure 3.5, Wisconsin Historical Society, WHi-3519

Figure 3.6, Charles E. Brown Papers, Box 21, Wisconsin Historical Society Archives

Figure 3.7, from *Wisconsin Archeologist* 12, no. 4 (1914), reproduced with permission of Wisconsin Archeological Society

Figure 3.8, Wisconsin Historical Society, WHi-38944

Figure 3.9, base relief map by Mapping Specialists, Ltd.

Figure 3.10, drawing by Robert Birmingham

Figure 3.11, base relief map by Mapping Specialists, Ltd.

Figure 4.1, base relief map by Mapping Specialists, Ltd.

Figure 4.2, from Brown, "Undescribed Groups of Lake Mendota Mounds"; reproduced with permission of the Wisconsin Archeological Society

Figure 4.3, from Brown, "Undescribed Groups of Lake Mendota Mounds"; reproduced with permission of the Wisconsin Archeological Society

Figure 4.4, map by Amy Rosebrough, Wisconsin Historical Society

Figure 4.5, Wisconsin Historical Society, WHi-39018

Figure 4.6, map by Amy Rosebrough, Wisconsin Historical Society, with additions by Robert Birmingham

Figure 4.7, photo by Robert Birmingham

Figure 4.8, reproduced with permission of James Stoltman, Department of Anthropology, University of Wisconsin–Madison

Figure 4.9, map by Amy Rosebrough, Wisconsin Historical Society, and Robert Birmingham

Figure 4.10, reproduced with permission of James Stoltman, Department of Anthropology, University of Wisconsin–Madison

Figure 4.11, Charles E. Brown Papers, Box 21, Wisconsin Historical Society Archives

Figure 4.12, photo by Robert Birmingham

Figure 4.13, map by Amelia Janes based on mapping by T. H. Lewis

Figure 4.14, Charles E. Brown Papers, Box 21, Wisconsin Historical Society Archives

Figure 4.15, map by Amelia Janes based on information from Brown, "Undescribed Groups of Lake Mendota Mounds"

Figure 4.16, from Brown, "Undescribed Groups of Lake Mendota Mounds"; reproduced with permission of the Wisconsin Archeological Society

Figure 4.17 above, photo by Robert Birmingham

Figure 4.17 below, drawing by Robert Birmingham

Figure 4.18, map by Amy Rosebrough, Wisconsin Historical Society

Figure 4.19, map by Amy Rosebrough, Wisconsin Historical Society, and Robert Birmingham

Figure 4.20, Wisconsin Historical Society, WHi-5569

Figure 4.21, from Lewis Notebook 24, Northwestern Archaeological Survey, Minnesota Historical Society

Figure 4.22, map by Amy Rosebrough, Wisconsin Historical Society, based on maps by A. B. Stout and Charles E. Brown

Figure 4.23 above, Wisconsin Historical Society, WHi-39005

Figure 4.23 below, photo by Robert Birmingham

Figure 4.24, photo by Kevin Birmingham

Figure 4.25, photo by Kevin Birmingham

Figure 4.26, both from Brown, "Undescribed Groups of Lake Mendota Mounds"; reproduced with permission of the Wisconsin Archeological Society

Figure 4.27, map by Amy Rosebrough, Wisconsin Historical Society, based on notes by Lewis and Brown.

Figure 4.28, drawing by Amy Rosebrough, Wisconsin Historical Society, based on maps by Charles E. Brown and Robert J. Salzer in Salzer and Johns, *Report of the Dane County Identification Project*

Figure 4.29, Charles E. Brown Papers, Box 21, Wisconsin Historical Society Archives, with additions by Robert Birmingham

Figure 4.30, from Brown, "The Heim Effigy Mound"; reproduced with permission of the Wisconsin Archeological Society

Figure 5.1, map by Amy Rosebrough, Wisconsin Historical Society, and Robert Birmingham

Figure 5.2, drawing by Robert Birmingham

Figure 5.3, from Brown, "Lake Wingra"; reproduced with permission of the Wisconsin Archeological Society

Figure 5.4, Wisconsin Historical Society, WHi-38942

Figure 5.5, from Brown, "Lake Wingra"; reproduced with permission of the Wisconsin Archeological Society

Figure 5.6, from Brown, "Lake Wingra"; reproduced with permission of the Wisconsin Archeological Society

Figure 5.7, from Brown, "Lake Wingra"; reproduced with permission of the Wisconsin Archeological Society

Figure 5.8, map by Amy Rosebrough, Wisconsin Historical Society

Figure 5.9, photo and drawing by Robert Birmingham

Figure 5.10, from *Wisconsin Archeologist* 25, no. 2 (1944), reproduced with permission of Wisconsin Archeological Society

Figure 5.11 above and below, photos by Robert Birmingham

Figure 6.1, base relief map by Mapping Specialists, Ltd.

Figure 6.2, map by Earth Information Technology

Figure 6.3, from Lapham, *The Antiquities of Wisconsin*; reproduced with permission of the University of Wisconsin Press

Figure 6.4, from Brown, "Lake Monona"; reproduced with permission of the Wisconsin Archeological Society

Figure 6.5, from Brown, "Lake Monona"; reproduced with permission of the Wisconsin Archeological Society

Figure 6.6, from McLachlan, "The Mounds of the Lake Waubesa Region," with additions by Robert Birmingham; reproduced with permission of the Wisconsin Archeological Society

Figure 6.7 above and below, photos by Robert Birmingham

Figure 6.8, from McLachlan, "The Mounds of the Lake Waubesa Region"; reproduced with permission of the Wisconsin Archeological Society

Figure 6.9, photo by Robert Birmingham

Figures 6.10, photo by May Lou Burczyk

Figures 6.11, photo by May Lou Burczyk

Figure 7.1, base relief map by Mapping Specialists, Ltd.

Figure 7.2, from McLachlan, "The Mounds of the Lake Waubesa Region"; reproduced with permission of the Wisconsin Archeological Society

Figure 7.3, drawings by Robert Birmingham

Figure 7.4, Charles E. Brown Papers, Box 21, Wisconsin Historical Society Archives

Figure 7.5, Wisconsin Historical Society, WHi-39007

Figure 7.6 above, from Lewis Notebook 27, Northwestern Archaeological Survey, Minnesota Historical Society

Figure 7.6 below, map by Amy Rosebrough, Wisconsin Historical Society, based on notes from T. H. Lewis

Figure 7.7, from McLachlan, "The Mounds of the Lake Waubesa Region"; reproduced with permission of the Wisconsin Archeological Society

Figure 7.8, map by Amy Rosebrough, Wisconsin Historical Society, and Robert Birmingham, based on maps by McLachlan and Lewis

Figure 7.9, from McLachlan, "The Mounds of the Lake Waubesa Region"; reproduced with permission of the Wisconsin Archeological Society

Figure 7.10, from McLachlan, "The Mounds of the Lake Waubesa Region"; reproduced with permission of the Wisconsin Archeological Society

Figure 8.1, base relief map by Mapping Specialists, Ltd.

Figure 8.2, Wisconsin Historical Society, WHi(X31)394

Figure 8.3 above, from McLachlan, "The Lake Kegonsa Region"; reproduced with permission of the Wisconsin Archeological Society

Figure 8.3 below, from Brown, "Waukesha County"; reproduced with permission of the Wisconsin Archeological Society

Figure 8.4, from Lewis Notebook 32, Northwestern Archaeological Survey, Minnesota Historical Society

Figure 8.5, from McLachlan, "The Lake Kegonsa Region"; reproduced with permission of the Wisconsin Archeological Society

Figure 8.6, from McLachlan, "The Lake Kegonsa Region"; reproduced with permission of the Wisconsin Archeological Society

Figure 8.7, from McLachlan, "The Lake Kegonsa Region"; reproduced with permission of the Wisconsin Archeological Society

Figure 8.8, from Lapham, *The Antiquities of Wisconsin*; reproduced with permission of the University of Wisconsin Press

Figure 8.9, corrected map by Amy Rosebrough, Wisconsin Historical Society

Index

Index

WISCONSIN LAND AND LIFE

Spirits of Earth: The Effigy Mound Landscape of Madison and the Four Lakes
Robert A. Birmingham

A Thousand Pieces of Paradise: Landscape and Property in the Kickapoo Valley
Lynne Heasley

A Mind of Her Own: Helen Connor Laird and Family, 1888–1982
Helen L. Laird

North Woods River: The St. Croix River in Upper Midwest History
Eileen M. McMahon and Theodore J. Karamanski

Buried Indians: Digging Up the Past in a Midwestern Town
Laurie Hovell McMillin

Wisconsin Land and Life: A Portrait of the State
Edited by Robert C. Ostergren and Thomas R. Vale

Door County's Emerald Treasure: A History of Peninsula State Park
William H. Tishler